DEBATING
CALViNISM

DAVE HUNT & JAMES WHITE

Multnomah® Publishers *Sisters, Oregon*

DEBATING CALVINISM
published by Multnomah Publishers, Inc.
© 2004 by Dave Hunt and James White
International Standard Book Number: 1–59052–273–7

Cover design by Kevin Keller/Design Concepts
Interior design & typeset by Katherine Lloyd, The DESK
Cover images by Digital Vision

Unless otherwise indicated, Scripture quotations used by James White are from
New American Standard Bible® (NASB) © 1960, 1977, 1995
by the Lockman Foundation. Used by permission.

Scripture quotations used by Dave Hunt are from
The Holy Bible, King James Version (KJV)

Multnomah is a trademark of Multnomah Publishers, Inc.,
and is registered in the U.S. Patent and Trademark Office.
The colophon is a trademark of Multnomah Publishers, Inc.
Printed in the United States of America

For information:
MULTNOMAH PUBLISHERS, INC.
POST OFFICE BOX 1720
SISTERS, OREGON 97759

Library of Congress Cataloging-in-Publication Data
Hunt, Dave.
    Debating Calvinism : five points, two views / by Dave Hunt and James White.
        p. cm.
Includes bibliographical references and index.
    ISBN 1-59052-273-7 (pbk.)
    1. Calvinism. 2. Reformed Church--Doctrines. I. White, James R.
(James Robert), 1962-   II. Title.
    BX9422.3.H86 2004
    230'.42--dc22
                                                                    2003016084

04 05 06 07 08 09 10—10 9 8 7 6 5 4 3 2 1

CONTENTS

Part II: Calvinism Denied

PREFACE

What did you do to be saved? What has God done?
Christians from every age of history have taken aim at
answering these questions from the Scriptures. And some of
these voices have rung out louder than others: Augustine, Pelagius,
Arminius, Calvin, Erasmus, Luther, Whitefield, Wesley. We've heard their
names, but have we listened to their words? Have we measured their arguments by the *God-breathed words* of the Bible?

Reader, you will find in our debate that the issues surrounding the vital
teachings of the Bible concerning our own salvation—what theologians call
the doctrines of soteriology—are still very dear to Christians of today. The
passion of our debaters is undeniable. Their positions are entrenched and
heavily fortified. Indeed, we might easily have had their names conjoined on
the cover with *versus* rather than the tamer *and*.

The issue at hand is "Calvinism" insomuch as that system is codified in
five main points: total depravity, unconditional election, limited atonement,
irresistible grace, and perseverance of the saints. And yet surely both James
White and Dave Hunt would readily admit that the issue runs deeper than
these five points, to a way of thinking about God and how He works the
impossible wonders of grace.

The format of this debate is largely standard, though most debates are done in live, public forums. Each author contributes seven chapters offered to substantiate his opening position statement. Following each chapter, a response, defense, and final remarks are given in turn. The constraints here are quantities of words, not minutes. As a reader, consider yourself at an advantage to glean and consider and reconsider the arguments at your leisure. *Why can't he get it?* you may find yourself asking. Or perhaps, *How could I have missed that all along?*

Our hope is that of Spurgeon, that publishing such a forum might "thrust forward before the minds of Christians, precious truths, which but for it, might have been kept in the shade."[1]

---

1. Charles H. Spurgeon, "God's Will and Man's Will," sermon preached 30 March 1862.

{ Introduction }

CALVINISM AFFIRMED

by James White

I n the late summer of 2000, I interviewed Dave Hunt on KPXQ radio in Phoenix. Mr. Hunt had just published an article in the *Berean Call* attacking the Reformed position. The article misquoted Matthew 23:37 and presented the "standard" objections to Calvinism, objections based primarily upon evangelical/Arminian traditions and common misconceptions concerning the actual beliefs of Calvinists. I had written a full-length response to Norman Geisler on the same topic in *The Potter's Freedom*, but Dr. Geisler had declined every opportunity for dialogue, especially public dialogue and debate. I knew Dave Hunt would not decline such an invitation.

When we began the program, I noted that both Dave Hunt and I engage in public, formal debates with Roman Catholic apologists. I also noted that I had recently debated Robert Sungenis, a Catholic apologist, on the topic of justification by faith. Here is how the first question and response between Dave Hunt and me went:

White: One of the key issues that came out there…this is one of the main reasons I contacted you, one of the main reasons I wrote you the letter…is the issue of monergism versus synergism; that is, the idea that there is one force that brings about salvation, over against a synergistic

viewpoint that views it as a cooperation, a cooperative effort between two forces, man and God. And the reason I brought that up…is that Mr. Sungenis, in representing the Roman Catholic perspective, very strongly attacked the Reformed emphasis upon the sovereignty of the grace of God…. In light of your article, and the fact that…you reject the concept of irresistible grace…you and I are responding to one of the key issues of the Reformation in a different way. In essence, my first question to you would be: Do you feel that the Reformers Martin Luther and John Calvin were in error in emphasizing the deadness of man in sin and the absolute necessity—not just necessity, but sufficiency—of the grace of God to bring a person to salvation?

Hunt: Well, first of all, James, I'm very ignorant of the Reformers. I have not had time to read them. There are truckloads, I guess, of their writings. I like to just kinda' pretend that we're back there in the days of the apostles before all of these things were written. And I like to go to the Bible. So whether the Reformers said this or that, I don't know.[1]

Mr. Hunt went on to say that we should go to the Bible, and I surely agreed with that. But I was surprised that he was unaware of the issue Luther had described as the very hinge upon which the entire Reformation turned; namely, the freedom of God and the *sufficiency* of the grace of God in salvation. This was even more surprising due to the fact that Mr. Hunt's attacks upon the Reformed faith parallel those of Roman Catholics. When it comes to the issues of the freedom of God, the efficacy of grace, and the will of man, Mr. Hunt's evangelical tradition stands side by side with Rome in denying the heart of the Reformation.

It was most surprising, then, to hear only a few months later that Mr. Hunt was writing a book about this very subject, especially in light of his own confession of ignorance of the topic. I informed him that, in light of the errors of understanding he had enunciated during the radio program, I felt it was out of line for him to be publishing on the topic.

The publication of *What Love Is This?* prompted me to write an open letter, which was posted on our website and very quickly distributed to a very wide audience.[2] The book was disappointing on every level. The tenor was harsh. The attacks upon historic figures were unfair and unkind, revealing a bias that no honest historian should abide. The misuse of sources was rampant and included numerous errors in understanding even of my own work, which played a prominent role in Mr. Hunt's broadside at "Calvinism." The same misconceptions spoken in self-professed ignorance in August of 2000 were now being promoted under the banner of research and argumentation in print. But most importantly, I noted the continued enshrinement of tradition over sound exegesis of the Scriptures.

Some may question the wisdom of engaging in a point-counterpoint debate with Mr. Hunt on this topic. Allow me to say that I do so first and foremost out of love for God's truth and God's people. As an elder in a Reformed Baptist Church,[3] I believe it is my duty to "refute those who contradict" (Titus 1:9) and give an answer for my faith. As an apologist, I must be consistent in my stance as well. If I point to Rome's teaching that the grace of God is *necessary* but not *sufficient* to save, and identify this as a gross error that denies God His true glory in salvation, must I not likewise point out this error when it is propounded under the name of evangelicalism? How can I consistently call Rome to the final authority of Scripture and insist that it test its traditions by God's Word when evangelicals go about blind to their own traditions, refusing to test them by Scripture, in essence abandoning *sola scriptura?* It would surely be more popular to refrain from pointing out these errors, but for the one who seeks God's approval there is no other choice.

Dave Hunt does not understand the Reformed faith, and his book is filled with numerous straw-men caricatures that have nothing to do with the reality of it. It is not as if Mr. Hunt had not been warned that he was going to put in print many errors that would be quickly documented and refuted. I, along with others, can prove that we gave him that brotherly warning. But he has refused to take heed, so now the issue is the impact of the publication and dissemination of error on the wider audience of the church.

TRADITION VERSUS *SOLA SCRIPTURA*

In our radio conversation, Mr. Hunt at one point made a very important statement. When I pointed out that he was simply responding to the Scripture passages I was raising on the basis of his "traditions," he said to me, "James, I have no traditions." I replied that we all have traditions and that the man who thinks he has none is the man who is the most enslaved to them. To truly practice *sola scriptura* we must test our traditions by the ulti-mate authority of God's Word, even if they are beliefs we have held for many years and have had pounded into our heads in sermon after sermon. That is what this debate is really about.

I am Reformed because of one thing: Consistently, honestly, and thoroughly read, God's Word, the Bible, teaches that God is sovereign over all things, that man is a fallen creature, and that God saves perfectly in Jesus Christ. It is the consistent application of *sola scriptura* (Scripture alone) and *tota scriptura* (all of Scripture) that leads inevitably to the doctrines of grace. When we use consistent, proper, unvarying exegesis of the text of the Bible, we are led to believe Reformed theology concerning the grand work of God in the gospel of Jesus Christ. I do not believe the doctrines of grace because of Augustine or Calvin or Jonathan Edwards or Charles Spurgeon or Benjamin Warfield or R.C. Sproul. I rejoice in their company and am thankful for the testimony of men of God down through history. But first and foremost, I believe in the doctrines of grace because of the exegesis of the text of the God-breathed Scriptures, the Holy Bible. This is the firm foundation of Reformed theology, and it is what must be dealt with by anyone who would seek to truthfully convince men that the doctrines of grace are not divine truth.

In this exchange I will be challenging Mr. Hunt to test his traditions, not merely reiterate them. I have chosen to present the positive case for the doctrines of grace based upon the text of Scripture. The reader is encouraged to hold both sides to the same standards. Who presents consistent arguments? Who presents a biblically based position that provides a consistent and *sound* exegetical basis for the assertions made? Does one side simply state basic assumptions over and over again, while refusing to respond to a critique of those presuppositions?

THE BIBLE VERSUS PERSONALITIES

In his book, Mr. Hunt focused on attacking Christian men of the past personally; specifically, John Calvin, Martin Luther, and Augustine of Hippo. Seemingly, he believes that if a teacher of the past held to doctrines he disagrees with, everything that person believed was wrong. Amazingly, he hands all of history to the Roman Catholic Church, making Augustine a Roman Catholic (although Augustine would have had no concept of the phrase and, as we shall see, held to all sorts of beliefs contrary to Roman Catholicism)—

and then he asserts that Calvinists are in essence crypto-Catholics!

This charge is made in ignorance of the facts; indeed, it is Mr. Hunt's position that stands in harmony with Rome on the key points of debate (the nature of grace and the will of man). But these specifics aside, is it a valid argument to attack these men, allege they taught various forms of errors and were somehow mean-spirited and unkind, and on this basis seek to bias the reader against an entire theological position? Does it somehow *mean something* that the Roman Catholics who engaged in the Inquisition would agree with Mr. Hunt on the "free will of man"? Or does a meaningful argument have to provide more than just a vague allegation of a connection to carry weight with the person who thinks clearly and weighs facts honestly?

The very term *Calvinism* is a strange fact of history, for Calvin is in no way the originator of "the doctrines of grace." His name became connected with the view simply because of the unrelenting consistency of his writing on the subject, not because he taught on it more often than anyone else. Indeed, the section on prayer in *The Institutes of the Christian Religion* is longer than that on predestination, and Luther spoke more often on the subject than Calvin did. Hence, the issues of God's freedom in salvation and man's inability are not to be decided by reference to John Calvin, or to Augustine before him, but simply on the basis of the examination of the text of Scripture. Hence, all the time Mr. Hunt spends going after Calvin and Augustine is irrelevant to the real issue.[4]

GOD'S CHARACTER, GOD'S LOVE

Mr. Hunt certainly has one advantage in this exchange. In the place of sound biblical teaching, modern evangelicals have adopted sentimental traditions regarding God's character and love. Hence, the mere repetition of those traditions is often enough for those whose traditions do not conform to the Word of God. Reformed believers know the meaning of the motto *semper reformanda,* "always reforming." It is a lifelong duty to conform one's beliefs to the Word of God, to always be growing in the grace and knowledge of Jesus Christ. And when it comes to the issue of God's character and love, one must allow the Bible to define one's beliefs.

In the articles he has written since he initially began addressing this issue only a few years ago, in his book, in his talks, and in the encounter he had with Dr. Joseph Pipa of Greenville Presbyterian Seminary, Mr. Hunt repeatedly asserts that Calvinists deny God's omnibenevolence. His belief seems to be that unless God loves each and every creature *in the same way,* He is not "all loving." There can be no distinctions in God's love. Patiently withholding judgment from a wicked man cannot be included in God's "love" unless He does everything in His power to save that person, even if the person is utterly undeserving and justly condemned. For Mr. Hunt, God must love every person equally, try to save every person equally, and leave the results up to men (which is why he denies the freedom of God in election and regeneration). This means that God's love for the apostle John in heaven will be equal to, and completely undifferentiated from, the love He will have for Adolf Hitler as he undergoes God's wrath in hell for eternity. God's love can admit of no degrees, no differentiation, for if it does, God is not "all loving."

Of course, we see from the start that this makes God less than the creature, man. We rightly and properly discriminate in our love. Men are to love their wives as Christ loved the church. I am not to love my neighbor's wife as Christ loved the church. The love I have for someone other than my wife is of a different nature, substance, and intensity. The same is true for my children and my family. This is why the Lord said that, in comparison to the love we have for Him, our love for family and friends must be *different*. We are expected to recognize this basic fact. Even the Bible refers to the "apostle whom [Jesus] loved" (John 19:26), showing that the Lord, though He loved all the apostles with divine and perfect love, *had a special love for John*. It is obvious that the love God showed Moses is substantially different than the love He showed Pharaoh. No one can possibly argue that God expended the same effort to redeem the Assyrians that He expended to redeem Josiah or Isaiah or Ezekiel.

God is not less than His creature, man, and since it is proper for man to differentiate in the nature, extent, and purposes of his love for others, so too God demonstrates different kinds of love toward His creation. Indeed, consider even the phrase "as Christ loved the church." Do we not have to see that Christ's love for the church is of a completely different nature and purpose than His love for anything else?

We need to point out the results of Mr. Hunt's assertions. In his system, God's love cannot be redeeming love, since man must have the final say in the matter. Hence, God must love everyone equally, and try to save each one equally, and fail with regularity to do so. Indeed, we must conclude that God will be eternally unhappy, since He will love those in hell with the very same kind of undifferentiated love He has for the myriad redeemed surrounding His throne. Surely we cannot even begin to consider such an obviously unbiblical concept. It is a tradition—a very popular tradition indeed—to deny God the same freedom in His love that we have as His creatures. But it is a tradition that must be rejected upon biblical examination.

Recognizing this truth completely undercuts the primary thesis of Mr. Hunt's attacks on Reformed theology. When faced with exegetical truths for which he has no answers, Mr. Hunt makes reference to the "impossibility" of the Reformed interpretation because "it violates what we *know* of God's love." As soon as a person realizes that God will not be spending eternity in agonized disappointment, weeping endlessly over the objects of His undifferentiated, unending, "I tried but failed" love, the main plank of Mr. Hunt's anti-Reformed platform collapses.

Unfortunately, Mr. Hunt constantly misrepresents the Reformed position by stating that "God has predestined billions to go to hell without any chance of being saved." The wonder of God's act of predestination is not that He justly condemns rebel sinners who love their sin and spit in His face on a daily basis. The wonder is that He actually quells the rebellion in the hearts of innumerable rebel sinners and solely from grace works the miracle of regeneration, removing their hearts of stone and giving them hearts of flesh.

Yes, God's decree includes the punishment of the wicked, all to His glory, but (unless your tradition denies to God the ability to love freely) simple fairness demands that the whole of the truth be stated: God is under no obligation to extend His grace to the rebel sinner, and every single person who enters into eternal punishment would, were they given the opportunity, *freely choose to remain under punishment* rather than bow the knee in loving adoration of the God they hate. The idea that those who are punished are innocent victims or denied a "chance" is scandalously false. The thrice-holy God is under no obligation to grant "chances" in the first place, and to base one's entire argument upon a tradition that says otherwise is the fatal flaw of the anti-Reformed polemic.

CONCLUSION

I invite the reader to place his or her traditions squarely on the table. It can be uncomfortable to admit the role of tradition in one's thinking, but the reward is great. The Christian who constantly seeks to be conformed to the truth of God's Word will have confidence in that truth. May God grant us all the desire to believe everything He has revealed, and only what He has revealed, in the Word.

---

1. You can listen to the discussion at www.straitgate.com/jwdh1.ram
2. aomin.org/DHOpenLetter.html
3. www.prbc.org
4. I will gladly refute the calumnies launched at these men but only for the sake of truth. The attacks are irrelevant to the actual debate.

CALVINISM DENIED

by Dave Hunt

Never forget that the ultimate aim of Calvinism (as with all of James White's erudite arguments and references to original Greek and Hebrew) is to prove that God does not love everyone, is not merciful to all, and is pleased to damn billions. If that is the God of the Bible, Calvinism is true. If that is not the God of the Bible, who "*is* love" (1 John 4:8, emphasis added), Calvinism is false. The central issue is God's love and character in relation to mankind, as presented in Scripture.

I never wanted to engage in public debate about Calvinism. But we at the *Berean Call* began to receive numerous questions about this subject from readers telling us of church splits and family breakups. Many mentioned that R. C. Sproul is on the radio daily across the country, promoting Calvinism. Were Calvinists becoming more aggressive, or was I just awakening?

I went from never having heard of John Piper to being asked questions about his teaching from such remote places as Mongolia. Piper's assertions could hardly be ignored: "The doctrines of grace (*T*otal depravity, *U*nconditional election, *L*imited atonement, *I*rresistible grace, *P*erseverance of the saints [TULIP]) are the warp and woof of the biblical gospel."[1] Do non-Calvinists, then, not understand "grace" and the "gospel"?

Before Piper, John H. Gerstner had already written that "Calvinism is just another name for Christianity."[2] How, then, could non-Calvinists be Christians? Even earlier, in a book I had often recommended, Jay Adams had written, "As a *reformed* Christian, the writer believes that counselors *must not* tell any unsaved counselee that Christ died for him.... No man knows except Christ himself who are *his elect for whom he died*" (emphasis added).[3] Jay was a *reformed* Christian! What was that?

Somehow I had missed the fact that Calvinists claimed not only grace and the gospel as their own—but the entire Reformation as well! Calvinist churches were "reformed churches," and Calvinism was "Reformed theology." In his introduction to *The New Geneva Study Bible*, R. C. Sproul assures readers that its Calvinistic notes are "based on Reformed principles" that convey "Reformation truth" in order to "present the light of the Reformation afresh."[4] The Reformation was Calvinism? But John Calvin was eight years old when Martin Luther nailed his Ninety-Five Theses to the door in Wittenberg.

Furthermore, millions of biblical Christians resisted Rome for fifteen hundred years before Luther or Calvin. Albigenses, Waldenses, Bogomils, Paulicians, Baptists, and those who simply called themselves "Christians" or "brethren" traced their doctrines back to the apostles and never obeyed the popes. Derisively called Anabaptists for centuries, they rejected a state church (which Calvinists and Lutherans retained), recognized the Bible as their only authority, and were persecuted and martyred by the Roman Catholic Church.

Because these Christians rejected infant baptism, Calvinists and Lutherans joined Rome in persecuting, burning, and drowning them. And today's Calvinists ignore the role of these heroes of the faith in breaking the yoke of Rome. It is unconscionable for Calvinists to give the impression that the Reformation was the sole means of deliverance from Roman Catholicism, much less that Calvinism *was* the Reformation. E. H. Broadbent writes:

> In the report of the Council of the Archbishop of Cologne...to the Emperor Charles V [early sixteenth century], it is said that the Anabaptists call themselves "true Christians," that they desire community of goods, "which has been the way of Anabaptists for more than a thousand years, as the old histories and imperial laws testify."
>
> The Parliament at Speyer...stated that the..."Anabaptists" had already been condemned many hundreds of years ago and "by common law forbidden." For more than twelve centuries baptism in the way taught and described in the New Testament had been made an offense against the law, punishable by death.[5]

Even in Protestant Switzerland, Calvinism was only part of the Reformation. Bern forbade its pastors to preach on predestination or pronounce excommunications, two trademarks of Calvinism. In 1558, "the Calvinist pastors and professors of Lausanne were expelled from their homes [in] the controversies between the Bernese and the Genevan theologians."[6]

Calvin often complained of opposition and of the rumor that everyone in Geneva "kissed his slippers."[7] He defended himself with characteristic railings against Protestant critics such as Bolsec, Trolliet, and Castellion, calling them "dogs" and "serpents."[8] In February 1555, Calvin's supporters gained the absolute majority on the council. On May 16 there was an attempted uprising because Calvin had excluded certain libertarian civic officials from the Lord's Supper.[9] Leaders of the rebellion who fled to Bern were sentenced to death in absentia. Four who failed to escape were beheaded, quartered, and their body parts hung in strategic locations as a warning.[10] Evoking the phrase "henchmen of Satan," which he had used years earlier against Anabaptists, Calvin justified this barbarity by saying, "Those who do not correct evil when they can do so and their office requires it are guilty of it."[11]

From early 1554 until his death in 1564, "no one any longer dared oppose the Reformer openly."[12] Calvin's opponents had either been silenced, expelled, or had fled from Geneva, but opposition continued from without. Calvin did not emulate Christ by suffering insult without reviling in return (1 Peter 2:23) but outdid his opponents in the use of abusive language. In a sermon on October 16, 1555, he referred to his enemies as "all that filth and villainy...mad dogs who vomit their filth against the majesty of God and want to pervert all religion. Must they be spared?"[13] All knew the answer!

Today, non-Calvinists are accused of rejecting "the great Reformation creeds." But these creeds, such as the Westminister Confession, were forced on Independents, Baptists, and Brethren by a Calvinist state church.[14] Historian David Gay writes:

> The Puritans...set up the Westminister Assembly [to impose] upon England...one Established Church...with no dissent [allowed].... They were greatly disturbed by the rapid growth of the Baptists...hated them and...included no Baptists in their Assembly.... Even as godly a man as Samuel Rutherford [declared], "There is but one true Church and all who are outside it are heretics who must be destroyed...."

Baillie…complained of the Independents…they "will admit of none to be members of their congregations of whose true grace and regeneration they have no good evidences."

Baillie admitted that if this principle were applied to the Reformed Churches—Presbyterians in particular—only about one in forty members would remain!… [And] the Baptists…insisted on marks of regeneration *before they baptised and welcomed any into membership.…* The Westminster Assembly [established] a State Church which embraced all—the regenerate and unregenerate—to the extent that "nearly the whole population might be included in the Church, even though few of them might have an experimental knowledge of the gospel."(emphasis added)[15]

The inflated claims of today's Calvinists are not new. Benjamin Warfield long ago declared that "Calvinism is evangelicalism in its purest and only stable expression."[16] Loraine Boettner, leading critic of Roman Catholicism, long claimed that the Five Points of Calvinism present "what the Bible teaches concerning the way of salvation."[17] Such assertions could not remain unchallenged.

Beginning an intensive study of Calvinism, I noticed that nowhere in the many volumes of Calvin's writings and sermons does he tell us when, why, and how he, a Roman Catholic from the cradle, became a Christian. In fact, Calvin never documented an experience of being born again of the Holy Spirit through believing the gospel. He considered that new birth unnecessary for all who had been baptized into the Roman Catholic Church in infancy and had confirmed their baptism. Consequently, today's ex-Catholics would not accept Calvin into their ranks; and were Calvin alive today, he would reject them as he did the Anabaptists he banished from Geneva in 1537.[18]

Calvin considered himself to have been a Christian from the moment of his infant baptism:

At whatever time we are baptised, we are washed and purified once for the whole of life.... We must recall...our baptism...so as to feel certain and secure of the remission of sins.... It wipes and washes away all our defilements.... God in baptism promises remission of sins.... Let us therefore embrace it in faith."[19]

Calvin trusted in his baptism as proof that he was one of the elect,[20] and he denounced the Anabaptists who, like today's evangelical ex-Catholics, were baptized *after* believing the gospel:

Such in the present day are our Catabaptists, who deny that we are duly baptised, because we were baptised in the Papacy by wicked men and idolaters; hence they furiously insist on anabaptism. Against these absurdities we shall be sufficiently fortified if we reflect that...baptism is...of God, by whomsoever...administered.... Be it that those who baptised us were most ignorant of God and all piety...[baptism] certainly included in it the promise of forgiveness of sin....Thus it did not harm the Jews that they were circumcised by impure and apostate priests.[21]

Rejection of infant baptism was one of the two charges for which Michael Servetus (prosecuted by Calvin the lawyer) was burned at the stake.

Of Servetus, Calvin wrote, "One should not be content with simply killing such people, but should burn them cruelly."[22] Many historians agree that the "most hateful feature...of popery adhered to him [Calvin] through life—the *spirit of persecution*." (emphasis added)[23]

Calvin accused Servetus of "specious arguments" against infant baptism. But the latter's main objections (in spite of his other faults) were actually quite sound. Calvin's derisive response, purged of that unchristian "biting and mocking tone of ridicule that would never leave him,"[24] is condensed as follows:

> Servetus [argues] that no man becomes our brother unless by the Spirit of adoption...only conferred by the hearing of faith.... Who will presume...that [God] may not ingraft infants into Christ by some other secret method?... Again he objects, that infants cannot be...begotten by the word. But what I have said again and again I now repeat...God takes his own methods of regenerating...to consecrate infants to himself, and initiate them by a sacred symbol.... Circumcision was common to infants before they received understanding....
>
> Doubtless the design of Satan in assaulting paedobaptism with all his forces is to...efface, that attestation of divine grace...that from their birth they have been...acknowledged by him as his children.[25]

Here, as elsewhere, Calvin promotes the error of baptismal regeneration, of salvation by "some secret method...of regenerating" without "the hearing of faith [of the gospel]," the error that children of the elect are automatically children of God, and the error of equating circumcision with baptism: "The promise...is one in both [circumcision and baptism]...forgiveness of sins, and eternal life...i.e., regeneration.... Hence we may conclude, that...baptism has been substituted for circumcision, and performs the same office."[26]

Nothing more than this section of his *Institutes* is needed to disqualify Calvin as a sound teacher of Scripture and to call into question his entire concept of salvation. His sacramentalism mimics Roman Catholicism:

> We have...a spiritual promise given to the fathers in circumcision, similar to that which is given to us in baptism...the forgiveness of sins and the mortification of the flesh...baptism representing to us the very thing which circumcision signified to the Jews
>
> We confess, indeed, that the word of the Lord is the only seed of spiritual regeneration; but we deny...that, therefore, the power of God cannot regenerate infants.... But *faith*, they say, *cometh by hearing*, the use of which infants have not yet obtained....
>
> Let God, then, be demanded why he ordered circumcision to be performed on the bodies of infants.... By baptism we are ingrafted into the body of Christ (1 Corinthians xii.13) [Therefore] infants...are to be baptized.... See the violent onset which they make...on the bulwarks of our faith.... For...children...[of] Christians, as they are immediately on their birth received by God as heirs of the covenant, are also to be admitted to baptism.[27]

This same baptismal regeneration, contempt for believers' baptism, and blindness concerning the difference between circumcision and baptism is still found among Calvinists today. Under the heading, "Infant Baptism," *The New Geneva Study Bible* echoes Calvin:

> Historic Reformed theology contests the view that only adult, believer's baptism is true baptism, and it rejects the exclusion of believers' children from the visible community of faith.... Rather, the scriptural case for baptizing believers' infants rests on the parallel between Old Testament circumcision and New Testament baptism as signs and seals of the covenant of grace.[28]

On the contrary, baptism belongs to the New Covenant and is only upon confession of faith in Christ (Acts 8:37); circumcision was under the Old Covenant and without faith. Neither one saves the soul. Moreover, not only did circumcision *not* effect regeneration, forgiveness of sins, or salvation, but it couldn't even be a symbol thereof, since it was only for males. How could women be saved? And it was for *all* male descendants of Abraham. Even Ishmael, a rank unbeliever, was circumcised, as were millions of Jews who never had the faith of Abraham but rebelled against God and are now in hell.

If, as Calvin taught, circumcision effects "forgiveness of sins, and eternal life...i.e., regeneration,"[29] how could Jews who were circumcised be lost, and why did Paul cry out to God "for Israel...that they might be saved" (Romans 10:1)? Why was he so concerned for the salvation of circumcised Jews that he said, "I could wish that myself were accursed from Christ for my brethren, my kinsmen according to the flesh: who are Israelites" (Romans 9:3–4)? Clearly, circumcision did not provide "forgiveness of sins and eternal life." Nor does baptism! In chapter 10 we will see the connection between

Calvin's erroneous teaching concerning salvation of infants and his insistence that everyone must be regenerated before believing in Christ.

What then of Calvin's declaration that "baptism has been substituted for circumcision, and performs the same office"? [30] And what of the many pronouncements of judgment upon duly circumcised Jews? God speaking through Israel's own prophets declared repeatedly:

I sent unto you all my servants the prophets, rising early…saying, Oh, do not this abominable thing that I hate [burning incense unto other gods]. But they hearkened not…. Wherefore my fury and mine anger was poured forth. (Jeremiah 44:4–6)

God's condemnation of millions of Jews, in spite of their having been circumcised, refutes Calvin's unbiblical statements about circumcision. Moreover, if only the elect have salvation and if they can never be lost, and if circumcision brought salvation, how could millions of circumcised Jews be condemned?

Most of Calvin's "Reformation" errors came from the influence of Augustine. John Piper, one of America's leading Calvinists, writes:

The Standard text on theology that Calvin and Luther drank from was *Sentences* by Peter Lombard. Nine-tenths of this book consists of quotations from Augustine…. Luther was an Augustinian monk, and Calvin immersed himself in the writings of Augustine, as we can see from the increased use of Augustine's writings in each new edition of the *Institutes*…. Paradoxically, one of the most esteemed fathers of the Roman Catholic Church "gave us the Reformation."[31]

What, then, of the boast that Calvinism *is* the Reformation? In chapter 8 we will consider Augustine's influence upon John Calvin.

1. John Piper, *TULIP: The Pursuit of God's Glory in Salvation* (Minneapolis, Minn.: Bethlehem Baptist Church, 2000), back cover.
2. John H. Gerstner, *Wrongly Dividing the Word of Truth: A Critique of Dispensationalism* (Brentwood, Tenn.: Wolgemuth & Hyatt, 1991), 107.
3. Jay E. Adams, *Competent to Counsel* (Grand Rapids, Mich.: Baker, 1970), 70.
4. R. C. Sproul, gen. ed., *The New Geneva Study Bible* (Nashville, Tenn.: Thomas Nelson, 1995), Introduction, iv–v.
5. E. H. Broadbent, *The Pilgrim Church: Tracing the Pathway of the Forgotten Saints from Pentecost to the Twentieth Century* (Grand Rapids, Mich.: Gospel Folio, 1999), 172.
6. Francois Wendel, trans. Philip Mairet, *Calvin: Origin and Development of His Religious Thought* (Grand Rapids, Mich.: Baker, 2000), 100.
7. John Calvin, *Lettres françaises*, ed. J. Bonnet (Paris: C. Meyrueis, 1854), 1:351, 2:19.
8. Calvin, *Lettres,* 2:20, 229, passim.
9. Wendel, *Calvin*, 98–101; Bernard Cottret, *Calvin: A Biography* (Grand Rapids, Mich.: Eerdmans, 2000), 195–8.
10. Wendel, *Calvin*, 100; Cottret, *Calvin*, 198–200.
11. Cottret, *Calvin*, 200.
12. Amédée Roget, *L'Église et l'État a Genève du temps de Calvin. Étude d'histoire politico-ecclésiastique* (Geneva: J. Jullien, 1867), n.p.
13. Cottret, *Calvin*, 235.
14. G. T. Bettany, *A Popular History of the Reformation and Modern Protestantism* (London: Ward, Lock & Bowden, 1895), 416–22.
15. David Gay, *Battle for the Church, 1517–1644* (Brachus, 1997), 438–9, 451–3.
16. Benjamin B. Warfield, *Calvin and Augustine*, ed. Samuel G. Craig (Phillipsburg, N.J.: Presbyterian & Reformed, 1956), 497.
17. Loraine Boettner, *The Reformed Faith* (Phillipsburg, N.J.: Presbyterian & Reformed, 1983), 24.
18. Cottret, *Calvin*, 129.
19. John Calvin, *Institutes of the Christian Religion*, tr. Henry Beveridge (Grand Rapids, Mich.: Eerdmans), 1998, IV: xv, 3, 17.
20. Calvin, *Institutes,* IV: xv, 1–6; xvi, 24, passim.

21. Ibid., IV: xv, 16.
22. Ronald H. Bainton, *Michel Servet, hérétique et martyr* (Geneva: Droz, 1953), 152–3; letter of 26 February 1533, now lost.
23. William Jones, *The History of the Christian Church*, 5th ed. (Church History Research & Archives, 1983), 2: 238.
24. Cottret, *Calvin*, 78.
25. Calvin, *Institutes,* IV: xvi, 31.
26. Ibid., IV: xvi, 4.
27. Ibid, IV: iii–xvi, viii, x, xvii–xxxii, 22.
28. Sproul, gen. ed., *New Geneva Study Bible,* 38.
29. Calvin, *Institutes,* IV: xvi, 4.
30. Ibid.
31. John Piper, *The Legacy of Sovereign Joy: God's Triumphant Grace in the Lives of Augustine, Luther, and Calvin* (Wheaton, Ill.: Crossway 2000), 24–5.

Part I
{ Calvinism Affirmed }

- Chapter One -

GOD'S ETERNAL DECREE

by James White

God is all-sufficient, and all life, glory, goodness and blessedness are found in Him and in Him alone. He does not stand in need of any of the creatures that He has made, nor does He derive any part of His glory from them. On the contrary, He manifests His own glory in and by them. He is the fountain-head of all being, and the origin, channel and end of all things. Over all His creatures His is sovereign. He uses them as He pleases, and does for them or to them all that He wills. His sight penetrates to the heart of all things. His knowledge is infinite and infallible. No single thing is to Him at risk or uncertain, for He is not dependent upon created things. In all His decisions, doings and demands He is most holy. Angels and men owe to Him as their creator all worship, service and obedience, and whatever else He may require at their hands.[1]

Thus the 1689 Baptist Confession of Faith describes the great foundational truths of the biblical revelation of God. God is the Creator, and therefore He is King over all that He has made. The King rules over His creation. This is the divine truth of God's sovereignty: His right to rule over what He has made. Those who love their king and are subject to Him find His sovereignty a great comfort and delight. Those who are in rebellion against Him fight and chafe against this divine truth. Much can be determined concerning our true subjection to God by asking if, in fact, we love God as He has revealed Himself to be, the divine ruler over all things, or whether we seek to "edit" Him down to a more "manageable" and "manlike" deity.

THE FREE AND PROPER KINGSHIP OF GOD

Modern men struggle with the biblical teaching of God's sovereignty. One of the reasons may have to do with the fact that we do not have many true kings today. Instead, many transfer their ideas of democracy to God's rule, thinking that God is limited in what He can do by what man "agrees" to allow by his "free will." The truth is that the Bible speaks much of free will—God's free will, that is, not man's. The utter freedom of God to do with His creation as He sees fit, not as His creatures see fit, is a constant theme. God's purpose rules over all, not just in the "big things" but in all things. This is the basis of the Christian doctrine of God's eternal decree: that in creating all that exists, God does so for a purpose, that being His own glorification. His decree is *personal* in that it is focused upon His own intent and purpose.[2] The biblical testimony speaks for itself:

Our God is in the heavens;
He does whatever He pleases. (Psalm 115:3)

Whatever the LORD pleases, He does,

In heaven and in earth, in the seas and in all deeps. (Psalm 135:6)

The lot is cast into the lap,

But its every decision is from the LORD. (Proverbs 16:33)

Many plans are in a man's heart,

But the counsel of the LORD will stand. (Proverbs 19:21)

Man's steps are ordained by the LORD,

How then can man understand his way? (Proverbs 20:24)

The king's heart is like channels of water in the hand of the LORD;

He turns it wherever He wishes. (Proverbs 21:1)

"Since his days are determined,

The number of his months is with You;

And his limits You have set so that he cannot pass." (Job 14:5)

These passages from the Psalter and the Wisdom Literature show us how *basic* this truth is for the child of God. And when God engages in a demonstration of the foolishness of idolatry by proving He is the only true God, His sovereignty over creation comes out with force:

"It is I who have declared and saved and proclaimed,

And there was no strange god among you;

So you are My witnesses," declares the LORD,

"And I am God.

Even from eternity I am He,

And there is none who can deliver out of My hand;

I act and who can reverse it?" (Isaiah 43:12–13)

The One forming light and creating darkness,

Causing well-being and creating calamity;

I am the LORD who does all these. (Isaiah 45:7)3

"Declaring the end from the beginning,

And from ancient times things which have not been done,

Saying, 'My purpose will be established,

And I will accomplish all My good pleasure.'" (Isaiah 46:10)

Who is there who speaks and it comes to pass,

Unless the LORD has commanded it?

Is it not from the mouth of the Most High

That both good and ill go forth? (Lamentations 3:37–38)

Space prohibits further testimony, though the list of such passages goes on almost indefinitely. The complete freedom of God, combined with God's role as the divine King who rules over His creation, provide the irrefutable foundation of God's sovereign decree.

THE COUNSEL OF HIS WILL

When Paul extolled the grace of God in salvation in the opening of his letter to the Ephesians, he included these words in his discussion of God's predestination of a specific, elect people unto salvation: "We have obtained an inheritance, having been predestined according to His purpose who works all things after the counsel of His will." (Ephesians 1:11)

God's work of salvation in Jesus Christ is grounded in the truth that He is sovereign over all things. The certainty of the inheritance that is ours in Christ is based upon the fact that God's purpose will never fail, and His purpose is grounded in the more basic truth that He "works all things after the counsel of His will." This is the positive way of stating what Paul said in Romans 9:11 ("So that God's purpose according to His choice would stand, not because of works but because of Him who calls") and 2 Timothy 1:9 ("[He] has saved us and called us with a holy calling, not according to our works, but according to His own purpose and grace which was granted us in Christ Jesus from all eternity").

God's purpose, God's will, is the basis upon which God acts. He works *all things* in accordance with the counsel of His will. Man's will cannot thwart or destroy His purpose, and this truth is stated here in Ephesians in the context of salvation itself. In light of the context, the "all things" cannot be limited to the physical creation but must include the work of salvation itself. The inheritance, predestination, and all that is associated with it in the preceding verses, must be included in the "all things" that are done in accordance with God's purpose. *The very foundation upon which the certainty of the gospel rests is the divine attribute of sovereignty and active rulership over the creation.* Without this truth, one is left with the religions of men: God offers, God tries, but in the final analysis, men dispose.

Does the King Reign over the Sons of Men?

Many are willing to confess God's sovereign rule over such things as earth-quakes, floods, or other "acts of God." Yet the fortress of man's pride, his "free will," is strictly off-limits. But does the Bible provide any basis for lim-iting God's sovereignty and leaving man in a position of autonomy, with God merely "foreseeing" what His free-willed creature will do? It certainly does not. Instead, we are provided with numerous examples of God accom-plishing His will despite not only the individual "freewill" decisions of men but also the combined "freewill" decisions of entire nations. The Psalmist was speaking the truth when he said:

> The LORD nullifies the counsel of the nations;
> He frustrates the plans of the peoples.
> The counsel of the LORD stands forever,
> The plans of His heart from generation to generation.
> (Psalm 33:10–11)

By repeating the same phrases, the Scriptures communicate a basic truth. As Sproul has put it, "God is free. I am free. If my freedom runs up against God's freedom, I lose. His freedom restricts mine; my freedom does not restrict his."[4] When the counsel of the nations is opposed to God's counsel, God's counsel stands forever, and the nations' counsel is nullified. This truth extends to the most personal level, the actions of men and women. In fact, it extends to the very commission of sin itself. Remember what God said to Abimelech regarding Abraham's wife, Sarah:

God said to him in the dream, "Yes, I know that in the integrity of your heart you have done this, and I also kept you from sinning against Me; therefore I did not let you touch her." (Genesis 20:6)

God revealed to Abimelech that He had kept him from sinning. Consider what this means. God prevented Abimelech from committing an act of sin. If God could keep him from sinning in this instance, could He not have kept him from sinning in any other given instance? Of course. And yet, He had not done so. Why? He had a purpose in restraining Abimelech in this instance. And if He has a purpose in this instance, does He not have a purpose in all instances, with each and every person? Surely.

God could, if He chose, restrain all evil this very moment. Indeed, I believe that God is preventing the expression of the *vast majority* of evil that fills the hearts of men. This "common grace" makes it possible for us to live our lives and preach the gospel, for if God were to allow the evil that fills the hearts of men to come to free and unrestrained expression, this world would self-destruct in a fireball of sinful violence. But if God does *not* restrain any particular act of evil, does it not inevitably follow that He has a purpose in it? And does this not mean that God's eternal decree, by which He acts in this world, includes the existence of evil for a purpose, one that leads to God's glorification through the work of Jesus Christ in redeeming a people unto Himself?

This is not speculation, but a certain biblical fact based on more than Genesis 20:6. Consider this amazing promise from God's law:

I will drive out nations before you and enlarge your borders, and no man shall covet your land when you go up three times a year to appear before the LORD your God. (Exodus 34:24)

All the men of Israel were to go up to appear before the Lord. But how could this be, when Israel was surrounded by enemies? If the pagan neighbors across the river saw the men leaving, would they not swoop down and take advantage of the situation? God promised that if Israel would be faithful in keeping His law, no one would even *covet* their land while they were gone. Surely this means that God has the power to stop even the internal sinful desire of covetousness. So why does God not stop all coveting, since it is obviously in His power to do so? The only answer is that He has a purpose in what He allows. And surely one must immediately ask the obvious question: What about the "free will" of the pagans that had been coveting the land, but stopped coveting it when the faithful Israelites left to go appear before the Lord? Was this not a "violation" of their "free will"? Such passages force us to recognize the difference between the biblical concept of man's creaturely will and the philosophical concept of autonomy that is held in the majority of man's religions, in Roman Catholicism, and in most non-Reformed Protestant theologies.

"COMPATIBILISM"

If, as we have seen, the Bible teaches the absolute sovereignty of God over His creation and that He has a purpose He is accomplishing in all that happens as part of His divine decree, what of the obvious fact that man makes choices and God holds him accountable for them? Despite the constant misrepresentation of the opponents of God's sovereignty, to fully appreciate the biblical evidence is to recognize that God's decree does not make Him the author of sin. As the 1689 Confession says:

From all eternity God decreed all that should happen in time, and this He did freely and unalterably, consulting only His own wise and holy will. Yet in so doing He does not become in any sense the author of sin, nor does He share responsibility for sin with sinners. Neither, by reason of His decree, is the will of any creature whom He has made violated; nor is the free working of second causes put aside; rather it is established.[5]

The biblical relationship of God's sovereign decree to the creaturely will of man has been aptly called "compatibilism," the belief that these two things are not contradictory but compatible with one another, when viewed properly. This truth is presented in numerous passages of Scripture, such as Genesis 50:20, where Joseph, in the presence of his brothers, refers back to their betrayal of him: "As for you, you meant evil against me, but God meant it for good in order to bring about this present result, to preserve many people alive."

One sinful action (the betrayal and sale of Joseph into slavery) is in view: Joseph's brothers meant their actions for evil. But in direct parallel, God meant the same action for good. Due to the intention of the hearts of Joseph's brothers, the action in the human realm was evil. The very same action as part of God's eternal decree was meant for good, for by it God brought about His purpose and plan. One action, two intentions, compatible in all things. Joseph's brothers were accountable for their intentions; God is to be glorified for His.

The longest, clearest presentation of compatibilism is found in God's use of Assyria as an instrument of judgment on the rebellious people of Israel:

"Woe to Assyria, the rod of My anger

And the staff in whose hands is My indignation,

I send it against a godless nation

And commission it against the people of My fury

To capture booty and to seize plunder,

And to trample them down like mud in the streets.

Yet it does not so intend,

Nor does it plan so in its heart,

But rather it is its purpose to destroy

And to cut off many nations."...

So it will be that when the Lord has completed all His work on

Mount Zion and on Jerusalem, He will say, "I will punish the fruit

of the arrogant heart of the king of Assyria and the pomp of his

haughtiness." (Isaiah 10:5–7, 12)

In one passage we have God's holy intention of judging His people through the means of Assyria—yet God holds Assyria accountable for her sinful attitudes in being so used! God judges them on the basis of their *intentions*, and since they come against Israel with a haughty attitude that does not recognize God's power and authority, they too are judged. This is compatibilism with clarity: God uses the sinful actions of the Assyrians for the good purpose of judging His people, and yet He judges the Assyrians for their sinful intentions. God's action in His sovereignty is perfectly compatible with the responsible, and culpable, actions of sinful men.

By far the greatest example of compatibilism is found in the sacrifice of the Lord Jesus Christ. The early church confessed:

Truly in this city there were gathered together against Your holy servant Jesus, whom You anointed, both Herod and Pontius Pilate, along with the Gentiles and the peoples of Israel, to do whatever Your hand and Your purpose predestined to occur. (Acts 4:27–28)

One action, the great sacrifice of the Son of God, is in view. Herod, Pontius Pilate, the Gentiles, and the Jews were all gathered together against Jesus. Their actions were obviously sinful. Their intentions were evil. Yet, the Word of God is clear: They did what they did because God's hand and purpose *predestined* it to take place. Were they accountable for their intentions and desires? Of course. But was the certainty of the Cross and the sacrifice of Christ ever dependent upon man's will? Never. It happened according to the predestined plan of God and is therefore completely to His honor and glory. One action, part of the divine decree, sinful on the part of the intentions of the men involved, and yet fully in harmony with the holy purpose of God, to His glory and praise. Man's will, God's sovereign decree, compatible with one another. This is the biblical teaching.

CONCLUSION

The truth of God's eternal decree flows from the fact that God is the Creator of all things and that everything He does (including the act of creation) is done for a purpose. In the final analysis, all things lead to the glorification of God. This would not be true if, in fact, God does not sovereignly reign over His creation, working all things in accordance with His will. As we will see, this divine truth forms the necessary basis for the truth of salvation by grace alone through faith alone in Christ alone.

1. *A Faith to Confess: The Baptist Confession of 1689 Rewritten in Modern English* (New York: Carey Publications, 1997), 2:2.
2. Hence the error of identifying God's eternal decree with "fatalistic determinism," which, by nature, is impersonal.
3. *Well-being* is the Hebrew term *shalom*, and *calamity* is the term *rah*, often translated as "evil." The combination of the two terms communicates the same truth as Ephesians 1:11: Whatever takes place does so for a purpose, for it is according to God's decree.
4. R. C. Sproul, *Chosen by God* (Chicago: Tyndale, 1986), 43.
5. *A Faith to Confess: The Baptist Confession of 1689 Rewritten in Modern English*, 3:1.

Response, by Dave Hunt

White begins his treatise with a ringing tribute to God's sovereignty. The Calvinist knows little else. John MacArthur Jr. calls Calvinism "the branch of evangelicalism most strongly committed to the sovereignty of God."[1] Another Calvinist writes, "The all-out emphasis on the almighty sovereignty of Jehovah God is the truth and beauty of Calvinism."[2] Another declares, "Only the Calvinist...recognizes God's absolute sovereignty."[3]

White quotes the 1689 Baptist Confession of Faith in praise of God's sovereignty. But where is God's love? Not once in the nearly thirteen hundred pages of his *Institutes* does Calvin extol God's love for mankind. This one-sided emphasis reveals Calvinism's primary defect: the unbiblical limitations it places upon God's most glorious attribute. How could God, who *is* love, damn billions He could save? That isn't explained. Something is radically amiss at the very foundation of this unbiblical doctrine.

Calvinists exult in a "sovereignty" that has chosen a select group alone to salvation and predestined the rest of mankind to eternal torment. But doubts of whether one is among the elect plague even leading Calvinists. White seems confident that he at least is one of the elect, and he glories in his own salvation. Missing is Paul's concern for the lost (Romans 9:1–3).

White says that the litmus test of one's "true subjection to God [is] if, in fact, we love God as He has revealed Himself to be, the divine ruler over all things." In fact, it is not God's sovereign power or rulership but His love that moves us to love Him: "We love him, because he first loved us" (1 John 4:19).

God commands all mankind to love Him. But how could that be required of those He doesn't love and has predestined to eternal torment? Such an idea is both unbiblical and repugnant to the conscience. If all men are required to love God, and if we can only love Him because He first loved us, God must love all men.

Love is not only an *attribute* of God but also the very essence of His being: "God is love" (1 John 4:8). The word *love* occurs 310 times in Scripture, while the mercy and compassion flowing from His love are mentioned hundreds of times. In stark contrast, the sovereignty that so rejoices the Calvinist, though a great truth, is not one of God's attributes. The word *sovereignty* isn't even found in Scripture.

Of course, God created and is the supreme ruler of His universe. And the fact that He effects His will in spite of man's proud ambitions and rebellion is a precious truth often declared. Nowhere in Scripture, however, do we find Calvinism's extreme sovereignty, which allows man no freedom of choice. That man is able to rebel and to disobey God's commands in spite of God's supremacy is taught repeatedly in Scripture. God's sovereignty is fully exercised despite man's free will, but never in denial of it.

This overemphasis upon God's sovereignty to the denial of man's will not only makes God the author of sin but also creates numerous additional contradictions and redundancies. The Baptist Confession exults that God's "sight penetrates to the heart of all things." Penetrates to the heart of what He Himself *causes*? What is the point?

White accuses non-Calvinists of editing God down "to a more 'manageable' and 'manlike' deity." On the contrary, our God-given consciences recognize that Calvinism libels the God of Scripture by denying His love for all.

MacArthur claims that "the fact that God…pleads with sinners to repent—proves His love toward them."[4] Only a Calvinist could believe that God loves those He has predestined to eternal suffering! And wouldn't it be mockery for God to plead with them to repent when He withholds from them the grace to do so?

There is neither a biblical nor rational reason why God in His sovereignty could not give to all mankind the power of choice. Nor does sovereignty prevent God from loving all and providing salvation for all who choose to receive it, as the Bible declares. Yet Calvinists reject this clear teaching of Scripture.

White derides man's free will as that by which "God is limited in what He can do." On the contrary, God sovereignly endued man with a free will so that he could love God and his fellows from his heart. Man's will is no threat to God's sovereignty. Instead, it brings greater glory to God, who wins the love and praise of those who are free to choose otherwise.

White quotes several Scriptures declaring that God does "whatever He pleases" (Psalm 115:3) and that "the counsel of the LORD will stand" (Proverbs 19:21). None of them, however, eliminates human choice or denies that all men can either receive Christ or reject Him. That the Lord can turn the king's heart "wherever He wishes" (Proverbs 21:1) does not say that He causes the king's every thought, word, and deed. God's sovereignty is more glorious in ruling over men with free will than over puppets with no choice.

If God, as Calvinism teaches, foreordained every thought, word, and deed of mankind, He is the instigator and perpetrator of evil, His commands and judgment are a pretense, and man is blameless. If God *causes* all, how can He be righteous and man guilty of the wickedness God causes him to do? In fact, God doesn't even tempt anyone to sin (James 1:13–14).

White gives the example of God preventing Abimelech from sinning. But this special case offers no proof that God ever *caused* anyone to sin, much less that He is the cause of all sin. Furthermore, the pagan king's heart was innocent in that instance. He sincerely thought that Sarah was Abraham's sister and acted "in the integrity of [his] heart." As soon as he knew the facts, he gave Sarah back to Abraham. Yet, White concludes that God could just as well have kept Abimelech from *ever* sinning and that He could do the same for everyone. In fact, He has done it for no one, "for all have sinned" (Romans 3:23). Abimelech's heart was not *always* innocent (Jeremiah 17:9). Nor does this incident teach that God could change the heart that is willfully set on sin, much less that He could do so for entire nations, as White erroneously concludes in his eisegesis.

White claims that God's sovereignty would be limited if man were free to choose salvation for himself. Then he contradicts himself by quoting Sproul: "God is free. I am free…. His freedom restricts mine; my freedom does not restrict his." Which is it?

In further contradiction, White says that as proof that man is not free, "we are provided with numerous examples of God accomplishing His will despite…the individual 'freewill' decisions of men." As we've just seen, the example he offers of Abimelech does not at all prove that man is not free to choose. Furthermore, for God to effect His will in spite of man's free choice is far more glorifying to Him and His sovereignty than if He would only be able to do so by denying man any freedom to choose.

The example White then gives of God preventing Israel's neighbors from attacking her while the males were worshiping in Jerusalem is no better. There is no suggestion that God changed hearts so that Israel's enemies loved her and desired to bless her. To prevent the actual deed but leave hearts unchanged does not prevent sin. For God to "restrain all evil" from being committed would not, as White erroneously contends, prevent the sinful desire in the heart. Nor is this the "'violation' of the 'free will'" that White suggests. The will of those nations was not changed from evil to good; they were simply restrained from fulfilling their evil intent.

Such attempts to justify Calvinism only increase the reproach it lays on God. We have quoted leading Calvinists to the effect that God is the cause of the evil in each heart. If so, in preventing evil, wouldn't God be restraining Himself? What is the point, and how would that bring Him glory? The sovereignty White elevates above all else turns out to rule over a theater of meaningless marionettes.

White then insists that God's decreeing sin "does not make Him the author of sin." As one writer insisted in a letter to me, "Calvinists indeed teach that God foreordains sin, that God decrees sin, that God is the cause of sin, but they also teach that this does not make God the author of sin."[5] My reply was simple:

Webster's *New Universal Unabridged Dictionary* defines author as "one who produces, creates, or brings into being; the beginner, creator, or first mover of anything." By this definition, Calvinism's God is unquestionably the author of sin! Can you explain how God can foreordain, decree, and cause sin without being its author? Calvinists cannot escape the logical consequences of their teaching by simply denying it to be so.[6]

White attempts to avoid the embarrassment of God causing sin by introducing what he calls "compatibilism" through the example of Joseph's brothers selling him into Egypt: "The action was evil [but] as part of God's eternal decree was meant for good." There is no escaping Calvinism's teaching that by "God's eternal decree" He *caused* the evil in the brethren's hearts and *caused* them to execute their evil deeds. So compatibilism is no escape.

Furthermore, the Bible does not say that God *decreed* that Joseph's brothers would hate him, desire to kill him, sell him into Egypt, and then lie to their father. It is clear that their evil intent came from jealous hearts. God foreknew their hearts and restrained and channeled their wicked desire to accomplish His will. This is all the text implies. White is guilty of reading into it a Calvinist meaning that isn't there.

Next, White offers the example of God using Assyria to discipline Israel. Absolutely. But the passage doesn't say that God *caused* Assyria to have this wicked desire. It says only that He foresaw, allowed, and used the Assyrians' wicked intention. The evil came from their own hearts, but God restrained it and used it for His purposes.

White's next example is Christ's crucifixion. Once again he goes beyond the text, which says only that God foreknew the evil in everyone's hearts and the actions they would take and that He used them to fulfill His preordained purpose. It does not say that God decreed or caused the evil intentions and actions of Pilate and Christ's crucifiers.

White says that God "has a purpose in what He allows." Of course—but *allows?* Isn't that a contradiction of Calvinism's claim that God decrees and causes everything that happens? Does He *allow* what He decreed? Such slips of the pen and tongue are difficult to avoid, given the contradictory nature of Calvinism. He *allows* man to act on his own initiative.

The intention of the heart and deeds of men are not caused by God but are under His control and used to fulfill His will.

White concludes this treatise on sovereignty with the statement that God works "all things in accordance with His will." In fact, Paul says, the *counsel* of his will (Ephesians 1:11). There is a difference between God's will and the *counsel* of His will. Sin is not His will, but He *allows* it. It makes no sense that He would *allow* what He has *caused*. The only reason He *allows* sin is to let man exercise freedom of choice, without which we could not love God or one another. Otherwise, *allows* is meaningless.

1. John MacArthur Jr., *The Love of God* (Dallas: Word, 1996), 17.
2. David J. Engelsma, *Hyper-Calvinism and the Call of the Gospel* (Reformed Free Publishing Association, 1980), 133.
3. Leonard J. Coppes, *Are Five Points Enough? The Ten Points of Calvinism* (Denver, Colo.: self-published, 1980), 15.
4. MacArthur, *Love of God*, 15.
5. *Berean Call*, June 2002, Q&A section.
6. Ibid.

Defense, by James White

At this point in the discussion the two sides have made their major presentations. In fact, the reader might find it useful to read this discussion "horizontally"; that is, read the fourteen "opening statements" and the initial replies to them first, and then go back to pick up the shorter presentations. The major issues are addressed as fully as they are going to be in the first two sections of each chapter unit. One cannot develop any serious points in only a few paragraphs; hence, the final presentations, on my part at any rate, will be focused upon correcting factual errors, misrepresentations, and the like.

The reader should also note if either side simply repeats assertions already addressed. In chapter 9, for example, I address the issue of God's love fully in my rebuttal section. In a serious debate, Mr. Hunt's references to the love of God *after* that portion should take into consideration all relevant and sound argumentation contained therein.[1] Any references that do not, in fact, respond to the information in the rebuttal but simply repeat the same arguments without taking into consideration facts that have been properly introduced in response, should be dismissed as refuted and irrelevant.

In Hunt's response to my presentation of God's sovereignty over creation, we find three examples of ad hominem argumentation within the first three paragraphs. He raises issues far outside the subject of the presentation to which he is supposed to be responding, and he completely misrepresents the position he is arguing against. He misrepresents the Reformed position by stating that those who will justly experience the wrath of God in eternity do so "without any choice." Every single person thusly punished *chose* to sin freely, without external compulsion; they *chose* their rebellion and loved their sin, and if they were given the choice in eternity to either love God completely or return to punishment, every one of them would march right back into punishment.

Focusing only on the relevant statements, we note that Hunt does not seem to be familiar with the term *compatibilism,* the oft-used description of how the decree of God interfaces with the will of man. The reader is encouraged to reread the discussion of Genesis 50:20, Isaiah 10, and Acts 4:27–28, and then compare Hunt's replies. The fact that God's intentions are good and holy in saving many alive in the selling of Joseph into slavery is completely ignored; and even though the biblical text says that God *intended* the action in order to save many lives, Hunt is forced to deny the plain meaning of the words, *without offering any basis in the text for doing so.* He simply says, "The Bible does not say that God *decreed* that Joseph's brothers...sell him into Egypt." Hunt is right that the evil intent came from their hearts, but he is wrong to deny the clear role the Bible assigns to God's intentions, God's purposes. How can God be glorified for saving the lives of His people through Joseph's work in Egypt if it were not a part of His plan, a part of His decree? Hunt does not tell us.

One of the many examples of eisegesis is found in these comments on Acts 4:27–28:

Once again he goes beyond the text, which says only that God foreknew the evil in everyone's hearts and the actions they would take and that He used them to fulfill His preordained purpose. It does not say that God decreed or caused the evil intentions and actions of Pilate and Christ's crucifiers.

This is a nonresponse. Where does *foreknew* appear in the text? Luke's words are "to do whatever Your hand and Your purpose predestined to occur"(Acts 4:28). What occurred was the greatest sinful act of all human history. It was predestined to happen. God's intentions were good; men's were evil. God's decree took place; man is properly accountable. Compatibilism is demonstrated from Scripture; the tradition of human autonomy is illustrated in Hunt's response. When one side is constantly reduced to "it doesn't say that," instead of "the text positively asserts this," the specter of tradition-trumping exegesis of the text is close at hand.

Indeed, the greatest problem here is that Hunt did not choose to present a positive defense of his own beliefs. We surely know what he does *not* believe and what he thinks the text *cannot possibly mean*, but we cannot test his position for consistency because he has not deemed it necessary to offer it. Is he saying that man's actions determine the future and that God merely knows what will happen? So it just "happened" to turn out for the best? Did God merely cast the cosmic dice and roll snake eyes? If God created this universe, knowing what would happen, as Hunt seems to believe (he constantly speaks of God's foreknowledge but does not give us a ground upon which to understand how God has such knowledge), how is He not responsible for that creation and the events that take place in time? And truly, if He created knowing what would happen, but has no decree, no purpose, how is that *better* than saying that He has a purpose in all things?

Hunt's objections to the sovereignty of God over all things seem to be just as relevant against his own assertions.

"The LORD has made everything for its own purpose, even the wicked for the day of evil" (Proverbs 16:4). Men may not like the truth that God is the potter, we the clay, and that He has a purpose for all He has done, but it is surely the testimony of Scripture itself. *Soli Deo Gloria!*

---

1. In this very response, Mr. Hunt says that "Calvinism libels the God of Scripture by denying His love for all." The recognition that God has the ability to differentiate in the kinds of love He shows, just as man can, fully refutes this objection. If Hunt repeats this objection without recognizing that it has been refuted, the reader can know that no reply will be forthcoming from him.

J. WHITE

Final Remarks, by Dave Hunt

White writes, "Those who love their king…find His sovereignty a great comfort." What comfort have those whom the "king" has "pleasure to doom…to destruction"?[1] Do Calvinists care? How could they? He claims that "God could…restrain all evil." Why doesn't He? Any kind person would if he could. Calvinism repudiates the compassion of God and man.

Eze 33:11 as I Live saith the Lord

For believing that God desires "all men to be saved" (1 Timothy 2:4), I'm accused of denying His freedom "to do with His creation as He sees fit." Of course, God "does whatever He pleases" (Psalm 115:3), but it doesn't please Him to damn *anyone*.

White denies that Calvinism assigns to hell multitudes who are without any choice. Those predestined to hell have a choice? He says they "chose to sin freely." But "the sinner's will is…free in only…the direction of evil"[2]; "every unsaved person is…free to go…only…down"[3]; "men do nothing save…what [God] decreed[4]…even sin"[5]; and "there aren't any…free decisions."[6]

I believe that God offers salvation to all. White says I deny "the freedom of God in election and regeneration." No, Calvinism denies God's freedom by limiting those to whom He can offer salvation. But God wants "the wicked [to] turn from his way and live" (Ezekiel 33:11).

"The Father loves the human race[7]…[but] the elect alone are they whose eyes God opens."[8] *What love is this?* White argues that free will gives man "the final say." No, God makes the rules; man just responds. White says the belief that God is obligated "to grant 'chances'" is "the fatal flaw of the anti-Reformed polemic." God is not obligated—but He *loves* all.

As for my "vague allegation of a connection" between Augustine and Catholicism, Warfield called him "the founder of Roman Catholicism,"[9] and Piper calls him "one of the most esteemed fathers of the Roman Catholic Church."[10] White says that the lives of Calvin and Augustine are "irrelevant to the real issue," but lives reflect doctrine (2 Timothy 3:10). Every man will be judged by his works (Matthew 16:27; 1 Corinthians 3:13; James 2:17–20).

1. John Calvin, *Institutes of the Christian Religion*, tr. Henry Beveridge (Grand Rapids, Mich.: Eerdmans, 1998), III: xxiii, 1.
2. Arthur W. Pink, *The Sovereignty of God* (Grand Rapids, Mich.: Baker, 1986), 135.
3. E. Best, *Free Grace Versus Free Will* (Houston, Tex.: W. E. Best Books Missionary Trust, 1977), 20.
4. Calvin, *Institutes*, I: xviii, 1.
5. Edwin H. Palmer, *The Five Points of Calvinism* (Grand Rapids, Mich.: Baker, 1999), 24–5, 82, 97–100, 116.
6. John Piper and Pastoral Staff, *TULIP: What We Believe about the Five Points of Calvinism* (Minneapolis, Minn.: Desiring God Ministries, 1997), 22.
7. John Calvin, trans. William Pringle, *Commentary on a Harmony of the Evangelists* (Grand Rapids, Mich.: Baker, 1979), 123; cited with approval in John MacArthur Jr., *The Love of God* (Dallas: Word, 1996), 17.
8. Ibid., 125; cited in MacArthur, *Love of God*, 18.
9. Benjamin B. Warfield, *Calvin and Augustine*, ed. Samuel G. Craig (Phillipsburg, N.J.: Presbyterian & Reformed, 1956), 313.
10. John Piper, *The Legacy of Sovereign Joy: God's Triumphant Grace in the Lives of Augustine, Luther, and Calvin* (Wheaton, Ill.: Crossway 2000), 24–5.

D. HUNT

Final Remarks, by James White

M r. Hunt writes, "God could…restrain all evil." Why doesn't He? Any kind person would if he could. Calvinism repudiates the compassion of God and man." We have seen clear biblical teaching that God does in fact restrain evil (Genesis 20:6), yet He does not restrain all evil, and He has a purpose in the evil that is a part of His decree (Genesis 50:20; Acts 4:27–28).

So what is Mr. Hunt saying? That God *cannot* restrain the evil of man? Or that He *will not*? We are not told. If He cannot, He was foolish in creating man; if He will not and has no eternal decree to give purpose to evil, He is careless and monstrous. While God says that men are like "grasshoppers" before Him (Isaiah 40:22), in Mr. Hunt's traditions, man's will controls God's desires, even to the point of controlling the greatest work of God, that of creating a special people in Christ Jesus.

Spurgeon summed up this section of our debate long ago:

There is no attribute of God more comforting to His children than the doctrine of Divine Sovereignty. Under the most adverse circumstances, in the most severe troubles, they believe that Sovereignty hath ordained their afflictions, that Sovereignty overrules them, and that Sovereignty will sanctify them all. There is nothing for which the children of God ought more earnestly to contend than the dominion of their Master over all creation—the kingship of God over all the works of His own hands—the throne of God, and His right to sit upon that throne.

On the other hand, there is no doctrine more hated by worldlings, no truth of which they have made such a football, as; the great, stupendous, but yet most certain doctrine of the Sovereignty of the infinite Jehovah. Men will allow God to be everywhere except upon His throne. They will allow Him to be in His workshop to fashion worlds and to make stars. They will allow Him to be in His almonry to dispense His alms and bestow His bounties. They will allow Him to sustain the earth and bear up the pillars thereof, or light the lamps of Heaven, or rule the waves of the ever-moving ocean; but when God ascends His throne, His creatures then gnash their teeth; and when we proclaim an *enthroned God,* and His right to do as He wills with His own, to dispose of His creatures as He thinks well, without consulting them in the matter, then it is that we are hissed and execrated, and then it is that men turn a deaf ear to us, for God on His throne is not the God they love. They love Him anywhere better than they do when He sits with His scepter in His hand and His crown upon His head. But it is God upon the throne that we love to preach. It is God upon His throne whom we trust.[1]

---

1. Charles H. Spurgeon, "Divine Sovereignty," sermon preached 4 May 1856.

J. WHITE

MAN'S INABILITY

by James White

The Bible presents a strong contrast between God *who is able* to save, and to save perfectly through Jesus Christ (Hebrews 7:25), and man, who is *unable* to make even the first move toward God due to the corruption of his nature, his slavery to sin, and his hatred of God. But since the biblical teaching is so contrary to the inclinations of man, it is far more common to hear the traditions of men, which extol man's ability and insist that though he is dead in transgressions, a slave to sin, and an enemy of God, he is able by the exercise of his will to frustrate the intentions of the triune God in saving him. The Father may decree his salvation, the Son may die to obtain his redemption, and the Spirit may exercise His divine power in bringing conviction and enlightenment, but all of this, tradition tells us, is not enough to bring about salvation unless the will of the creature cooperates. This is called "synergism," the belief that God's grace cannot save unless joined in the effort by the will of man. Over against this tradition of men, the Bible proclaims the all-sufficiency of God's grace and perfect power in what is called "monergism," the belief that His is fully able to save without the aid of His creatures.

We have already seen the first element of the Bible's teaching of monergism in the absolute freedom of God. The second divine truth that leads inexorably to the truth of monergism is the slavery of man to sin: Outside of the miracle of divine grace changing a God-hater into a God-lover, no man would ever be saved. The 1689 London Confession summarizes the Bible's teaching in these words:

1. In the natural order God has endued man's will with liberty and the power to act upon choice, so that it is neither forced from without, nor by any necessity arising from within itself, compelled to do good or evil.

2. In his state of innocency man had freedom and power to will and to do what was good and acceptable to God. Yet, being unstable, it was possible for him to fall from his uprightness.

3. As the consequence of his fall into a state of sin, man has lost all ability to will the performance of any of those works, spiritually good, that accompany salvation. As a natural (unspiritual) man he is dead in sin and altogether opposed to what is good. Hence he is not able, by any strength of his own, to turn himself to God, or even to prepare himself to turn to God.

4. When God converts a sinner, and brings him out of sin into the state of grace, He frees him from his natural bondage to sin and, by His grace alone, He enables him freely to will and to do what is spiritually good. Nevertheless certain corruptions remain in

the sinner, so that his will is never completely and perfectly held in captivity to what is good, but it also entertains evil.

5. It is not until man enters the state of glory that he is made perfectly and immutably free to will what is good, and that alone.[1]

The debate is rarely over the fact of universal sinfulness but rather over the *results* of sin in the life of mankind. No man is a neutral moral agent, uncommitted with regard to God's truth or law. All are rebels, each one of the sons of Adam an enemy of God. Man is not a blank slate, waiting for good or evil to come and write upon it. No, the terms used to describe man are vivid, if uncomfortable for us to consider:

As it is written,
"There is none righteous, not even one;
there is none who understands,
there is none who seeks for God;
All have turned aside,
Together they have become useless;
There is none who does good,
There is not even one.
Their throat is an open grave,
With their tongues they keep deceiving,
The poison of asps is under their lips;
Whose mouth is full of cursing and bitterness;
Their feet are swift to shed blood,
Destruction and misery are in their paths,
And the path of peace they have not known.
There is no fear of God before their eyes." (Romans 3:10–18)

Such lengthy descriptions of the depravity of man may not be enjoyable reading, but they are necessary for us to ponder repeatedly, since it is the bent of our nature to exalt our capacities, not to honestly recognize our limitations. But while many are willing to confess the universal *existence* of sin, it is the universal *debility* sin brings that is so offensive to the world's religions and the natural man. Paul asserts that there are none who seek after God. In the midst of describing man's sin, he speaks of the result: Men do not seek God and have no fear of God before their eyes. Yet, if there is no God-seeker, how can anyone be saved? Because there is a sinner-seeker, a Savior, who saves His people perfectly—Jesus Christ! That is the vast difference between man's religions and the Christian faith: One is focused upon man and his abilities (synergism); one upon God and His (monergism).

UNABLE TO DO WHAT?

When the Bible speaks of man's *inabilities*, what, specifically, is he unable to do? A number of things are to be noted. For example:

> Can the Ethiopian change his skin
> Or the leopard his spots?
> Then you also can do good
> Who are accustomed to doing evil. (Jeremiah 13:23)

Those who are accustomed to doing evil can no more simply decide to do good than a leopard can simply "choose" to change its spots. Why? Because a leopard's spots are part of its *nature*, and sinners, fallen sons and daughters of Adam, likewise share his corrupted nature. The nature must be changed before true good can be done. This is especially true of *spiritual good*, as Paul explained to the congregation at Rome:

> Those who are according to the flesh set their minds on the things of the flesh, but those who are according to the Spirit, the things of the Spirit. For the mind set on the flesh is death, but the mind set on the Spirit is life and peace, because the mind set on the flesh is hostile toward God; for it does not subject itself to the law of God, for it is not even able to do so, and those who are in the flesh cannot please God. (Romans 8:5–8)

Paul speaks of two groups: those according to the flesh and those according to the Spirit. Some mistakenly think he is talking about two groups of Christians here, but that is manifestly untrue. Those who are according to the Spirit are those he goes on to describe as the sons of God.[2] Those who are according to the flesh experience only death, not life. These are unregenerate people, the ones outside of Christ. And what do the Scriptures tell us about them? We are told that their minds are "hostile toward God." The term translated *hostile* is a strong word that can signify hatred. Their rebellious hearts are not neutral toward God; they are hostile, at odds, at war. Such people are not subject to the law of God (and hence will never repent, which involves just such a submission).

But note the two statements: The mind set on the flesh is an enemy and does not subject itself to the law of God (willful and wanton rebellion), *but* at the same time, it is not able to do so! The inability of the fleshly mind to subject itself to the law of God *does not take away its guilt*. It does not *want* to be subject and is not *able* to be subject. This is a vitally important truth.

It follows, then, that those who are in the flesh "cannot please God." Literally, they are "unable." They lack the capacity, the power, the ability to please God. Those who promote the autonomous will of man and place the final choice of salvation in the hands of man must explain how such a person, enslaved to evil, an enemy of God, incapable of doing what is pleasing to Him, could in fact exercise saving faith and repentance, something that is obviously pleasing to God.

DEAD IN SIN

One of the most forceful pictures of man's sinfulness is the Bible's teaching that he is "dead in sin":

> You were dead in your trespasses and sins, in which you formerly walked according to the course of this world, according to the prince of the power of the air, of the spirit that is now working in the sons of disobedience. (Ephesians 2:1–2)

> When you were dead in your transgressions and the uncircumcision of your flesh, He made you alive together with Him, having forgiven us all our transgressions. (Colossians 2:13)

All believers who are now alive in Jesus Christ were once dead in their trespasses and sins. But what does it mean to be "dead in sin"? It obviously does not mean that man's spirit ceases to exist or that man's will is no longer active. But given the Bible's teaching that man is incapable of doing what is pleasing to God and that he is the enemy of God outside of Christ, we can see that spiritual death involves the inability to will and do what is good and pleasing in God's sight. As one is in rebellion against the source of all true life, the result is called spiritual death—a death that only the miracle of regeneration, being "born again," can remedy. Those who are dead in sin can indeed understand the facts of the gospel message, but they will always respond in the same fashion: with rebellion, rejection, or suppression. Until God takes out the heart of stone and gives a heart of flesh (Ezekiel 36:26), or causes His Spirit to make those dead bones come together into living beings (Ezekiel 37:1–14), men are dead in their trespasses, incapable of doing what is pleasing to God. As Paul elsewhere expressed it:

A natural man does not accept the things of the Spirit of God, for they are foolishness to him; and he cannot understand them, because they are spiritually appraised. (1 Corinthians 2:14)

There is a fundamental *incapacity* in the natural man. He *does not accept* the things of the Spirit of God (willful rejection), for they are foolishness to him. [3] Why are they foolishness? Because he is not a spiritual man. He *cannot* (not "does not" or "normally chooses not to") understand them. This is another phrase of *inability*, just as in Romans 8:7. This is not to say that there are not unregenerate, unsaved men who understand the outlines of Christian theology, for example, or the claims of the Christian faith. What it does mean is that there is no unregenerate man who *spiritually* accepts, understands, and knows the things of God. They exist on a level he cannot access, the spiritual level, and he is spiritually dead. But if true saving faith is focused upon the spiritually understood truths of Christ's perfect and substitutionary sacrifice and His resurrection from the dead, how can the natural man have this kind of faith?

JESUS ON MAN'S INABILITIES

Jesus answered that question for us. Elsewhere we will look more closely at John 6 and its incredible testimony to the sovereignty of God in salvation, but for the moment we introduce Christ's own teaching as testimony to this divine truth:

> Jesus answered and said to them, "Do not grumble among your-selves. No one can come to Me unless the Father who sent Me draws him; and I will raise him up on the last day." (John 6:43–44)

In this section of the discourse in the synagogue in Capernaum, Jesus is explaining the unbelief of those Jews who had seen Him and yet did not cling to Him in true faith. While they are even said to have been seeking Him, He knew they did not have saving faith. He knew this because He knew that the Father had not given them to Him, that they were not of His sheep. In explaining their unbelief, He speaks of the very same *inability* we have seen testified to elsewhere in Scripture, but here the inability is very clearly defined: No person has the ability to come to Christ in faith unless God first effectively draws that person.[4] This is not some general drawing, but a specific action of God the Father whereby He draws a particular people to the Son *and* raises them up at the last day as a result. Outside of this divine action, man *lacks the ability to come to Christ*. This is the plain teaching of inspired Scripture. All references, then, wherein it is *implied* that such a freedom exists must be interpreted in the light of the plain teaching of Jesus Christ that man lacks this capacity. *Inferences* cannot be used to contradict direct, plain, clear teachings, and yet doing so is absolutely necessary for those who seek to present man as the final arbiter of salvation.

It was not only in Capernaum that the Lord taught His doctrine of man's incapacity. It was part of the very core of His message, especially when faced with the unbelief of the Jews. How could the very ones to whom the Scriptures had been entrusted reject the Messiah Himself? The answer is not found within the rebel sinner, but in the free grace of God. Jesus said to some who had claimed faith in Him:

> "If you continue in My word, then you are truly disciples of Mine; and you will know the truth, and the truth will make you free." They answered Him, "We are Abraham's descendants and have never yet been enslaved to anyone; how is it that You say, 'You will become free'?" Jesus answered them, "Truly, truly, I say to you, everyone who commits sin is the slave of sin." (John 8:31–34)

Slavery is the direct opposite of freedom.[5] When faced with the reality of their slavery and need, these surface-level believers rebelled. Why do men defend the philosophically derived concept of human autonomy when the incarnate Son taught so plainly that everyone who sins is the slave of sin and in need of being set free? It is significant that it was to these same men that Jesus said:

> "If God were your Father, you would love Me…. Why do you not understand what I am saying? It is because you cannot hear My word. You are of your father the devil, and you want to do the desires of your father…. But because I speak the truth, you do not believe Me…. If I speak truth, why do you not believe Me? He who

is of God hears the words of God; for this reason you do not hear them, because you are not of God." (John 8:42–47)

Again the words of *inability* leap out at us. These men "cannot" hear Christ's word. They *want* to do the desires of their father, the devil, and they do not believe the truth. And why do they not believe? Because they lack a fundamental ability to "hear the words of God." Most people would say that people do not hear the words of God because they simply choose not to, and surely that is true to a point. Outside of the grace of God, none ever *would* choose to do so! But Jesus is more to the point. He says that they cannot hear them because they are not "of God." One must belong to God, be one of Christ's sheep, to hear His word and therefore believe.

CONCLUSION

The idea that the fallen creature has the ability to control God's free and sovereign work of salvation does not find its origin in the exegesis of inspired Scripture, but in the philosophies and traditions of man. This idea must be inserted into the text through the process of eisegesis. It will never be derived *from* the text through proper exegesis. It is, quite simply, a tradition of men (Matthew 15:1–6). The Bible is plain: Fallen man is unable to come to Christ, unable to do what is good in God's sight, unable to free himself from the shackles of sin. God must move in grace, not simply to make all men able to come, but to actually *draw* a people unto Christ and *save them.*

1. *A Faith to Confess: The Baptist Confession of 1689 Rewritten in Modern English* (Carey Publications, 1997), 9.
2. It should be noted that if people are Christians, they are adopted into the family of God. Without adoption, there is no true salvation. It is not something only "special" Christians experience.
3. These are defined in context not as a part of some superspiritual knowledge given only to a few but as the content of the entirety of apostolic preaching: "the things which we speak" (1 Corinthians 2:13), including both the basic message of the gospel and the wisdom spoken among the mature (2:1–6).
4. As will be noted later, only those the Father sovereignly gives to the Son come to the Son, and the Father draws to the Son only those so given. Also, the Father raises up all who are drawn to the Son. These exegetical facts undercut every attempt to remove the testimony of this passage.
5. These men had a "one-time" faith in Christ rather than the normative ongoing faith that in John's Gospel signals true salvation.

Response, by Dave Hunt

The Bible always presents two sides to salvation: God's sufficiency and man's responsibility; God's love and provision and man's repentance and faith; God's drawing of man and man's seeking of God. To support Calvinism's denial of human ability and responsibility, White gives a few favorite proof texts while ignoring a plethora of passages that present the other side. He offers inferences but *not one* Scripture that clearly states that unregenerate man is *unable* to believe the gospel.

Moreover, the Scriptures he cites often present both sides, one of which he ignores. He quotes, for example, Hebrews 7:25: "He is able also to save them to the uttermost that come unto God by him." White emphasizes Christ's ability "to save" but neglects entirely man's responsibility to "come unto God."

Criticizing non-Calvinists for their supposed bondage to traditions that "extol man's ability," White gives us Calvinist traditions that glory in man's alleged inability. Ability? Inability? *Believing* in Christ and *receiving* from Him the free gift of eternal life require *no ability*—a child can believe.

He claims that free will would allow man "to frustrate the intention of the triune God in saving him." Why would God be any more "frustrated" by man's rejection of the gospel than by man's continual rejection of His Law? God said, "I have nourished and brought up children, and they have rebelled against me" (Isaiah 1:2). Was God "frustrated"? Indeed, if Calvinism is true and God decrees all, why is He complaining?

White claims that non-Calvinists believe that God cannot save without the "aid of God's creatures." What *aid*? Believing the gospel doesn't "aid" God. Everyone, including the elect, *must* believe to be saved (Romans 1:16) or to please God (Hebrews 11:6).

Instead of Scripture (there is none), White offers the 1689 London Confession as proof that "man has lost all ability to will the performance of any of those works, spiritually good, that accompany salvation." What "works, spiritually good…accompany" salvation? None. The works follow salvation (Ephesians 2:10). Salvation is "through faith" (Ephesians 2:8), and faith is the opposite of works: "To him that worketh not, but believeth…his faith is counted for righteousness" (Romans 4:5).

The Confession says that man is unable "by any strength of his own, to turn himself to God." Of course. Coming to God is not a matter of "strength" but of the heart's desire and faith. Hundreds of Scriptures call upon the unregenerate to come to God and testify that it is possible:

If…thou shalt seek the LORD thy God, thou shalt find him, if thou seek him with all thy heart (Deuteronomy 4:29); If ye seek him, he will be found of you (2 Chronicles 15:2); This poor man cried, and the LORD…saved him out of all his troubles (Psalm 34:6); Thou, O Lord, art…plenteous in mercy and truth (Psalm 86:15); Ye shall seek me, and find me, when ye shall search for me with all your heart (Jeremiah 29:13); It is time to seek the LORD (Hosea 10:12); Seek ye the LORD, all ye meek of the earth (Zephaniah 2:3); Come unto me…all…and I will give you rest (Matthew 11:28); "The publican…smote upon his breast, saying, God be merciful to me a sinner. I tell you, this man went down to his house justified" (Luke

18:13–14); If any man thirst, let him come unto me, and drink (John 7:37); [The gospel] is the power of God unto salvation to every one that believeth (Romans 1:16); [God] is a rewarder of them that diligently seek him (Hebrews 11:6); Whosoever will, let him take the water of life freely (Revelation 22:17).

Such Scriptures would mock us if Calvinism were true. In fact, they declare the universal capability of the "wicked [to] forsake his way, and the unrighteousness man his thoughts...[to] return unto the LORD" (Isaiah 55:7). But White persists with another favorite proof text, Romans 3:11: "There is none who understands...who seeks for God." As the many Scriptures that White avoids make clear, this is the *willful*, but not the *necessary*, condition of man.

White omits that Paul is quoting Psalm 14 and that five Psalms earlier David writes, "Thou, LORD, hast not forsaken them that seek thee" (Psalm 9:10) and ten later, "This is the generation of them that seek [God], that seek thy face" (Psalm 24:6). Similar Scriptures abound:

When they...did turn unto the LORD...and sought him, he was found of them (2 Chronicles 15:4); All Judah...sought him with their whole desire; and he was found of them (2 Chronicles 15:15); Thou...hast prepared thine heart to seek God (2 Chronicles 19:3); He began to seek after the God of David his father (2 Chronicles 34:3); I sought the LORD, and he heard me" (Psalm 34:4).

If the unregenerate man is unable to seek God, scores of Scriptures that urge man to do so and declare that many have sought and found Him are a gross deception. The entire Bible would then mock God by depicting Him as endlessly pleading for repentance from those unable to repent, those He has predestined to eternal doom. And it would mock the nonelect by offering a salvation they cannot receive.

White cites Jeremiah 13:23 as proof that "those who are accustomed to doing evil can no more simply decide to do good than a leopard can... change its spots." Yet many sinners have been able to quit a life of crime or drunkenness. Salvation comes about not by the sinner changing his behavior but by believing the gospel. Moreover, Jeremiah is not referring to all mankind, but only to Israel, especially to Judah and Jerusalem (verses 9–11, 13, 19, 24–27), a vital fact White ignores.

White misapplies Romans 8:6–8 when he says, "Those who are according to the flesh experience only death, not life. These are unregenerate people... outside of Christ." In fact, Paul is speaking to Christians: "*Brethren...if ye live after the flesh, ye shall die; but if ye through the Spirit do mortify the deeds of the body, ye shall live*" (Romans 8:12–13, emphasis added). The terms "not after the flesh, but after the Spirit" (vv. 1, 4), "carnally minded... spiritually minded" (v. 6), "carnal" (v. 7), and "in the flesh" (v. 9), do not refer to the unsaved. Telling Christians that they cannot please God while walking after the flesh, Paul urges them to walk after the Spirit.

White insists that the unregenerate person will never repent or exercise saving faith and in fact is unable to do so because his fleshly mind lacks "the capacity, the power, the ability to please God." But the unsaved person is never called upon to "please God." White argues that if the unregenerate could believe the gospel, they would be pleasing God without the power of the Spirit. But the non-Calvinist does not deny the work of the Holy Spirit in bringing the sinner to salvation.

Unable to find even one Scripture declaring in plain language the *inability* of unregenerate people to repent and believe the gospel (and ignoring the numerous Scriptures declaring that they can and calling upon them to do so), White argues that believing the gospel is impossible for the spiritually dead because "they will always respond [to God]...with rebellion [and] rejection." But he fails to cite a Scripture that says so. And why the spiritually dead can actively disbelieve and rebel but cannot believe is not explained.

Of course, "only the miracle of regeneration...can remedy" spiritual death. But Peter says that sinners are "born again...by the word of God... which by the gospel is preached" (1 Peter 1:23, 25). Clearly those dead in sin can and must believe to be regenerated.

From Ezekiel 36 and 37, White "proves" again that "men are dead in their trespasses, incapable of doing what is pleasing to God." But "these bones are the whole house of Israel" (37:11), and the context is not regeneration of sinners but Israel's restoration at the second coming of Christ (Ezekiel 39:7, 22, 27–29; Zechariah 12:10–14:11).

As further proof of the "inability" of the spiritually dead to believe the gospel, White quotes 1 Corinthians 2:14 that the "natural man" can neither accept nor understand "the things of the Spirit of God." In fact, the "things of the Spirit of God" are not the gospel but "the deep things of God" (v. 10) that are known to "no man, but the Spirit of God" (v. 11). These things "are freely given to us of God...[who] have received...the Spirit who is of God"(v. 12). Paul is encouraging Christians that the deep things of God will be revealed to those who "have the mind of Christ" (v. 16).

Referring to John 6:43–44 ("No one can come to me unless the Father... draws him; and I will raise him up on the last day"), White reiterates his theme of the sinner's alleged inability to believe the gospel. But this declaration no more says that sinners "lack the ability to come to Christ" than the rule that no one can board an airliner without a ticket proves that all men lack the ability to walk aboard. Nor does Christ say that the Father draws only the "elect" or that all are "effectively" drawn (a word White inserts in the text) or that all who are drawn are raised up on the last day.

Christ says that "those who come to me" must be drawn by the Father and will be raised up by Him on the last day. He is teaching not human *inability* but that His Father is in charge. Christ clearly equates believing with "coming" to Him, the responsibility for which scores of passages place upon man. Like other Calvinists, here and in *The Potter's Freedom,* White avoids Scriptures such as "Strive to enter in at the strait gate" (Luke 13:24).

For White, John 8:34 ("Everyone who sins is the servant of sin") becomes further "proof" of the sinner's *inability* to do "works pleasing to God." That men serve sin does not prove that they cannot repent and turn to Christ when convicted by the Holy Spirit. White quotes John 8:43: "You cannot hear My word." This is not a statement of inability but of unwillingness. If they were *unable* to hear His word, they would be *unable* to hear this statement, and He would be wasting His time talking to them. No, He condemns their *unwillingness* to believe the truth (8:45).

White then sums up his arguments with the false implication that non-Calvinists teach that "the fallen creature has the ability to control God's free and sovereign work of salvation." *Control?* Does a woman "control" a man because she can either accept or reject his proposal of marriage? Love must be reciprocal, and neither lover "controls" the other. When God pleaded with Israel to repent and His judgment fell upon them when they refused, did Israel thereby "control" God? No, God is in control. He makes the rules

80

RESPONSE, BY DAVE HUNT

and brings blessing to those who obey and judgment on those who disobey.

White insists that non-Calvinists deny that "fallen man is…unable to do what is good in God's sight, unable to free himself from the shackles of sin." No, we agree. Salvation, however, is not by sinners doing good works or freeing themselves from sin. Salvation is a free gift of God's grace received by faith in Christ. And that is why we cannot agree that "fallen man is unable to come to Christ."

Coming to Christ is simply believing on Him. The invitation, "Come unto me" is given to *all* who under sin's burden are "weary and heavy laden." Is that condition exclusive to the elect? The invitation implies ability to respond on the part of those invited—an ability that Scripture repeatedly affirms for all who submit to the convicting, wooing, and drawing of the Father through the Holy Spirit.

Defense, by James White

In the face of the overwhelming and consistent testimony of Scripture, Dave Hunt actually has the temerity to state that I offered "*not one* Scripture that clearly states that unregenerate man is *unable* to believe the gospel." To say this, Hunt has to first dismiss Romans 8:7–8 by ignoring the exegesis I offered, which shows that his explanation is faulty (he does not even note the argumentation presented). Likewise, he dismisses 1 Corinthians 2:14 as being about "the deep things of God" rather than the gospel (again failing to respond to the contextual argumentation presented). Finally, he turns the phrase "is not able" in John 6:44 and 8:34 into "is not willing," an understanding completely contradicted by every rule of sound hermeneutics and grammar. Only after all these actions can Hunt say that I have not provided a single Scripture. Would it not be far more meaningful and honest to say, "I disagree with the interpretations offered, and here is why"?

The power of human tradition must again be seen, for its ability to overrule even the most basic rules of grammar and meaning must be recognized. In John 6:44, Jesus says, "No one can come to Me." The Greek is *oudeis dunatai elthein:* "There is not one able to come." *Dunatai* means "able, capable," and *oudeis* means "no one." How much plainer can this be? Jesus is talking about the unbelief (v. 36) that manifests itself right before Him (vv. 41–42). The subject is coming to Christ in faith for eternal life.

Every single aspect of the passage speaks to the same truth: People do not have the capacity in and of themselves to come to Christ for salvation until something divine happens; i.e., the drawing of the Father, which despite Hunt's constant denial, is limited to the elect, for they are the ones raised up on the last day. And in John 8:43 we have "are not able to hear," and those who cannot hear the words of Christ will not, of course, cling to Him in faith. They cannot understand, let alone believe. Can Hunt's traditions survive this biblical examination?

With reference to John 6:44 he writes, "He is teaching not human *inability* but that His Father is in charge." Well, the Father is surely in charge, but how can Jesus say "no man is able" and *not* be addressing human *inability?* Where does such a statement come from? It does not come from the Bible. It comes from tradition, as Hunt's next statement demonstrates. Rightly recognizing that Jesus is talking about believing in Him but adamantly refusing to allow Scripture to define the order of salvation and the nature of saving faith, he says, "the responsibility for [believing] scores of passages place upon man."

Do you see what is being said? "I interpret the commands of God to repent and believe to mean that all men can do this. Therefore, when I encounter a passage that says they cannot, the passage must be understood in light of my preexisting belief." So we fly from John 6 and 8 to Luke 13:24, where Jesus, answering the question, "Are there just a few who are being saved?"(v. 23) replies, "Strive to enter through the narrow door; for many, I tell you, will seek to enter and will not be able." Of course, Hunt quotes only the first phrase, and he reads into it an ability to do something outside of the gracious enablement of the Father. But obviously Jesus is speaking in a parable (vv. 25–30) regarding the judgment of God upon

84

Israel and the nature of the kingdom, including Gentiles. Ironically, Jesus says that others will seek to enter and "will not be able" because God will exclude them. Not able! There's that phrase again! And these words are uttered in reference to whom? Those who will hear the Lord say, "DEPART FROM ME, ALL YOU EVILDOERS" (v. 27).

And what of the words of John 8:43, "You cannot hear My word"? Tradition speaks again: "That men serve sin does not prove that they cannot repent and turn to Christ when convicted by the Holy Spirit." The one who sins is the slave of sin, Jesus said (v. 34). Slaves do not "choose" to be free. Another must free them. The conviction of the Holy Spirit must include His freeing us from the power of sin, which is what He does when He raises us to spiritual life. And when faced with the plain words *you cannot hear,* we discover that words are malleable things that can change meaning when necessary to protect the tradition of libertarian free will: "This is not a statement of inability but of unwillingness. If they were *unable* to hear His word, they would be *unable* to hear this statement, and He would be wasting His time talking to them."

Such interpretation leaves one breathless. The text says "cannot," but Hunt says that "it must mean "will not," because if it really means they could not hear, Jesus was wasting His time since they couldn't hear Him." It is painfully obvious that Jesus is using *hearing* in the same way He uses it in John 6: "This is a difficult statement; who can listen to (literally, "hear") it?" (v. 60). This is hearing joined with spiritual understanding and acceptance, as in John 6:45, where the elect "hear" and "learn" from the Father. Those who are not Christ's sheep *cannot hear the voice of the Shepherd.* Hunt offers commentary that has no connection whatsoever with the point of the text, as it ignores the use of "hear" in John and turns "cannot hear" into "are not willing."

We yet again have a clear, concise, documentable example of eisegesis in its purest form: the insertion of a foreign concept into the text in violation of its original language and context. The foreign concept is derived from Mr. Hunt's tradition of libertarian free will, not from the sacred text.

Final Remarks, by Dave Hunt

Despite White's denial, Romans 8 is clearly addressed to Christians. Claiming "the overwhelming and consistent testimony of Scripture," he cites only a few select verses. None of them states clearly that the natural man is unable to seek and find the Lord, that God draws only an elect to Christ, or that regeneration is required before saving faith.

I agree that man can do *nothing* apart from the "enablement of the Father." We differ on *what* enablement for *whom*. Yes, slaves of sin can't free themselves, but they can seek freedom. Romans 3 quotes Psalm 14, but other Psalms have men seeking God.

White says that the unregenerate are "incapable of even the first move toward God…filled with enmity and hatred toward His holy standards"[1] and can only "respond to God in a universally negative fashion."[2] Yet even Gentiles respect and obey God's holy standards and judge one another by His Law written in their consciences (Romans 2:14–15). Paul testified that he was "blameless" under the Law before he was saved (Philippians 3:6). The rich young ruler could say, "Master, all these [laws] have I observed from my youth. Then Jesus, beholding him, loved him" (Mark 10:20–21).

I don't "insert a foreign concept into the text…derived from [my] tradition." I look to the entirety of Scripture as the only interpreter of any text. The Father's drawing in John 6 cannot contradict the scores of verses that call all to repent and come to Him and testify that this is possible. I cite many (e.g., Deuteronomy 4:29, 2 Chronicles 15:2), and White avoids them all!

In view of such verses, "no man can" in John 6:44 means permissibility, not incapacity. Christ repeatedly calls all to believe on Him. Spurgeon condemned Calvinism's telling sinners "that it is not their duty to...believe in Christ...[and] that God hates some men...simply because he chooses to do so."[3]

I fail "to respond to contextual argumentation" with regard to 1 Corinthians 2:14? White gives none; he merely quotes the verse. The context shows that "the deep things of God" (v. 10) taught by the indwelling Spirit of God (vv.11–13) are not the gospel to the unsaved.

The "shall not be able" (Luke 13:24) is not because of innate inability. The door has been shut, and it is *too late* to enter. Christ's enjoinder, "strive to enter in," refutes Calvinism. Nor is the subject "the judgment of God upon Israel" but personal salvation: "Are there few that be saved?" (v. 23).

The Old Testament sacrifices pointing to Christ were for all Israel. White avoids them because they don't support *even one* of Calvinism's five points. All Israel kept the Passover and all were delivered from Egypt—without being regenerated. Christ's teaching on the serpent lifted up (John 3:14–17) conclusively refutes Calvinism.

---

1. James R. White, *The Potter's Freedom: A Defense of the Reformation* (Amityville, N.Y.: Calvary Press, 2000), 75.

2. Ibid., 98.

3. Charles H. Spurgeon, "The Minister's Farewell," *The New Park Street Pulpit* (London: Passmore & Alabaster, 1860), 6: 28–9; sermon preached 11 December 1859.

D. HUNT

Final Remarks, by James White

his chapter has provided us with one of the clearest examples of tradition overthrowing the text of Scripture. Mr. Hunt believes firmly in libertarian free will. He refuses to accept the fact that there is a general call of God that goes to all men (we preach the gospel to all men, not knowing who the elect are, for we have not been given that ability) and a specific call that results, unfailingly, in justification and glorification (Romans 8:30).

With his tradition firmly in place, Hunt falls upon the text of John 6:44. Every one of his many attempts to overthrow the text has been refuted. So finally we have the real admission: "No man can" *cannot* mean "unable" since *that contradicts his understanding of "all these other verses."* But what if Hunt has misunderstood all these other verses? What if Deuteronomy 4:29 is talking to God's people and is not positing a universal ability contrary to the plain meaning of Romans 3:11? And what if, in his rush to defend libertarianism, Hunt has, in fact, destroyed Paul's argument in Romans 3, leaving Paul liable to refutation on the very doctrine of justification itself? What if he has ignored the contexts of these passages in service of his tradition? What then?

Hunt's admission that he "interprets" the words "no man is able" as "men are unwilling" because of his *understanding* is a clear admission of eisegesis based upon tradition, the constant issue we have encountered throughout this discussion. There is simply no difference between this kind of "interpretation" and that promoted by the very groups Mr. Hunt opposes, wherein they follow their own traditions and extra-Scriptural authorities. When the uncontested, established meaning of the very words of the text are overthrown, the serious student of Scripture must ask why. And there is one answer here: man's traditions.

Why is the clear testimony of Scripture, as we have presented it, so offensive to man's religions? Spurgeon was correct:

The fact that conversion and salvation are of God, is an humbling truth. It is because of its humbling character that men do not like it. To be told that God must save me if I am saved, and that I am in his hand, as clay is in the hands of the potter, "I do not like it," saith one. Well, I thought you would not; whoever dreamed you would?"[1]

We conclude with the words of Charles Hodge:

No more soul-destroying doctrine could well be devised than the doctrine that sinners can regenerate themselves, and repent and believe just when they please.... As it is a truth both of Scripture and of experience that the unrenewed man can do nothing of himself to secure his salvation, it is essential that he should be brought to a practical conviction of that truth. When thus convinced, and not before, he seeks help from the only source whence it can be obtained.[2]

---

1. Charles H. Spurgeon, "High Doctrine," (sermon preached) 3 June 1860.
2. Charles Hodge, *Systematic Theology* (Grand Rapids, Mich.: Eerdmans, 1960), II: 277.

J. WHITE

- Chapter Three -

UNCONDITIONAL
ELECTION

by James White

Before the world was made, God's eternal, immutable purpose, which originated in the secret counsel and good pleasure of His will, moved Him to choose (or to elect), in Christ, certain of mankind to everlasting glory. Out of His mere free grace and love He predestinated these chosen ones to life, although there was nothing in them to cause Him to choose them.[1]

Unconditional election is simply the recognition of the biblical teaching that God is free in the matter of salvation. He chooses to exercise mercy and grace toward undeserving creatures solely on the basis of "the good pleasure of His will" (Ephesians 1:5). There is nothing in the creature that merits, earns, or attracts His favor. His election is *unconditional* in that it is based solely on His purpose and His pleasure and not in anything whatsoever in the creature.

This belief, of course, is most unpopular, since it leaves no room for man's accomplishments, works, rituals, sacraments, or (and this is the main issue), the exercise of his allegedly autonomous will. In biblical theology, it is God's free will, not man's, that determines the outcome of the work of salvation. As with each of the doctrines of grace, the foundation is to be found in the careful, fair, contextual exegesis of the inspired Scriptures.

EPHESIANS 1 AND
GOD'S ETERNAL PURPOSE IN CHRIST

Few passages of Scripture reach to the heights of divine revelation regarding God's eternal purpose in Christ as does Ephesians 1. Paul begins in eternity past and moves with resolute purpose to eternity future, all in the scope of the first two chapters of the epistle. And while the subject matter is truly exalted, the meaning of the text is clear and compelling. This passage, along with Romans 8–9, presents in uncompromising language the truth of God's eternal, unconditional, gracious predestination of a particular people to salvation.

The apostle begins by blessing God for all the spiritual blessings He has poured out upon His people (v. 3). He then writes, "just as He chose us in Him before the foundation of the world, that we would be holy and blameless before Him" (v. 4). God the Father chose a particular and personal people in Christ Jesus before time itself. It was God's choice. God was the active agent. The direct object of His eternal choice is "us." Why emphasize this? Because many try to circumvent the passage by saying that God has simply chosen *to save* or to *make salvation possible*, but the passage nowhere teaches this. He chose *a people*, not *a plan*. He chose *us* in union with Jesus Christ.

This choice is unto salvation, as obviously only the redeemed are to be "holy and blameless before Him." And, of course, unless one inserts some concept *into* the passage from outside, it is clearly the author's intention to place this decision completely outside the realm of human activity by placing it in the timeless realms of eternity. This election unto salvation is plainly unconditional, for how could those who do not yet exist fulfill the necessary conditions for their election?

The apostle continues, "In love He predestined us to adoption as sons through Jesus Christ to Himself, according to the kind intention of His will, to the praise of the glory of His grace, which He freely bestowed on us in the Beloved" (vv. 5–6). Again the Father is the active agent. His action of predestination is not a mere passive choosing to implement a plan of salvation: He predestines *us* to adoption as sons. Again, all believers are adopted into the family of God: Any person who is not a child of God has not experienced redemption. So again we see that election is personal and that it is salvific. This election, as with the entirety of the work of salvation, is accomplished in and through Jesus Christ.

In the next two phrases we have the clearest answer to the "why?" question man always poses in light of the truth of God's free choice of an elect people. Why one man and not another?[2] Man's religions and traditions put the answer to that question firmly in the realm of human choice and accomplishment, but the Bible gives a very different answer. Upon what basis does God choose one and not another? "According to the kind intention of His will." It is God's will, God's purpose, God's intention that determines the issue.[3] How else could it be in light of the next phrase, "to the praise of the glory of His grace"? If the crux of the matter lies in man's successful accomplishment of works of righteousness, or even in the exercise of "free will" to effectuate God's grace, how can the very next phrase speak of the praise of the glory of His grace? And this is not merely some "prevenient grace" that may or may not accomplish God's intended end; this grace is freely bestowed not upon all men but upon *us* in the Beloved, that is, in Jesus Christ. This is salvific grace, grace that leads to salvation, and it is found only in Jesus Christ. This is borne out by the next words: "In Him we have redemption through His blood, the forgiveness of our trespasses, according to the riches of His grace which He lavished on us" (vv. 7–8).

That full and complete salvation is in view is unquestionable. The grace that marks God's eternal predestination of this elect people is said to be given to us in Jesus Christ (v. 6), and it is in Him that we have redemption and forgiveness, and that in accordance with the riches of His grace, which He lavished on us. Surely we cannot miss the *particularity* of these words, for no person who stands screaming his hatred at God from the parapet of hell itself could ever say that the riches of God's grace in Christ Jesus had been lavished upon him. No, these words are specifically and clearly about the elect, those chosen by God before the foundation of the world. They, and they alone, experience the sovereign grace that brings redemption in the blood of Jesus Christ, the forgiveness of their sins. [4]

Paul then goes on to speak of the centrality of Christ and how the Father's will and purpose is found solely in His Son. It is the Father's intention to "sum up" all things in Christ. He then says, "In Him also we have obtained an inheritance, having been predestined according to His purpose who works all things after the counsel of His will" (vv. 10–11). The apostle describes God as working "all things after the counsel of His will." This is a truth that human religion cannot abide. Surely the Scriptures do not mean *all things!* Surely this just means that God created all things but now sort of lets them run on their own, does it not? No, God is the one who works *all things* after the counsel of His will. Let the questions come, the God of the Bible is more than able to answer the most difficult ones men can ask.

This all-sovereign God has predestined a particular people, so that as a result of that divine action, they receive an inheritance. The inheritance refers to all the divine benefits given to the redeemed, although Paul limits it specifically to God's work of salvation.[5] Why is any person who possesses the righteousness of Christ and the peace that comes with that perfectly accomplished salvation enjoying fellowship with God? Is it because he has believed? Yes. Because he has repented? Yes. But behind every single action of man there lies a truth that shatters the ego of the creature and exalts the eternal God in whose hand salvation lies: In the final analysis, I have peace with God because God in eternity past chose this undeserving sinner and placed His grace and love upon me. There can be no other consistent, biblical, and God-glorifying answer.[6] This is sovereign freedom, divine grace, and it leads inexorably to the truth of unconditional election.

UNCONDITIONAL ELECTION ILLUSTRATED

It is said almost in passing. Luke is narrating the events of Paul's ministry in Pisidian Antioch. The Jews are stirred to jealousy and anger by his preaching and begin opposing the gospel proclamation. Paul announces that the gospel is coming to the Gentiles, and Luke comments: "When the Gentiles heard this, they began rejoicing and glorifying the word of the Lord; and as many as had been appointed to eternal life believed" (Acts 13:48).

The "surface meaning" of the text is clear: When Paul announces that the message of eternal life is for all men, including the Gentiles, there is rejoicing, and on the part of some, belief in the truth. But it is Luke's comment on who believes that makes Acts 13:48 so relevant to our discussion of unconditional election. He says that those who had been appointed to eternal life believe. This divine appointment obviously precedes and brings about the act of faith. God has appointed them to eternal life, and they believe. Obviously, this statement touches upon not only unconditional election, but upon irresistible grace as well.

A survey of published English translations shows that there really is no question about how this passage should be translated. Luke's use of the Greek verb in the rest of his writings and the construction found here both defy the attempt to remove Acts 13:48 from the list of verses testifying to God's unconditional election.[7] Some have suggested that the translation should be "judged themselves worthy" of eternal life and hence believed. Others join the *New World Translation* of Jehovah's Witnesses in suggesting that these Gentiles "had disposed themselves" to eternal life.[8]

The problem with all of these is that they ignore the actual text. Acts 13:48 uses a construction that indicates that the action had been taken in the past and was completed in the past.[9] Are we to seriously suggest that, contrary to all biblical teaching about the enmity that exists on the part of the unregenerate man, these Gentiles had, at a time in the past, "disposed" themselves to eternal life, so that when they heard that the apostles were turning to them, this past action of "disposing" themselves caused them to believe? Are we to believe that this passage alone, contrary to all of Luke's uses of the relevant terms, conveys this wildly unusual meaning? This is a tremendous example of *eisegesis*, the reading into the text of a meaning that is totally foreign to its original context.

FURTHER WITNESSES

Space permits but a brief review of some of the other biblical witnesses to the truth of unconditional election. John testified to this truth when he wrote:

> As many as received Him, to them He gave the right to become children of God, even to those who believe in His name, who were born, not of blood nor of the will of the flesh nor of the will of man, but of God. (John 1:12–13)

We note that God begets His children freely and without reference to accomplishment or worthiness or even "foreseen faith." Every possible aspect of human action is denied a place in bringing about the new birth, *including the will of man*. If it is argued that it is John's intention in this passage to present an order (contrary to the order he establishes elsewhere, such as in 1 John 5:1) in which the human action of "receiving" Christ leads to being born from above, we respond by noting that the description in verse 13 is of those who receive Christ. They do so *because* they are born of God. It is not John's intention to say that those who believe in His name do so *to become* born again but, instead, that those who are born of God believe in Christ (which explains why others do *not* believe in Him). We do not become children of God by "enabling" Him to adopt us—as if it is *our* action that determines our entrance into the family of God! God is the one who chooses, in grace, to bring people into the wonderful status of children and heirs, and as we saw in Ephesians, He does so freely. The freedom of this choice on God's part is illustrated in the words of Jesus as well:

All things have been handed over to Me by My Father; and no one knows the Son except the Father; nor does anyone know the Father except the Son, and anyone to whom the Son wills to reveal Him. (Matthew 11:27)

Do men have an unfettered, natural ability to come to know the Father? No, not outside of the Son's choice to reveal the Father to them, and we know, in light of the revelation of the Father's will for the Son, that Jesus will reveal the Father perfectly to all those who are given to Him (John 6:39). Such freedom on God's part precludes any idea of conditions on the part of man that determine the work of God in salvation.

But surely, if the words of inspired Scripture in Romans 9 do not speak with sufficient clarity to the topic, what could?

So then it *does not depend* on the man who wills or the man who runs, but on God who has mercy. So then He has mercy on whom He desires, and He hardens whom He desires. (Romans 9:16, 18, emphasis added)

The manifold attempts to get around this passage are far beyond our scope at this point.[10] Suffice it to say that the attempt to turn this passage into a mere commentary on national privilege completely and utterly misses the point of Romans 9:5–6 and the intensely personal application of 9:10–24. In verse 16 the application is *personal* and *singular,* not national. When the passage is allowed to speak for itself, it speaks of unconditional election in the plainest of terms. It is God's mercy, not man's will or effort, that determines the outcome of salvation. And verse 18 is just as compelling, for the English masks the strength of the apostle's teaching. Literally the passage says, "He *mercies* (active verb, God the subject) whom He desires and He *hardens* (active verb, God the subject) whom He desires." The parallel is undeniable: In the act of "mercying" as well as "hardening," God, and God alone, is the determining agent. His choice is not determined by human action. It is, therefore, unconditional.

CONCLUSION

To confess unconditional election is simply to confess both the freedom and grace of God as well as the depravity and sinfulness of man. Those who seek to set up conditions that must be met do so at the cost of God's freedom and the truth of man's depravity. Every works-oriented system must deny God His kingship over the creature and must give to man abilities and powers beyond his sinful state, so that in the final analysis God's power can be "channeled" through human structures, whether they be rituals, sacraments, or even the very popular concept of "decisionalism," the idea that man, by his autonomous will, controls the very work of the triune God in salvation.

The Scriptures know nothing of such a concept. Instead, God's choice of a people unto salvation is free, based solely in His own will and purpose. As the apostle Paul expressed it so plainly, God "has saved us and called us with a holy calling, not according to our works, but according to His own purpose and grace which was granted us in Christ Jesus from all eternity" (2 Timothy 1:9). To the redeemed heart, these are words of life, for we know that God's will and purpose will always be accomplished (Psalm 135:6).

1. *A Faith to Confess: The Baptist Confession of 1689 Rewritten in Modern English* (Carey Publications, 1997), 3:5.
2. So often has the question been raised it has been dubbed the *crux theologorum*.
3. Should someone miss the glory of this statement by saying, "How can it be a good intention that millions perish?" the answer is clear: The good intention is the miraculous redemption of rebel sinners who once reveled in their sin and their rebellion but are then changed and made new. The emphasis in this and other passages is not on the just condemnation of sinners but on the miraculous redemption of them.
4. This should be kept in mind when considering the nature of the atonement, especially when pondering its scope and intention.
5. Note Galatians 3:18, Colossians 1:12, and Ephesians 1:14 and 18.
6. Indeed, all other answers must at some point be "because I was better than those who did not believe."
7. Specifically, it is a periphrastic construction. Almost none of the sources that seek to present an alternative translation of the passage deal with the fact that it is a periphrastic, not a stand-alone construction.
8. Mr. Hunt joins this group, though he does not deal with any of the relevant issues (i.e., Luke's usage or the periphrastic construction) and in fact errs in stating that "the Liddell and Scott Greek dictionary offers a number of alternate meanings, but 'ordain' or 'foreordain' is not one of them" (Dave Hunt, *What Love Is This?* [Sisters, Ore.: Loyal, 2002], 210). A quick glance at Liddell and Scott, however, reveals that under section III, number 2, we have, "to appoint, ordain, order, prescribe," with an almost identical participial form cited as an example. Further, Liddell and Scott is not a *koine* Greek lexicon. Lexicons of the language of the New Testament are far more relevant to the proper translation of the passage.
9. That is, a pluperfect tense meaning to a periphrastic construction using a perfect passive participle with an imperfect form of *eimi*.
10. The majority of these attempts are fully refuted in John Piper, *The Justification of God: An Exegetical and Theological Study of Romans 9:1–23* (Grand Rapids, Mich.: Baker, 2000).

Response, by Dave Hunt

White says that non-Calvinists rely on tradition, but he promotes a Calvinist tradition, "unconditional election," which he claims is simply the biblical teaching that God is free in the matter of salvation. Free? It limits salvation to an elect. Nor does he explain why God Himself doesn't love and do good to everyone, as Christ said we must in order to be "perfect, even as your Father who is in heaven is perfect" (Matthew 5: 48).

If Calvinism is true, there ought to be at least *one* Scripture that clearly states that God's love and grace are limited to a select group, but White can offer *none*. Yet *many* passages state clearly that God loves all, desires all to be saved, wants *none* to perish, and takes *no pleasure* in the death of the wicked—Scriptures that Calvinism attempts to explain away.

White says that God's choosing and election are unto salvation. Yet Christ said, "Have not I chosen you twelve, and one of you [Judas] is a devil?" (John 6:70). The disciples' choosing was unto service, not salvation. Judas is in hell. "Chosen [to] be holy and without blame" (Ephesians 1:4) describes not salvation but a special blessing for the saved.

White assures us that Ephesians 1 and Romans 8 and 9 present God's "predestination of a particular people to salvation." Yet salvation isn't the subject. Romans 8 is addressed to those "which are in Christ Jesus." It urges them to "mortify the deeds of the body...through the Spirit," which inwardly "beareth witness" that they "are the children of God" and recites the many blessings to which God has predestined those "whom he did foreknow." That foreknowledge is the basis of predestination is a vital truth that White repudiates.

Ephesians 1 is likewise written to "the saints...faithful in Christ Jesus" (v. 1). The only mention of salvation contradicts Calvinism: "In whom ye also trusted, *after* that ye heard...the gospel...*after* ye believed, ye were sealed with that holy Spirit of promise" (v. 13, emphasis added). In contrast, Calvinists claim that one is born of the Spirit *before* believing the gospel unto salvation.

As in Romans 8, Paul holds out to the saints at Ephesus the glory to which they have been predestined "before the foundation of the world." This is not predestination of certain sinners unto salvation but of the redeemed to "all spiritual blessings in heavenly places in Christ"—a bonus added to salvation.

Sinners could be saved from hell without being adopted into God's family and made "joint-heirs with Christ" (Romans 8:17). That God added these blessings is "to the praise of the glory of his grace." But White claims that in "the kind intention of His will," God predestined billions to eternal torment. What love and kindness is this?

White insists that "this choice is unto salvation, as obviously only the redeemed are to be 'holy and blameless before Him.'" It doesn't follow. That those God knew would receive Christ were predestined to be "holy and blameless before Him" and to receive other special blessings does not say that they were predestined to salvation, much less that redemption is only for a select group. Indeed, numerous Scriptures offer salvation to all mankind.

He then says, "This election unto salvation is plainly unconditional, for how could those who do not yet exist fulfill the conditions necessary for their election?" Election is not unto salvation but unto blessings, and foreknowledge is the basis. God knew from eternity past who would believe the gospel, and it was for these that God predestined special blessings: "Whom he did foreknow, he also did predestinate (Romans 8:29)…elect according to the foreknowledge of God the Father" (1 Peter 1:2).

White argues that "this grace is freely bestowed not upon all men but upon *us*." If "blessed *us*" (Ephesians 1:3, emphasis added) limits God's grace to an elect, Paul's declaration, "the Son of God, who loved *me*" (Galatians 2:20, emphasis added) means that Paul alone is loved.

White implies that non-Calvinists deny God's sovereignty. Not so. Free will does not detract from God's sovereignty or His grace. Yes, God works "all things after the counsel of his own will" (Ephesians 1:11), but White ignores the key word *counsel*. Contrary to Calvinism, which makes God its author, the evil and suffering in this world are not God's will but the result of man's rebellion: "They rebel against me" (Hosea 7:14). In the *counsel* of His will, God has given man a free will. That fact provides the only explanation for rampant wickedness ("Oh, do not this abominable thing that I hate" [Jeremiah 44:4]).

White's chief proof text is Acts 13:48: "As many as were ordained to eternal life believed," which as Laurence Vance notes, "every Calvinist [uses] to prove Unconditional Election."[1] In his book, White devotes four pages to it.[2] The Greek word translated "ordained" is *tetagmenoi*, a nominative case, perfect tense, passive voice participle of *tasso*. "*Ordained* to eternal life" is the translation found in all major translations. Yet none of the seven other usages of *tasso* in the New Testament connotes a divine decree from eternity past. Had that been what Luke meant, he would have used *prooridzo* (predestinated).

Salvation is promised to all ("Repent, and be baptized every one of you" [Acts 2:38]), contingent upon individual faith ("Believe on the Lord Jesus Christ, and thou shalt be saved" [Acts 16:31]). Never is there a hint of God predestining certain ones to heaven, sovereignly regenerating and irresistibly causing them to believe the gospel while withholding that grace from others. If that were the meaning of Acts 13:48, it would contradict all of Scripture.

The context is clear. In verse 46, Paul tells the Jews, "Seeing ye put it [the gospel] from you...we turn to the Gentiles." Verse 48 presents the contrast between the Jews who had rejected the gospel and the Gentiles who believed it. What influence persuaded the Gentiles? We are not told. The book of Acts provides several examples, but a sovereign decree is not among them.

For "further witness," White turns to John 1:12–13. Surely he can't seriously mean that "those who receive Christ...do so because they are born of God." The text says the opposite: "As many as received him, to them gave he power to become the sons of God, even to them that believe on his name: who were born...of God." Clearly, those who "received Him...[and] believe in His name" *become* the sons of God. White's reversal of this order is inexcusable.

That salvation and the new birth (which Spurgeon said are the same)[3] follow faith is incontestably established. Here are only a few examples:

> They that hear shall live (John 5:25); Ye will not come to me, that ye might have life (John 5:40); Every one who seeth the Son, and believeth on him, may have everlasting life (John 6:40); Believing ye might have life (John 20:31); "Believe...and thou shalt be saved (Acts 16:31).

White's final proof text is Romans 9, but he gives us no exegesis. Quoting Genesis 25:23, Paul writes, "The elder shall serve the younger" (v. 12). Clearly this has nothing to do with either Jacob or Esau as individuals (Esau never served Jacob during their lifetimes), much less with their predestination to heaven or hell. God tells Rebekah, "Two nations are in thy womb, and two manner of people." Thus it was the descendants of Esau (Edomites) who were subjugated by the descendants of Jacob, as archaeology, secular history and the Bible prove (e.g., 1 Samuel 14:47; 1 Kings 11:15–16; 2 Samuel 8:13–14; 2 Chronicles 20:22, 25:11).

Paul continues: "As it is written, Jacob have I loved, but Esau have I hated" (v.13) *Written* where? Not in Genesis but in Malachi 1:2–3, and not about salvation of individuals but concerning blessing and judgment upon the nations descended from Jacob and Esau: "Whereas Edom saith...we will...build...[the Lord says] they shall build, but I will throw down...[and] be magnified from the border of Israel" (vv. 4–5).

Nor does Paul deal with Pharaoh's salvation. If he were "totally depraved" and *unable* to do anything pleasing to God, why would God need to "harden" his heart? God did not make Pharaoh the evil man he was but raised him up at that time to manifest His power over the gods of Egypt, "that thou mayest tell in the ears of thy [descendants] what things I have wrought in Egypt and...know that I am the LORD" (Exodus 10:2).

Piper writes that "before the first active assertion of God's hardening in Exodus 9:12, there are two assertions that he [Pharaoh] hardened his own heart."[4] The Hebrew *kabed* indicates that Pharaoh hardened his own heart (Exodus 7:14; 8:15; 9:7, 34). The Hebrew *chazaq* indicates that God was simply giving Pharaoh the courage to continue his determined resistance (Exodus 4:21; 7:13, 22; 8:15; 9:12, 35; 10:20, 27; 11:10; 14:4, 8, 17.)

Pharaoh resisted not the gospel but the freeing of the Hebrew slaves. There is nothing about Pharaoh's salvation, yet this is a major Calvinist "election to salvation" proof text.

White exults that "God in eternity past chose this undeserving sinner and placed His grace and love upon me." He concludes: "To the redeemed heart these are words of life." But what if one is among those predestined to the lake of fire, of whom Calvin says God's "pleasure it is to inflict punishment"[5] by what Arthur Pink calls "his predestining grace"?[6] Though some have had troubling doubts about their own election, White seems confident that he is one of this select group. How does he know? And how can he assure others that they too are among the elect? Jay Adams says, "No man knows except Christ himself who are his elect for whom he died."[7]

White comments, "It is God's mercy, not man's will or effort, that determines the outcome of salvation." Absolutely. "Salvation is of the LORD" (Jonah 2:9). No man can either save himself or force God to save him. This is all Romans 9:16 says, not that some are predestined to salvation and others to damnation, as White claims. Christ is "the author of eternal salvation" (Hebrews 5:9). To those so predestined? No, but "unto all them that obey him," and the first step of obedience is to come unto Him in faith.

White concludes with the charge that making faith a condition of salvation is "at the cost of God's freedom and the truth of man's depravity." In fact the Calvinist limits God's freedom by not allowing Him to love all. Nor has White given any biblical proof that "depravity" equals "inability," making it impossible for a sinner to believe unto salvation. Incredibly, he brands the biblical requirement of faith for salvation ("Believe…and thou shalt be saved"[Acts 16:31]) a "works-oriented system," despite the fact that faith is the opposite of works and that the requirement of faith for salvation is

D. HUNT

stated repeatedly in Scripture. "Reformed theology" denying *sola fide?*

Rejecting the clear call to sinners to believe in order to be saved, White declares that the only basis for peace with God is to trust that you have been predestined to salvation. In footnote 6 he declares that a person who says he was saved by faith must say it was "because I was better than those who did not believe." On the contrary, Paul specifically says, "Boasting...is excluded...by the law of faith" (Romans 3:27).

1. Laurence M. Vance, *The Other Side of Calvinism* (Pensacola, Fla.: Vance, 1999), 345.
2. James R. White, *The Potter's Freedom: A Defense of the Reformation* (Amityville, N.Y.: Calvary Press, 2000), 186–90.
3. Charles H. Spurgeon, "The Warrant of Faith," in *The New Park Street Pulpit* (Pasadena, Tex.: Pilgrim Publications, 1978).
4. John Piper, *The Justification of God: An Exegetical and Theological Study of Romans 9:1–23* (Grand Rapids, Mich.: Baker, 2000), 163.
5. John Calvin, *Institutes of the Christian Religion,* tr. Henry Beveridge (Grand Rapids, Mich.: Eerdmans, 1998), III: xxiii, 1, 4.
6. Arthur W. Pink, *The Sovereignty of God* (Grand Rapids, Mich.: Baker, 1986), 52.
7. Jay E. Adams, *Competent to Counsel* (Grand Rapids, Mich.: Baker, 1970), 70.

Defense, by James White

I t must be noted that in his response, Mr. Hunt completely ignores the exegesis drawn directly from the text of Ephesians 1. Its clear testimony to the sovereignty of God in salvation is simply dismissed, almost without comment. This work is supposed to present a point/counterpoint debate on the same topics, and the topic in this presentation is the biblical basis of the belief in the unconditional electing grace of God, especially as found in Ephesians 1. Surely Mr. Hunt presents no positive exegetical foundation; hence, we must assume that the truth of unconditional election drawn from Ephesians 1 has been established.

Dave Hunt tells us that Ephesians 1 and Romans 8–9 are not about salvation. Christian theologians down through the centuries have believed otherwise, and when you find Paul speaking of "redemption" and "forgiveness of trespasses" (Ephesians 1:7) and justification (Romans 8:30) and "mercy" and hardening (Romans 9:18) in those very passages, it is hard to understand how he can make such a statement. That Paul is, in fact, speaking of salvation is plain beyond refutation. Yet, while these central texts on salvation are dismissed by Mr. Hunt, for some reason he cites John 6:70 and the choosing of Judas as relevant. Again Mr. Hunt violates all standard rules of hermeneutics: The choosing of Judas was to apostleship and to the role of His betrayer. It was *not* unto salvation. This has nothing to do, of course, with the passages that speak of election unto salvation. Only by insisting that all uses of the word *choose* have to bear the same meaning, even in different contexts, can Dave Hunt make this kind of error.

Hunt repeatedly asserts that election is never unto salvation but only to privileges and blessings. This assertion is repeated in his book and in talks he has given over the past few years. Yet, amazingly, despite its obvious centrality to the entirety of his position, Mr. Hunt does not provide an explanation of this text:

> We should always give thanks to God for you, brethren beloved by the Lord, because God has chosen you from the beginning for salvation through sanctification by the Spirit and faith in the truth. (2 Thessalonians 2:13)

Paul speaks of God choosing the believers at Thessalonica "from the beginning for salvation." There is a direct refutation of a claim Hunt makes repeatedly. The text shows that the work of the Spirit and our faith in God's truth are the *result* of that eternal choice. God ordains both the ends and the means, just as Reformed theology has taught all along. No reference is found to 2 Thessalonians 2:13 in the Scripture index of *What Love Is This?*

In my presentation, I noted Romans 9:16 and 18 as they relate to unconditional election and referred readers to the full treatment of the entire chapter offered by John Piper. Mr. Hunt says I offered no exegesis, and if he means by that I did not focus upon Romans 9, he is correct. I was presenting the verses that are relevant to *unconditional election*, the point of my presentation, and in reference to this I most assuredly did provide exegesis, pointing out the freedom of God in mercying and hardening based upon His own will, not man's. Hunt spends a great deal of time repeating assertions about Romans 9 that John Piper completely dismantled years ago, but he leaves the two verses I cited, the information I presented, and the point I made in reference to unconditional election *completely unmentioned and unanswered.*

Mr. Hunt asserts that I "repudiate" foreknowledge as the "basis" of predestination. As the careful reader knows, I have documented Mr. Hunt's misunderstanding of the terms related to this concept. Likewise, Mr. Hunt has failed to explain to us how God *has* foreknowledge or how this relates to His decree (or lack thereof). The basis of predestination is God's will and intention, as we proved in this presentation from Ephesians 1. Mr. Hunt may wish to assume a particular passive kind of "foreknowledge," so that God's actions are made dependent upon what He learns about man's actions in time, but simply *assuming* this does not *prove* it. God's election is in accordance with His foreknowledge. Hunt assumes that this means God elects based upon what He foresees in time. But if this idea is central to his argument, why does he not establish it through the exegesis of the text rather than just assuming it from his tradition? How can Hunt *prove* (given the importance of the subject) that "according to" means "on the basis of a passive taking in of events in time" rather than "in harmony with God's perfect knowledge of all things based upon His creative decree"?

Finally, Dave Hunt quotes the King James Version's (KJV) rendering of Ephesians 1:13 as if it were "the only mention of salvation" in Ephesians 1. We have already seen how this is utterly untrue (cf. verse 7). Hunt says that this text "contradicts Calvinism." Hunt is assuming, it seems, that being "sealed" with the Holy Spirit is identical to being regenerated by Him and that the verbs in verse 13 present a temporal succession of events. This is not the case. The string of aorist participles ("heard" and "believed") can be antecedent to (hence the translation "after") *or* contemporaneous with the action of the main verb (you were sealed). Hunt assumes a particular syntactical conclusion but does not even attempt to argue his case. Ephesians 1:4–11 has presented the freedom and eternality of God's will in saving His elect. In light of this, the contemporaneous translation of the participles and verbs in verse 13 fits the context best. The New American Standard Bible (NASB) accurately handles the text by rendering it:

> In Him, you also, after listening to the message of truth, the gospel of your salvation—having also believed, you were sealed in Him with the Holy Spirit of promise.

So we see nothing in this text that contradicts the Reformed perspective.

Final Remarks, by Dave Hunt

White says I offer no "point/counterpoint" exegesis of Ephesians 1 and Romans 8. In fact, I show that these texts are written to Christians and are not about getting saved but about the "spiritual blessings" to which God predestined believers. I show that Paul does not say that every evil event on earth is willed by God but is *allowed* in the *"counsel* of his will"—a huge difference. I deal with 2 Thessalonians 2:13 elsewhere.

White repeats that "God is free in the matter of salvation." He means free to *limit* salvation to the elect and damn the rest. But the Bible repeatedly says that God desires all mankind to be saved. That men reject Christ no more impacts God's sovereignty than does their habitual breaking of the Law.

I fail to deal with White's treatment of Romans 9:5–6 and 10–24? His "exegesis" overlooks the key passages in Genesis and Malachi to which I refer.

The phrase "creative choice," isn't found in Scripture. Nor does God "learn about man's actions" through "a passive taking in of events." God knows all from eternity! White repeats that I "fail to explain how God has foreknowledge." It is by the omniscience Calvinists deny, claiming that God can only know what He foreordains.[1] MacArthur says, "It's not that [God] merely sees what will happen in the future; rather He ordains it."[2]

By not allowing God to grant mankind the power of choice, the

Calvinist limits God and makes Him the cause of sin. God is robbed of the love and praise that can only come from man's heart. And all the references to "heart" (e.g., "Daniel purposed in his heart" [Daniel 1:8]; "Believe in thine heart" [Romans 10:9]) become meaningless.

As for John 1:11–13, clearly only those who have believed upon and received Christ "*become* the sons of God" (emphasis added). White claims that the reverse order is established "elsewhere, such as in 1 John 5:1." That verse could be taken either way. But he avoids 1 Peter 1:23–25, where very clearly we are "born again" (regenerated) *through believing the gospel.* Yet Calvinism says that faith *follows* regeneration.

That no one can know the Father or the Son without God's revelation does not limit this revelation to the elect. Scores of Scriptures express God's desire for the salvation of all.

Referring to "aorist participles" and "syntactical" rules in Ephesians 1:13 is impressive but can't change "after that ye believed, ye were sealed with that Holy Spirit of promise" into "after ye were sealed with the Holy Spirit, ye believed." Nor does the NASB help: "Having also believed [the gospel], you were sealed in Him with the Holy Spirit." Clearly, believing the gospel precedes the sealing with the Holy Spirit. White must therefore propose being regenerated by the Spirit without this sealing—unimaginable and unbiblical.

1. John Calvin, *Institutes of the Christian Religion*, tr. Henry Beveridge (Grand Rapids, Mich.: Eerdmans, 1998), III: xxiii, 6; Arthur W. Pink, *The Sovereignty of God* (Grand Rapids, Mich.: Baker, 1986), 249; David S. West, *The Baptist Examiner* (18 March 1989), 5.
2. John MacArthur Jr., *Saved Without a Doubt* (Chariot Victor, 1992), 58.

D. HUNT

Final Remarks, by James White

God's freedom in electing a people in Jesus Christ is central to His glory. As Paul said in Ephesians 1, God's choice of His people in eternity past is based upon the kind intention of His own will, to the praise of the glory of His grace. Mr. Hunt's facile response that this is not talking about salvation but merely "spiritual blessings" has already been demonstrated to be in error, though Mr. Hunt has not deigned to offer a response to that rebuttal. The language of redemption is all through Ephesians 1:4–11, and the idea that such things as "adoption" are mere "blessings" that not all Christians experience is a view far outside the pale of orthodoxy. In light of the fact that this is the only defense Hunt has offered, we are again left with tradition-driven eisegesis attempting to refute the uncontested language of the text.

As much as man wishes to claim the glory for his salvation, the glory belongs solely to God. Embrace the synergism of Hunt's tradition, and you are forced to divide the glory due to God alone between the Father, who tries so hard, the Son, who makes a theoretical salvation a mere possibility, the Spirit, who attempts to bring conviction to sinners, and the self-appointed redeemed, who demonstrate that in some way, shape, or form, they are "better" than those who are lost simply because they "do the right thing" while the others do not.

In June of 1735 the great preacher of Northampton, Jonathan

Edwards, spoke on the revealed truth of divine sovereignty. In his application he said:

It is from little thoughts of God, that you quarrel against his justice in the *condemnation of sinners,* from the doctrine of original sin.... What horrid arrogance in worms of the dust, that they should think they have wisdom enough to examine and determine concerning what God doth, and to pass sentence on it as unjust!... It is from mean thoughts of God, that you contend with him, because he bestows grace on some, and not on others.... But what a low thought of God does this argue! Consider what it is you would make of God. Must he be so tied up, that he cannot use his own pleasure in bestowing his own gifts? Is he obliged to bestow them on one, because it is his pleasure to bestow them on another? Is not God worthy to have the same right to dispose of his gifts, as a man has of his money? or is it because God is not so great, and therefore should be more subject, more under bounds, than men?...God is pleased to show mercy to his enemies, according to his own sovereign pleasure.... How unreasonable is it to think that God stands bound to his enemies! Therefore consider what you do in quarrelling with God, and opposing his sovereignty. Consider with whom you contend. Let all who are sensible of their misery, and afraid of the wrath of God, consider these things.

- Chapter Four -

JESUS TEACHES THE DOCTRINES OF GRACE

by James White

The strength of the Reformed faith (and the confidence of those who embrace it) is the exegesis of the inspired text of Scripture. As long as the Word of God remains with men, it will teach the sovereignty of God and the doctrines of grace. And one of the most compelling passages that will always testify to these divine truths is found in Jesus' sermon in the synagogue in Capernaum, recorded in John 6. Opponents of free grace have tried every conceivable means of getting around the plain teaching of this passage, but every single effort, no matter how ingenious, collapses upon consistent and fair exegetical examination. The simple fact is that Jesus taught the doctrines of grace while explaining the unbelief of the very men who had watched Him perform the miracle of the feeding of the five thousand. Sound hermeneutic principles demand that we allow the passage to define its own terms and that we follow its own order of presentation.[1]

THE CONTEXT

Jesus has fled the excited crowd of people who have seen His miraculous multiplication of the bread and fish and has gone to Capernaum. Some in the crowd seek after Him and find Him in the synagogue. In the ensuing dialogue, Jesus exposes their unbelief. They are seeking more miracles; they are not seeking a Savior from sin. He tells them that He is the bread of life and that if they come and believe in Him, they will not suffer spiritual hunger or thirst. But as soon as He makes this statement, He adds this vital insight: "But I said to you that you have seen Me, and yet do not believe" (John 6:36). Despite seeing Him and hearing His preaching, these men stand before Christ in unbelief. They refuse to truly *come* to Him in faith. Why?

GOD GIVES CERTAIN MEN TO THE SON

The explanation offered by the Lord focuses not upon the mass of unbelievers, but first upon those who actually do come to Christ. Jesus' words are sharp and clear:

God Convicts   Man Wills

"All that the Father gives Me will come to Me, and the one who comes to Me I will certainly not cast out." (John 6:37)

Jesus Saves!

Each word is vital. Jesus begins where Christian salvation begins (and ends!), with the Father. The Father gives a particular people to the Son. Why do I say a particular people? Because Jesus says that *all of them* will come to Him. We know that not all people come to Him; hence, this is a distinct group that does not embrace all of mankind. This divine and sovereign act of giving on the part of the Father *results in* an action on the part of those given: They unfailingly come to Christ. All who are given come. Not some, not most, but *all*. How can this be if, in fact, the coming is conditional upon human effort, desire, or choice? Obviously, it isn't. The giving of the Father is a sovereign and divine act that guarantees, beyond all question or doubt, the eventual coming of the individual person to Christ in saving faith. All come, because coming to faith in Christ is not the result of an autonomous human decision. Instead, as the Bible teaches, saving faith is a gift from God, given to His elect people, and when God in grace removes the heart of stone and gives a heart of flesh, making a person a new creature in Christ, that person will, without fail, cling to Jesus Christ and to Him alone.

It must be emphasized that in Jesus' teaching, the giving precedes and determines the coming. Jesus does not teach that all those that the Father somehow "foresees"[2] will come to Christ are given, but that all who are given come *as a result*. The divine order is clear: The Father sovereignly gives a people to the Son, and as a result of that giving, they come.[3] Men may try to turn the order around, but the text of Scripture simply does not allow it.

The one who, as a result of being given by the Father to the Son, comes to the Son will always find Him a perfect Savior who will never cast him out. Why? Jesus explains:

> "For I have come down from heaven, not to do My own will, but the will of Him who sent Me. This is the will of Him who sent Me, that of all that He has given Me I lose nothing, but raise it up on the last day." (vv. 38–39)

In these tremendous words the incarnate Son reveals that He has come from heaven to do the Father's will, and the Father's will is explicit: that of all that have been given to Him (the same group noted in verse 37) He lose *nothing*, but raise it up on the last day. If it is the Father's will that the Son save His people perfectly and without fail, it follows that the Son must have the capacity to save without the assistance, permission, or cooperation of man. And this is surely the case. The Son is fully capable of saving rebel sinners perfectly, of raising them up to eternal life on the last day. Few passages of Scripture express the security of God's people in their salvation with greater force than this one. To say that any of those given by the Father to the Son can ultimately be lost is to say that Christ can fail to do the will of the Father.[4]

In summary thus far, we see that the Father gives a particular group of people to the Son; all who are thus given come to the Son, without fail; the giving of the Father precedes and determines that coming (not, as is so often suggested, that the coming of someone in faith determines the Father's giving them to the Son, as if the human action determines the divine); and the Son is charged by the Father with the salvation of every single one of those given to Him by the Father (to "raise up on the last day" and to "give eternal life" are used interchangeably in this entire passage).

One might ask, "How is this relevant to explaining the unbelief of the Jews who were listening?" Their unbelief is explained with reference to the fact that God must graciously give a person to the Son. If a person does not receive this divine benefit, he will remain firmly attached to his sin and rebellion, and he will like these men ultimately walk away when faced with the claims of Christ (John 6:65–66).

It is only after firmly establishing the divine freedom of God in saving His people that Jesus affirms the result of God's election in the life of the redeemed:

> "This is the will of My Father, that everyone who beholds the Son and believes in Him will have eternal life, and I Myself will raise him up on the last day." (v. 40)

We immediately note three vital truths in the passage: 1) This is the "human side" of the expression of the Father's will (the "divine side" was in 38–39); 2) the actions of "beholding" and "believing" are present tense actions, which means they are ongoing actions, not one-time, surface-level responses (as the Jews had had upon seeing the miracle the previous day);[5] and 3) those who behold the Son and believe in Him are *the very same ones* seen in the preceding three verses, those who are given by the Father to the Son. It is simple eisegesis to remove this passage from its context, insert a concept of universal ability into "all the ones seeing/believing," and then read that concept back into verses 37–39 as if this somehow removes the particularity, the specificity of God's giving a people to the Son for salvation. Who will behold and believe in the Son? Those whom the Father gives the Son, *and no one else*, as we will see below.[6]

MAN'S INABILITY PROCLAIMED

Jesus' teachings on the freedom of the Father in giving men to the Son and the certainty of their coming to Christ as a result are not popular. The Jews grumble about the claims Jesus makes for Himself, for they can see that His teaching implies His divine origin and status. They have not come across the lake for *this* kind of teaching! Jesus does not seek to "woo" them to a "freewill decision," nor does He strike up a lengthy invitation hymn and try to over-come their stubborn rejection of truth through an emotional appeal. His words are unmistakable:

> Jesus answered and said to them, "Do not grumble among your-selves. No one can come to Me unless the Father who sent Me draws him; and I will raise him up on the last day. It is written in the prophets, 'AND THEY SHALL ALL BE TAUGHT OF GOD.' Everyone who has heard and learned from the Father, comes to Me." (vv. 43–44)

There is no reason for these unbelievers to grumble. Why? Because it is not within their capacity to come to Him in faith: As condemned sinners, they are dependent upon the grace of God for that. Jesus plainly states, "No one can come to Me." Literally, "No one is *able to come*." No one has the capacity, the ability, to simply come to Christ in faith. Why? The Bible's answer has already been seen: Man is dead in sin, enslaved to its power, an enemy of God, unable to do what is good. Only those the Father gives to the Son come to Him in faith, and that as a *result* of being given.

If Jesus had stopped with these words, there would be no gospel. But He did not. He said that no one has the ability to come to Him *unless the Father draws* him. And of course we are immediately told that God draws *all men* to Christ.[7] But the text does not allow this abandonment of the context. Remember, Jesus is explaining the *unbelief* of those who will walk away from Him by the end of His discourse. In context, the ones who are drawn in verse 44 are the ones the Father gives to the Son in verse 37, the ones Jesus raises up on the last day in verse 39, and the ones who, as a result of being given by the Father to the Son, believe in verse 40. The consistency of the text is a treasure to believers who seek to draw their beliefs solely from Scripture.

Jesus tells us two things about the one who is drawn. We are told that the one who is drawn lacks the ability, in and of himself, of coming to Christ. But, and this is most important, we also see that the one who is drawn by the Father *is also raised up by the Son.* There is no warrant anywhere in the text for introducing a disjunction between "unless the Father…draws *him*" and "I will raise *him* up on the last day." In the original language the first word "him" is separated from the second occurrence (in the identical form) by only two words, which in English we translate as "and I will raise." Given that the people drawn are, in fact, those given by the Father to the Son and that Jesus promises to raise those given to Him to eternal life, it follows that the very same "him" is in view in both occurrences in verse 44. *All those who are drawn by the Father to the Son are raised up by the Son on the last day.* This simple consideration closes the door on every effort to get around the necessary teaching of this passage.[8]

The fact that those who are drawn are *only* those given by the Father to the Son is borne out in verse 45, where everyone who has "heard and learned" from the Father comes to Christ. Consider the entire passage. Who comes to Christ? Those who 1) are given by the Father to the Son (v. 37); 2) behold and believe in Him (v. 40); 3) are drawn by the Father (v. 44); and 4) hear and learn from the Father (v. 45). To attempt to disrupt the flow of the text, introduce new groups, or in any way destroy the singular focus of Jesus' words is to show that we are not doing exegesis but are instead attempting to defend a tradition against the very inspired words of God in Scripture. We must let this passage teach what it teaches, no matter what our preconceptions might be.

THE RESULT

Preaching the truth is never popular. The result of Jesus' sermon was the founding of the Church Shrinkage Movement: He started with five thousand; He ended with a small, confused group. He simply refused to stop preaching the sovereignty of God. "He was saying, 'For this reason I have said to you, that no one can come to Me unless it has been granted him from the Father'" (v. 65).[9] Despite the negative response it garnered, He kept pressing this truth upon His listeners. And their response? The next verse says they walked away. They no longer followed after Him. But those who truly were given to Him, like Peter, confessed that He had the words of eternal life. What about us? Will we walk away from hard truths, or will we speak as Peter, knowing that Jesus has the words of eternal life? May God grant us grace to hear and obey His Word.

---

1. The vast majority of attempted ways out of the passage involve ignoring the text's own presentation and order, such as jumping to verse 40, interpreting it outside of its context, and then reading the interpretation back into verse 37 or forward into verse 44.
2. See the discussion on the actual biblical meaning of *foreknowledge* in my exegesis of Romans 8:28–34.
3. This is the verdict of the grammar of the passage in the original language as well.
4. Some, desperate to avoid the sovereignty of God in this passage, have suggested that Judas was "given" to the Son and hence the passage does not mean that Christ will save all who are given to Him. But this is manifestly untrue. Judas is always identified as the son of perdition, marked out in God's sovereignty for his role in the betrayal of Christ. Nowhere are we told that he was given to Christ in the same way Jesus refers to His elect people here in John 6. Just the opposite is in fact the case.
5. Specifically, these are present participles, emphasizing the ongoing nature of the faith of true believers in contrast to the temporary, noncontinuing belief that characterized the crowds.

6. Note also that this explains the confusion many have about why there are so many passages in the Bible in which God commands sinners to repent and calls for faith in His mercy and grace. Why have such invitations and calls for repentance if, in fact, God must first free the slave from the dungeon of sin? Because a slave, once set free, is still in need of direction as to what to do and where to go. Those passages serve two functions: For the believer they serve to give light and direction, assurance of God's acceptance, and guidance in the path of righteousness. For the unbeliever they show the power of sin and the fact that no man, outside of God's enablement, will even desire to do what is right in God's sight.

7. Normally based upon John 12:32, though that passage is patently not teaching any kind of universal drawing of every single individual. The passage is about the coming of Gentiles who are seeking Jesus, so that the "all men" is in reference to Jews and Gentiles, as it most often is in Scripture. Further, it is obvious that the cross of Jesus Christ repels unbelievers. It does not attract them. As Paul taught, the Cross is foolishness and a stumbling block. Hence, the obvious meaning, especially in light of Revelation 5:9, is that the "all men" of John 12:32 refers to those who are of every tribe, tongue, people, and nation.

8. Some have suggested amazingly facile ways around this simple truth. It has been suggested that just because someone has been drawn doesn't mean he will actually end up being saved. Yet, given the context, this would not only turn Jesus' argument on its head (that He is explaining the disbelief of the Jews and saying that maybe some of them are drawn by the Father to the Son but are just not "cooperating" is hardly in view in the passage) but would also require us to believe that the one who is raised up is someone different from the one who is drawn, an assertion without any basis whatsoever in the text. Such an assertion is a classic example of eisegesis: reading into the text something that is not there to begin with.

9. Mr. Hunt has erroneously asserted that the term *given* in the KJV (Greek: *didomi*) means that the ability has been given to the sinner to come to Christ (Dave Hunt, *What Love Is This?* [Sisters, Ore.: Loyal, 2002], 343–4). The periphrastic construction found here is best translated as *granted* or *enabled.* None of the examples offered in his book are even remotely relevant on a translational basis to the construction in John 6:65. Indeed, Mr. Hunt takes this error so far as to say that the real meaning of John 6:44, in light of this erroneous understanding of *didomi* in 6:65, is not that no man is able, but that all men are able if the Father draws them, and since He draws all, all men are able (p. 346). This is eisegesis in its fullest form.

Response, by Dave Hunt

From John 6:37, White deduces that "the Son must have the capacity to save without the assistance, permission, or cooperation of man." Even believing on Christ is disallowed "cooperation." Yet Spurgeon continually urged every unsaved person to believe.[1] We quoted Sproul: "The Reformed view [is] that before a person can choose Christ…he must be born again."[2] So the gospel is only for those who have already been saved! Spurgeon rejected this doctrine: "A man who is regenerated…is saved already, and it is…ridiculous…to preach Christ to him."[3]

If regeneration takes place by God's sovereign act without any faith on man's part, what does believing the gospel accomplish? Why would a regenerated child of God need to be saved? The biblical doctrine of salvation through faith in Christ contradicts so-called "Reformed theology."

Moreover, since this regeneration comes without any effort, understanding, or faith on the part of the elect, it could be true of infants. Why infant baptism? The elect don't need it, and it can't benefit the nonelect. And having been elected from eternity past, why would they need the gospel and "confirmation"?

Yes, Christ "is able also to save them to the uttermost," but only those who "come unto God by him" (Hebrews 7:25). All of Scripture teaches that salvation comes only by faith. White focuses on the one reference each in John 6 to the Father's drawing and giving but ignores the eleven references that describe man's responsibility:

"He that cometh to me and…that believeth on me" (v. 35); "Every one who seeth the Son, and believeth on him" (v. 40); "Every man…that hath heard, and hath learned of the Father, cometh unto me" (v. 45); "He that believeth on me" (v. 47); "If any man eat…my flesh, which I will give for the life of the world" (v. 51); "Whoso eateth my flesh, and drinketh my blood, hath eternal life" (v. 54); "The words that I speak…are spirit, and they are life" (v. 63).

Christ miraculously multiplied "five barley loaves and two small fishes" (6:9–10) to feed five thousand men plus women and children. They followed Him, hoping He would continue to feed them, just as God gave their ancestors manna to eat. Jesus used their hunger to illustrate faith as spiritual eating and drinking. This metaphor refutes White's idea that there is nothing man can do. The multitude willingly ate the multiplied loaves and fishes; the Father didn't cause them to eat. Yes, the Father draws to Christ, but man must willingly come and eat and drink by faith. This fact is taught in numerous Scriptures, which White's few proof texts cannot annul.

That the prodigal "came to himself [and] said…I will arise and go to my father" (Luke 15:17–18) contradicts White's entire thesis. So does the parable of the sower. In contrast to White's claim that salvation is "without the…cooperation of man," Christ declares that whether the seed ("the word of God" [Luke 8:11]) sprouts and bears fruit depends upon the soil; i.e., the heart. "[The] good ground are they who, in an honest and good heart, having heard the word, keep it, and bring forth fruit" (Luke 8:15). "By the way side" ground are those from whom the devil "taketh away the word out of their hearts" (Luke 8:12). Calvinism makes nonsense of good and bad soil and the devil taking seed from the heart. Scripture, however, emphasizes the attitude of the heart toward God and His Word: "Thou shalt love the LORD thy God with all thine heart, and with all thy soul, and with all thy might" (Deuteronomy 6:5). Isn't that human response? Consider the following:

> I command you…to love the LORD your God, and to serve him with all your heart (Deuteronomy 11:13); Take diligent heed…to love the LORD your God…and to serve him with all your heart and with all your soul (Joshua 22:5); [David] followed me with all his heart (1 Kings 14:8); Their heart was not right (Psalm 78:37); Thy word have I hidden in mine heart (Psalm 119:11); Thou triest the heart (Jeremiah 11:20); Search for me with all your heart (Jeremiah 29:13); Daniel purposed in his heart (Daniel 1:8);If ye will not lay it to heart (Malachi 2:2); If ye from your hearts forgive not (Matthew 18:35); Have ye your heart yet hardened? (Mark 8:17); O fools, and slow of heart to believe (Luke 24:25); Believe in thine heart (Romans 10:9).

Clearly, God does not sovereignly regenerate and cause man to believe, but man must choose from his heart. In response, Calvinists point to another proof text: "The king's heart is in the hand of the LORD…he turneth it whithersoever he will" (Proverbs 21:1).[4] White lists this among a number of Scriptures declaring that God does as He pleases, but not one of them denies human ability and responsibility to believe the gospel.[5] Indeed, the next verse says, "the LORD pondereth the hearts"—a meaningless statement if God decrees every thought, word, and deed. What would He ponder? In fact, King Solomon is expressing his commitment to the Lord.

In Luke 8:10, Christ is speaking in parables to the unbelieving multitude "that seeing they might not see, and hearing they might not understand."

So it is no surprise that they do not understand and that they turn away from Him. In this context, Christ says, "All that the Father giveth me shall come to me" (John 6:37). This is a statement of fact, not of cause and effect, and it must agree with all of Scripture concerning man's responsibility to come and believe.

Yes, the Father gives the redeemed to the Son (e.g., "my Father, who gave them me" (John 10:29); "all that he hath given me" (John 6: 39); "as many as thou hast given him" (John 17:2); "thou gavest them me" (John 17:6); "given me" (John 17:9, 11, 24); "the children whom God hath given me" (Hebrews 2:13). And the Father will bring "many sons unto glory" (Hebrews 2:10), having adopted them into His family as Christ's brethren and joint heirs (e.g., Romans 8:15–17; Galatians 3:26, 4:5–7; Ephesians 1:5; 1 John 3:1–2). But what does *giving* mean?

The Father "sent the Son to be the Saviour of the world" (1 John 4:14). To Him Christ prayed in Gethsemane, asking to be spared the agony of the Cross if it were possible for mankind to be saved any other way (Matthew 26:39). The Father "laid on him the iniquity of us all…[and was] pleased… to bruise him…[and to] put him to grief…[and to] make his soul an offering for sin" (Isaiah 53:6, 10). It is the Father "who justifies" (Isaiah 50:8; Romans 4:5; 8:33), whose justice must be satisfied for our redemption and who accepts the payment Christ made for sin (Romans 3:24–25).

The Father's "giving" to the Son is not the sovereign predestining of some for heaven and others for hell "according to the good pleasure of his will," as Calvin declared. [6] The Father can only justify "him who believeth in Jesus" (Romans 3:26). He can give to the Son only those who have come to Him in faith and accepted His sacrifice for their sins. Willing faith from the heart is vital.

D. HUNT

It is not the Father's giving of the elect to the Son that *causes* them to believe on Christ. Rather it is upon the basis of the Cross and the faith of those who "believe in Jesus" that the Father gives the redeemed to the Son in satisfaction of "the travail of his soul" (Isaiah 53:11). Only those who have "received him…[and] believe on his name" become the sons of God (John 1:12–13).

Yet to uphold Calvinism, White insists that "this divine and sovereign act of giving on the part of the Father *results in* an action on the part of those given: they unfailingly come to Christ." The context of John 6, Christ's metaphor, and all Scripture contradict this idea. Nor does the Father, who inhabits eternity (Isaiah 57:15), "give" the redeemed to the Son in time and space—a fact that destroys White's argument.

The redeemed have been seated in "heavenly places in Christ Jesus" (Ephesians 2:6) from eternity past. Likewise, by God's foreknowledge in eternity, the redeemed were given by the Father to the "lamb…foreordained before the foundation of the world" (1 Peter 1:19–20). Yet they had to believe on Christ to get saved. Thus, predestination/election is always according to foreknowledge.

In John 6, Jesus is offering Himself not to an elect but to the entire unbelieving multitude, showing again that the gospel is for all. Though He knows they will refuse to eat (i.e., believe), Christ says, "My Father giveth you the true bread from heaven…. I am the bread of life" (vv. 32, 35). The offer is to everyone, but the partaking is willingly from the heart.

White's interpretation of John 6:37 disregards the immediate context and the entire Bible. The hundreds (perhaps thousands) of Scriptures that call upon man to choose, to repent, to believe, to come, must all be set aside to allow a few proof texts to declare that no one has any choice and that faith is a gift only to a select group, who alone can come to Christ and believe on Him. Hundreds of passages showing God pleading with Israel and mankind to repent are non-sensical if there are those from whom He withholds the grace to repent and the faith to believe. The theory that God takes pleasure in damning billions nullifies hundreds of Scriptures stating that He loves all and that He has no pleasure in the death of the wicked. Hundreds of Scriptures indicating that man has a will and that he must believe in his heart, as well as examples of those who have done so, are set aside to maintain that man is *unable* to believe.

Verse 45 explains verse 37: "Every man...that hath heard, and hath learned of the Father, cometh unto me." This is misleading language if men are *unable* to hear, learn, and come to Christ by faith. The entire teaching of the Bible indicates that the Father's drawing and giving of the redeemed to Christ is the result of their hearing and learning from the Father through the gospel of God (e.g., Romans 1:1; 15:16; 1 Thessalonians 2:2, 8–9; 1 Timothy 1:11) and of Christ (Mark 1:1; Romans 1:16; 15:19; 1 Corinthians 9:12, 18). Those who believe the gospel come to Christ and will never perish.

The conclusion to which White's argument leads is that all who are not among the elect given by the Father to the Son are *unable* to come to Him, *unable* to believe on Him, *unable* to be saved. The only thing anyone can do is to hope that he is among the elect and that a bolt from the blue causes him to believe. And there is no purpose in trying to believe, because that would only lead to the delusion of thinking one is saved through fleshly effort. Is this good news? Hardly.

White concludes: "May God grant us grace to hear and obey His Word." *Grant us?* How can He grant grace to those He has from eternity past predestined to eternal torment? And if we have been predestined to heaven and all is God's doing, why do we need grace at all?

Yeah!

D. HUNT

1. Charles H. Spurgeon, "The Warrant of Faith," in *The Metropolitan Tabernacle Pulpit*, Newington, 20 September 1863, www.seegod.org/the_warrant_of_faith.htm; "Compel Them to Come In," in *The New Park Street Pulpit* (London: Passmore & Alabaster, 1859), 5: 20–2. In the preface he says, "The sermon entitled 'Compel them to come in' has been so signally owned of God, that scarcely a week occurs without some cases of its usefulness coming to light. The violent, rigid school of Calvinists will, of course, abhor the sermon."

2. R. C. Sproul, *Chosen by God* (Chicago: Tyndale, 1986), 72.

3. C. H. Spurgeon, "The Warrant of Faith."

4. James R. White, *The Potter's Freedom: A Defense of the Reformation* (Amityville, N.Y.: Calvary Press, 2000), 42–3.

5. Ibid., 41–51.

6. John Calvin, *Institutes of the Christian Religion*, tr. Henry Beveridge (Grand Rapids, Mich.: Eerdmans, 1998), 10.

Defense, by James White

D ave Hunt begins his response to my exegesis of John 6 in these words:

> From John 6:37, White deduces that "the Son must have the capacity to save without the assistance, permission, or cooperation of man." Even believing on Christ is disallowed "cooperation." Yet Spurgeon continually urged every unsaved person to believe.

Aside from the fact that Mr. Hunt has again misread the text he is replying to (the quoted words are about verses 38–39), the reader should note that even if the reference to Spurgeon were relevant (it is not), what does it have to do with the text? The only way to meaningfully respond to exegesis is to demonstrate errors from the grammar and context of the passage. Mr. Hunt offers no positive exegesis whatsoever. All we learn from his pen is what he feels the text *cannot* mean, not what it really *does* mean. But even here, Hunt errs again by setting up a straw man. Calvinists like Spurgeon call upon all men everywhere to believe and repent, just as the Word of God does. We do not know who the elect are; hence, we preach the gospel to every creature.

Mr. Hunt asks, "If regeneration takes place by God's sovereign act without any faith on man's part, what does believing the gospel accomplish?"

Again, faith and repentance are gifts given by God in regeneration, as we have shown exegetically elsewhere. <u>The preached Word is God's chosen means of bringing His elect unto Himself.</u>

But this section is supposed to be about John 6, so leaving aside all the many straw men and rabbit trails, did Mr. Hunt respond meaningfully to the exegesis of the text itself? No, he did not.

Hunt asserts that the eating of the food by the five thousand "refutes White's idea that there is nothing man can do." Eating physical food is not a spiritually relevant thing: These people refused to see their need of spiritual food, and Jesus said it was because they *could not do so* (6:44). It is simply amazing that Mr. Hunt would actually suggest that total depravity means men can do *nothing at all* —including eating physical food!

But most importantly, the reader must see the role of extrabiblical tradition in Hunt's attempt to explain verse 37. Remember, we noted the fact that according to the grammar of the text, the action of being given by the Father to the Son *precedes* the coming of those so given to Christ. It is the same thought as that expressed in the sentence "All those chosen by the coach will play in the game." The choosing of the coach precedes, and determines, who will play in the game. The inarguable assertion of Jesus is that those who come to Him *come because the Father has given them to the Son.* How does Hunt deal with this?

First, Hunt tells us that this is not a statement "of cause and effect." What in the text supports the assertion that the Father's giving to the Son does not bear a causal relationship to the coming of *all* those given to Christ? Hunt does not say. He simply makes the assertion without any textual support. He later says that "the context of John 6, Christ's metaphor, and all Scripture contradict" the idea of a causal relationship. Where does the text say this? This is wishful thinking based upon tradition, not exegesis. The point, therefore, is firmly established.

Mr. Hunt lists other Scriptures that speak of the Father giving men to the Son, some of which, such as John 17:9, stand in direct contradiction to his thesis. But then he says:

The Father's "giving" to the Son is not the sovereign predestining of some for heaven and others for hell "according to the good pleasure of his will," as Calvin declared.... He can give to the Son only those who have come to Him in faith and accepted His sacrifice for their sins. Willing faith from the heart is vital.

The reader will note that all Mr. Hunt does is repeat his traditions. No effort is made to connect these repeated assertions to the text of John 6. If this giving does not involve sovereign predestination, what *does* it involve?[1] Jesus Himself says it results in eternal life. If that is not election unto salvation, what is?

Hunt asserts that the Father, because He is eternal, "does not give the redeemed to the Son in time and space." This allegedly "destroys" my argument. Ironically, the verb *gives* in verse 37 is in the present tense: Every time a believer comes to Christ, he or she is "given." Verse 39 refers back to the eternal transaction of grace. In any case, Hunt's assertions are groundless. He is forced to retreat from John 6, grab his fully refuted theory of "foreknowledge," and read it back into the passage from outside—all to maintain his tradition of libertarian free will.

Dave Hunt cannot offer a positive, contextual exegesis of John 6. His tradition has no room for its teachings. He turns the passage on its head by stating that verse 37 should be interpreted in light of his own erroneous interpretation of verse 45. He misses the fact that the hearing and learning of verse 45 is "from the Father" and parallel with the drawing of verse 44.

Mr. Hunt's real beliefs come out in his closing remarks. He rightly sees that if what I am saying is true, God, and God alone, saves. While mocking the miracle of God's sovereign and gracious regeneration of His elect by referring to a "bolt from the blue," Hunt lets his real views out: If salvation is truly all of God, he will not believe it.

---

1. Note Hunt's continued and repetitive refusal to see that positive predestination to life is what is according to God's good pleasure, not the just punishment of the wicked.

J. WHITE

Final Remarks, by Dave Hunt

ike other Calvinists, White refers repeatedly to Calvinism as "the doctrines of grace" and "Reformed theology." The Reformation was all Calvinism? Many others were involved! Non-Calvinists embrace all that the Bible teaches about God's grace. We simply reject as unbiblical Calvinism's "grace," which is irresistibly applied to the elect and neglects all others.

White says that "this section is supposed to be about John 6" and faults me for citing other Scriptures. No, the debate is about *Calvinism*. He uses John 6 to defend it, and I can go to any Scripture to refute it because the Bible must be understood as a whole.

I "suggest that total depravity means men can do *nothing at all*—including eating physical food"? He can't be serious! Is he diverting attention from his lack of response to the parables of the prodigal son ("I will arise and go") and the seed sowed on good soil ("an honest and good heart"), which show man's part in receiving salvation?

He says, "Eating physical food is not a spiritually relevant thing." By analogy, it is. Christ often used the metaphor of eating and drinking to illustrate spiritual truth. In this passage, He refers to "that meat which endureth unto everlasting life" (John 6:27), "bread from heaven" (v. 32), and "the bread of life" (vv. 35, 48). Eating and drinking Christ by faith underlies this entire passage and is the Lord's major emphasis in illustrating that *man* must *believe* to be saved.

White claims that he exegetes this passage and that I don't. He puts all the emphasis upon the Father's drawing and giving men to Christ—mentioned three times: verses 37, 39, and 44. But he neglects entirely Christ's major emphasis upon human responsibility: hearing and learning of the Father, coming to Christ, seeing Him, eating and drinking of Him, and believing on Him are mentioned seventeen times. White's "exegesis" is far out of balance in this particular context, leading to conclusions that contradict the overall emphasis of the Bible.

Calvinism allows no cooperation or willingness on man's part; faith and obedience must be God's sole doing. This turns the entire Bible into a charade and mocks both God and man. What is the point of, "Choose you this day whom ye will serve" (Joshua 24:15) if there is no free will?

If Christ imposes this faith upon the elect without their choosing, why does He say to the woman, "Great is thy faith" (Matthew 15:28), or to the centurion, "I have not found so great faith...in Israel" (Luke 7:9), or to the two blind men, "According to your faith be it unto you" (Matthew 9:29)? What is the purpose of judgment, either for the saved or the damned, if everything is God's doing?

White claims that I wouldn't believe in a salvation that is "truly all of God." Of course salvation is all of God. But to be able to accept it by faith or reject it no more gives any credit to the believer than accepting a gift of a million dollars gives the recipient credit for earning the money.

Final Remarks, by James White

I have to trust that the careful reader by now has become fully aware of the fact that Mr. Hunt is not listening to the replies offered him. He has just stated that man *must* believe to be saved. Of course. No one has said otherwise. The issues have been man's capacity to exercise saving faith and the nature of regeneration, the gifts given by God to His people when he miraculously brings them to spiritual life. Despite the repeated correction of his misrepresentations of Calvinism, Dave Hunt remains doggedly impervious to instruction.

The words of the Lord Jesus in John 6 are clear and compelling. The plethora of failed explanations of the passage produced by those who oppose the message that offended so many in the synagogue in Capernaum (and evidently continues to offend today) is testimony to the force of the teaching and the clarity of the text. The person who eschews tradition and simply seeks to follow the reasoning of the incarnate Lord will hear His voice and will come to the conclusion that no man is able to come to Christ unless he is drawn by the Father *and* that this drawing is powerful, effective, and unfailing in its accomplishment.

Spurgeon so cogently observed:

I remember meeting once with a man who said to me, "Sir, you preach that Christ takes people by the hair of their heads and drags them to himself.''… But said I, while Christ does not drag people to himself by the hair of their heads, I believe that he draws them by the heart quite as powerfully as your caricature would suggest. Mark that in the Father's drawing there is no compulsion whatever; Christ never compelled any man to come to him against his will. If a man be unwilling to be saved, Christ does not save him against his will. How, then, does the Holy Spirit draw him? Why, by making him willing.… He goes to the secret fountain of the heart, and he knows how, by some mysterious operation to turn the will in an opposite direction, so that, as Ralph Erskine paradoxically puts it, the man is saved "with full consent against his will" that is, against his old will he is saved. But he is saved with full consent for he is made willing in the day of God's power.… It is quite true that first of all man is unwilling to be saved. When the Holy Spirit hath put his influence into the heart, the text is fulfilled—"draw me and I will run after thee." We follow on while he draws us, glad to obey the voice which once we had despised. But the gist of the matter lies in the turning of the will. How that is done no flesh knoweth; it is one of those mysteries that is clearly perceived as a fact, but the cause of which no tongue can tell, and no heart can guess.[1]

Misquote

_we_

---

1. Charles H. Spurgeon, "Human Inability," sermon preached 7 March 1858.

Chapter Five

THE GOLDEN
CHAIN OF REDEMPTION

by James White

I t has been rightly observed that "if the Epistle to the Romans may be likened to a great cathedral of Christian truth, then chapter eight is the highest of the towering spires of that divine revelation."[1] And the pinnacle of that tower is found the "golden chain of redemption," Romans 8:28–30. Since it is one of the clearest and most compelling passages in all of Scripture regarding the reality of God's absolute sovereignty in salvation, the exegesis of the passage in defense of the Reformed faith is most relevant to the topic of this work.

Called According to His Purpose

The passage begins with words known to almost any believer who has spent more than a brief time reading the Bible:

We know that God causes all things to work together for good to
those who love God, to those who are called according to His purpose.
(Romans 8:28)

As precious as these words are in providing comfort to believers, the
theology upon which they rest is far deeper than what is often admitted.
God causes all things to work together simply because He is *sovereign* over
human affairs. His will is being accomplished in the world, resulting in His
glory and honor. We know that those who are "in the flesh" (as opposed to
"in the Spirit") are enemies of God (Romans 8:7–8); they are not God-lovers
but God-haters. So this promise is for a specific group of people. And who
are they? Who loves God? All men, saved or unsaved? No, God-lovers are
limited to a particular group, "those who are called according to His purpose." The electing grace of God, based on His eternal purpose, flows
naturally from the assertion that He causes all things to work together for
His particular purpose in the lives of the elect. It should be emphasized that
the calling of the elect here noted is not based upon the fact that these are
God-lovers. Instead, those who are now loving God do so because they have
been called according to God's purpose. God's purpose results in their being
God-lovers, not the other way around.

THE GOLDEN CHAIN

The "golden chain of redemption" begins in Romans 8:29 and comprises a
chain of five verbs, all of which have God as the subject and the elect as their
object. The verbs are:

foreknew → predestined → called → justified → glorified

Each is an active verb in the past tense; that is, these are actions that are, from God's perspective, finished and certain, and the fact that they are active means that they are *divine actions*. These are things *God* does. We will see how important this is as we exegete the passage.

For those whom He foreknew, He also predestined to become conformed to the image of His Son, so that He would be the firstborn among many brethren. (Romans 8:29)

The main clause is the direct assertion of a positive act of predestination on the part of God the Father. The predestination is unto the fullness of salvation, of course, for only those who are forgiven, justified, and adopted are conformed to the image of Christ, and these are called Christ's "brethren," a term that in this context is reserved for believers.

The traditions of men attempt to short-circuit the entire passage by misdefining the first divine action on God's part. When Paul says that God "foreknew" those He then also predestines, calls, justifies, and glorifies, men immediately ignore the biblical meaning of the term, put a creation of philosophy in its place, and insist that all the actions God undertakes in this passage are based upon His responding to and acting in light of foreseen actions on the part of autonomous men. So often is the "God looked into the future and saw who would choose Him" statement made, that most accept it without any inquiry into its truthfulness. But the fact is that the text knows nothing of this "crystal ball" approach to God's decree of salvation.

The term translated *foreknow* is an active verb. The way it is portrayed in evangelical tradition would not be something God *does* but instead would involve God passively taking in knowledge from an outside source. When we examine the use of this word in Scripture, we discover that three times in the New Testament God is said to "foreknow."[2] And what is vitally important to understand is that *in none of these passages does God foreknow future events.* That is, the word does not refer to looking into the future and observing *events.* The direct object of "foreknow" when used of God is *always personal.* God foreknows the elect (Romans 8:29), His people (Romans 11:2), and Christ (1 Peter 1:20). These are all *personal objects,* never *events.* This means that, for the person who wishes to dismiss this section of Scripture using the "foreknowledge defense," the task is difficult indeed, for such a person will have to explain how this one usage is the exception, and why, in the context, it must bear a meaning seen nowhere else.[3]

But there is simply too much evidence against such an assertion. A full study of the term, its Old Testament background and uses, and the relevant lexical sources,[4] demonstrates that the verb speaks of a personal choice on the part of the subject. It refers to the choice to enter into relationship with someone. In this case, in eternity past God chose to enter into personal relationship with His elect people, even before bringing them into existence. The relationship is so personal, so intimate, that it is proper to speak of it in the sense of foreloving. God's eternal choice was to enter into a loving, intimate relationship with the elect. This results in His predestinating them to adoption as sons,[5] His calling them into relationship with Him in time, His justifying them by declaring them righteous, and His glorifying them in His presence for all eternity.

An important (and sometimes overlooked) truth that should be emphasized is that *all* who are foreknown are predestined. Not *some,* not *most,* but *all.* The object of each of these divine actions is identical. This is vital, for many systems of theology assume that a person can be, for example, called but not glorified. The introduction of human autonomy into the passage disrupts its message and coherence. Only a fully divine salvation can be described as this passage describes it:

> These whom He predestined, He also called; and these whom He called, He also justified; and these whom He justified, He also glorified. (Romans 8:30)

The "golden chain" continues with the application in time of the eternal and divine will. Those who have been predestined experience the results of that eternal action in time. God calls them into relationship with Jesus Christ. Of course, Paul is using the term more specifically than we find it, for example, in Matthew, "'For many are called, but few are chosen'" (Matthew 22:14). In Paul, "calling" can refer either to the actual call of God into union with Christ, or to the blessings that flow from that union, especially in ministry.[6] Here, given the connection to justification, this is the call into union with Christ. At God's time, in God's way, His eternal love for His people expresses itself in time in the divine action of calling each of those elect persons into union with Jesus Christ.[7]

Reformed theologians refer to this as "effectual calling." All the elect experience the divine calling of God, and, since the very same people are also justified, we see the outworking here of the truth Jesus announced in John 6:37: "All that the Father gives Me will come to Me." If the "calling" here is but a wooing, a general call to salvation that is rejected by many, the chain is broken. And if the autonomous will of man must be factored in, how can it be said that all who are called are also justified? Those who seek to find a place for human autonomy will find the links of the golden chain far too strong to be pried apart.

The plastic link of the autonomous will of man cannot be forged into the golden chain of God's work of redemption in Christ Jesus.

All who are called into union with Jesus Christ are then justified. Justification is a divine action, the forensic declaration of the divine Judge, based upon the finished work of Jesus Christ on behalf of the elect. But immediately we are struck with what this must mean. Are we not justified by faith (Romans 5:1)? Yes, Paul has already taught this divine truth in Romans. But if the apostle can teach that all who are called are justified, and all of those are glorified, does it not follow that human faith, which is surely taught as being the passive instrument or "means" of justification (by grace alone through faith alone), cannot be anything other than a divine gift, a divine certainty, something God does within us?

He is faith Himself

And such is indeed the biblical teaching. Saving faith is not the offspring of an autonomous will but the renewed ability and natural desire of a changed and regenerated heart, that of the new creature in Christ Jesus. So we see that by teaching that all who are called are also justified, Paul is precluding the very position of those who seek to limit God's freedom in salvation through the assertion of man's controlling will. The opponent of God's free grace in salvation must explain how the apostle can speak like this in light of their promotion of the autonomous will of man.

Finally, the apostle teaches the perfection of God's work of salvation: Every person who experiences the divine declaration of his righteousness will likewise experience the supernatural work of glorification. As we struggle here on earth with our failures and shortcomings, we find great solace in the truth that we do not bring about our own glorification. It, like all else in salvation, is God's work. He has promised that He will glorify every one of those He justifies. He will finish His work. This is why we must affirm without apology the truth of the perseverance of the saints. We persevere because it is God's will that we do so. We are secure in Christ. Only when we abandon biblical truth and allow for a gospel that is a mixture of Christ and man can we ever come to a position of believing that Christ can fail to save one who has been united with Him. As long as we remain faithful to the sure teaching of Scripture that "salvation is from the LORD" (Jonah 2:9) we will not be able to profess this synergistic, "God is dependent upon the creature" kind of theology that is so rampant in today's church.

THE GLORIOUS RESULT

The apostle builds upon the tremendous truth of the divine nature of salvation by asking what kind of response we can offer to the truth that God saves, and saves perfectly:

> What then shall we say to these things? If God is for us, who is against us? (Romans 8:31)

Paul asks who can be against "us." Who is the "us"? All men? No, as the context reveals, he speaks of the elect of God (v. 33). Who can stand against those God has foreknown, predestined, called, justified, and glorified? No power in creation can thwart God's purpose in bringing them into His presence!

> He who did not spare His own Son, but delivered Him over for us all, how will He not also with Him freely give us all things? (Romans 8:32)

Paul refers to the Father who "delivered over" His own Son. And for whom did He do this? The text is clear, "for us all." The "us" is limited by the context. In the very next phrase we see the same word, "us": "How will He not also with Him freely give us all things?" Have "all things" been given to the reprobate sinners who are even now undergoing the wrath of God? Has *Christ* been given over for them? Surely not. The Father freely gives "all things" to His people, and the "all things" encompass the "spiritual blessings in heavenly places" of which he speaks in Ephesians 1:3. Christ was given over in place of God's elect people, and His substitutionary atonement shows the fullness of the love of God the Father and His commitment to the redemption of His people.

> Who will bring a charge against God's elect? God is the one who justifies; who is the one who condemns? Christ Jesus is He who died, yes, rather who was raised, who is at the right hand of God, who also intercedes for us. (Romans 8:33–34)

Speaking from the context of the law court, Paul asks who can possibly act as prosecutor against God's elect people. Who can lodge a charge against the elect before the Judge of heaven? The question is rhetorical: No one can, for God the Father is the one who has made the forensic, legal declaration of their right standing before Him. How will He hear any further charge when He has already brought down the gavel and declared them "not guilty"? Who then would dare to contradict such a declaration on God's part? Who can utter a word of condemnation against the elect?

Paul then adds to this wondrously comforting truth by pointing to the Intercessor, the Mediator, the High Priest of the people of God, Jesus Christ, who died and was raised from death (hence accomplishing redemption [Romans 3:24–25]). He intercedes "for us." The "us" is again defined in the context. Not only does verse 33 identify the "us" as the elect of God, but the very nature of intercession likewise proves this point. As we will note in more detail under the topic of the atoning work of the Lord Jesus, His work of intercession is not separate from His work of atonement but instead involves the presentation of that finished work before the Father on behalf of those for whom the offering has been made. Christ's intercession, by definition and revelation, always avails before the Father. That is, Christ succeeds in His intercession, for the offering is perfect and satisfies God's wrath against sin. Therefore, as Hebrews 7:25 says, Christ "is able also to save forever those who draw near to God through Him, since He always lives to make intercession for them." Christ intercedes only for the elect of God. To say that He intercedes for those who perish is to say that He can fail in His intention to save, which is sheer folly. The great consolation found in Paul's words, which then leads to the ascription of praise found in Romans 8:35–39, is simply that God the Father and God the Son are inalterably *for* the elect of God, and hence their salvation, from beginning to end, is assured. This is their hope; this is their glory.

CONCLUSION

Romans 8:28–34 cannot be understood outside of the truth that God is indeed sovereign over all of His creation and that His greatest work, the redemption of a people for His own possession in Jesus Christ, is solely by His grace alone to His praise alone. It is not a cooperative effort, subject to failure due to man's involvement. Man appears in the golden chain of redemption solely as the object of gracious redemption. He nowhere inserts his allegedly autonomous will so as to control God's gracious work.

The apostle Paul will expand upon this theme in the next chapter, where he explains why it is that many Jews continue in stubborn rebellion against the truth that is in Jesus Christ. He will not wander off into some discussion of national privilege in Romans 9 but will instead explain his assertion in verse 6, "They are not all Israel who are descended from Israel." The passage remains intensely personal, using personal examples of God's electing grace in the history of His dealing with His people as support for Paul's thesis.

It should be remembered that Paul focuses upon the positive action of God's predestination in mercy of a people unto Himself long before he writes, "It does not depend on the man who wills or the man who runs, but on God who has mercy" (9:16) and "He has mercy on whom He desires, and He hardens whom He desires" (9:18). We miss the true biblical emphasis if we do not see this. The wonder is not that God passes by rebel sinners and shows His justice in their condemnation; the wonder is that in eternity past He foreknew a people, chose them in love, and decreed their eternal salvation in their perfect Savior, Jesus Christ.

---

1. Reference note on Romans 8 in *The New Scofield Reference Bible*.
2. We must distinguish between the verb here and God having *foreknowledge,* a noun. In Scripture the noun is used differently than the verb.
3. Of course, most often this meaning is simply assumed, not demonstrated or proven.
4. For a fuller discussion, including references to lexical sources, see my response to Norman Geisler in *The Potter's Freedom: A Defense of the Reformation* (Amityville, N.Y.: Calvary Press, 2000), 198–200.
5. All who are saved are adopted into the family of God. This is not some special "second blessing" or a benefit for "superChristians." A person who is not adopted is not a Christian.
6. For example, the call into union with Christ is seen in 1 Corinthians 1:2, 26; Ephesians 1:18; and 2 Timothy 1:9.
7. This is one of the great errors of the heresy of "inclusivism," for it is clearly God's stated purpose to save His people in Christ Jesus only so that all things resound to His glory in Christ.

Response, by Dave Hunt

White's foundation is again an extreme view of sovereignty: "His will is being accomplished in the world, all resulting in His glory and honor." In fact, most of what happens in the world is not in accordance with, but in defiance of, God's will. Certainly rebellion against God is not obedience to His will. Nor is the evil practiced by sinners with whom God is "angry...every day" (Psalm 7:11) to "His glory and honor."

Yes, the promise in Romans 8:28 is only for those "that love God...who are the called according to his purpose." White says, "Reformed theologians refer to this as 'effectual calling.'...[A]ll who are called are also justified." The word *effectual* is not there. These people love God because they have heeded His call, as He "foreknew" they would. The basis of being justified and glorified is not simply being "called" (which all are), but the predestination of those "whom he did foreknow" would respond to His call. White's reference to God's foreknowledge as a "'crystal ball' approach" borders on blasphemy.

Not every person who is "called" is saved and glorified ("Many are called, but few are chosen" [Matthew 22:14]), and not all chosen are glorified. God both called and chose all of Israel: "The LORD thy God hath chosen thee to be a special people unto himself" (Deuteronomy 7:6). But most of Israel rejected this call. They served false gods and God's judgment fell upon them. Yahweh asked unrepentant Israel, "Wherefore...[w]hen I called, was there none to answer?" (Isaiah 50:2); "I called you, but ye answered not" (Jeremiah 7:13). Judas, too, was not only called but chosen, yet he is in hell (John 6:70; Acts 1:17).

God's call to man through creation has "gone out through all the earth" (Psalm 19:4) so that all men "are without excuse" (Romans 1:20). God, "the fountain of living waters" (Jeremiah 2:13; 17:13), calls to "every one that thirsteth" to drink of the water of life (Isaiah 55:1). Proving that He is Yahweh, Christ calls, "If any man thirst, let him come unto me, and drink" (John 7:37); "Whosoever will, let him take the water of life freely" (Revelation 22:17). The invitation to love God, to heed His call, has always been open to all.

White claims that "God's purpose results in their being God-lovers, not the other way around." No, it is not God's sovereignty but His love that causes us to love Him (1 John 4:19). Nor does God create that love in us sovereignly. It must be the genuine response of our hearts: "Thou shalt love the LORD thy God with all thine heart" (Deuteronomy 6:5).

White manages to find "God's decree on salvation" and the "golden chain of redemption" (a favorite Calvinist term) in Romans 8. In fact, the subject is not redemption but the blessings to which God has predestined the redeemed He foreknew, the tribulations they will suffer in this life, and their eternal security in Christ.

White's insistence that "faith is...the renewed ability and natural desire of a changed and regenerated heart" is dealt with in my third chapter.

White says that "we do not bring about our own glorification." Who imagines that we do? He adds that it is unbiblical to believe "that Christ can fail to save one who has been united with Him." Who would disagree? His implication that non-Calvinists teach a "synergistic, 'God is dependent upon the creature' kind of theology" is absurd.

RESPONSE, BY DAVE HUNT

The fact that the "us" in "delivered him up for us all" refers to Paul and all true believers reading the passage does not limit salvation to a select group. Nor does it indicate that Christ did not die for all mankind. "Freely give us all things" does not limit the promise to a predestined elect. Any person reading this passage could claim this promise and, by faith, become a believer in Christ.

What we need from White (which he hasn't given us) is a clear statement that salvation is only for a select group. And it would have to be unequivocal to counter the numerous clear statements that God loves the whole world, that whosoever will may come, and that He is not willing that any should perish.

That no charge can be brought against "God's elect" for whom Christ died does not say that there is a select group for whom alone Christ died and who were sovereignly regenerated without faith and predestined to salvation. In the context of the entire book of Romans, one can only conclude that the "elect" are the "whosoever" who have believed the gospel.

White says that the word *us* in "who also intercedes for us" can only signify the elect because it would be "sheer folly" to imagine that Christ "intercedes for those who perish." Yet Christ from the cross interceded for those who crucified Him: "Father, forgive them (Luke 23:34). Of course, "for us" means the redeemed for whom He intercedes in this special way, but that does not say that the redeemed are those for whom alone Christ died.

Calvinists cannot admit that foreknowledge means to know in advance what man will do of his free will, because that would disprove their theory. Pink writes, "God foreknows what will be because He has decreed what shall be."[1] Calvin said, "God foreknew what the end of man was to be...because he had so ordained by his decree."[2] Piper says, "Foreknowledge is virtually

D. HUNT   155 the same as election.... He foreknows—that is, elects—a people for him-self."[3] Likewise, MacArthur says, "God's foreknowledge, therefore, is not a reference to His omniscient foresight but to His foreordination."[4] But what is "foreknowledge" if not "omniscient foresight"? Moreover, to know in advance is clearly different from ordaining in advance.

Romans 8:29 clearly distinguishes between foreknowledge and foreordi-nation: "For whom he did foreknow [*proginosko*], he also did predestinate." Without this distinction, Paul would be saying redundantly, "For whom he foreordained [i.e., predestined] he also predestined." First Peter 1:2 makes the same distinction: "Elect according to the foreknowledge [*prognosis*] of God." Is Peter really nonsensically saying, "Elect according to the election of God"?

Prognosis is found twice in the New Testament (Acts 2:23 and 1 Peter 1:2), and both times it is rendered "foreknowledge." *Proginosko* is found five times (Acts 26:5; Romans 8:29; 11.2; 1 Peter 1:20; 2 Peter 3:17). It is translated respectively: *knew* me from the beginning; *foreknow*; *foreknew*; *foreordained*; *know before*. First Peter 1:20 is an aberrant rendering in the KJV (the NASB has "foreknown"). Yet to save his theory, the Calvinist insists on "foreordained" for *all five passages*, in spite of the redundancy it produces.

Paul and Peter are both stating that foreknowledge is the basis of pre-destination and election. What would God know in advance that would cause Him to predestine certain people to heaven or hell? Nothing. Otherwise, unconditional election, a cornerstone of Calvinism, would be denied. The only reasonable answer is that those God knew from eternity past would believe the gospel were predestined to blessings. Nor do I think that God's omniscience is "God passively taking in knowledge from an out-side source," as White claims.

White declares that the object of God's foreknowledge "is *always*

D. HUNT

personal...never events" and "refers to the choice to enter into a relationship with someone." Both statements are false. God has no knowledge of future events—only knowledge of *people*? But prophecy is all about future *events*; e.g., "New things do I declare; before they spring forth I tell you of them" (Isaiah 42:9); "God...revealeth...what shall be in the latter days" (Daniel 2:28); "Known unto God are all his works from the beginning" (Acts 15:18). God's foreknowledge is limitless and involves all events that will ever occur, not just persons, and rarely does it foretell God's "choice to enter into a relationship with someone."

White attempts to turn foreknowledge into "foreloving." Other Calvinists attempt the same because to "know" in Scripture can mean sexual intercourse. But that kind of "knowing" could not be in advance, and God does not "know" man in that way. Yet Calvinists argue that "to 'foreknow' on God's part means to 'forelove.'"[5] Paul is using the biblical idiom of "know" for "love."[6] God's foreknowledge, then, is His eternal love for His chosen people.[7] Many times in Scripture "know" [is] practically synonymous with "love."[8]

Such attempts are completely without foundation. Of the approximately two hundred times *love* or *loved* are found in the New Testament, *not once* is it from *proginosko* or *prognosis*. John 2:24 declares that Jesus "knew all men," which, if *know* equals *love*, undermines the teaching that He loves only the elect.

White declares that *"all* who are foreknown are predestined [to salvation].... Not *some*, not *most*, but *all*."* On the contrary, Romans 11:2 tells us that God "foreknew" all Israelites, yet all Israel is not saved. In fact, a number of times God declares that He "foreloved" Israel; e.g., Deuteronomy 7:6–8; 1 Kings 10:9; Hosea 11:1, 4; Malachi 1:1.

Regarding Paul's statement that Christ "gave himself a ransom for all" (1 Timothy 2:6), Norm Geisler faults John Owen for justifying his "dubious view that 'all' doesn't mean 'all' here" by diverting "to other passages where 'all' does not mean the whole human race." White defends Owen, claiming that since "all" *sometimes* doesn't mean "all," non-Calvinists must prove that it does in any given context.[9] On the contrary, it is those who deny the normal understanding of a word who must justify a different meaning.

White argues that if salvation depended upon faith (as the Bible says it does), it would be "subject to failure due to man's involvement." Did God fail in His purposes for Israel? Wasn't the blessing He promised contingent upon Israel's obedience? Did He not say that His desire was to feed Israel with the finest of wheat and to subdue all her enemies? But they refused to obey (Psalm 81:10–16). Did He not say, "If ye be willing and obedient" (Isaiah 1:19)? Is White saying that God really desired and willed that Israel should rebel and be punished and cast out of her land and killed by the millions? Is that what God meant when He said, "I know the thoughts that I think toward you…thoughts of peace, and not of evil, to give you an expected end" (Jeremiah 29:11)?

White concludes with Calvinism's standard objection that if man had the power of choice, he would "control God's gracious work." But Scripture from Genesis to Revelation declares that man must be willing for God to work in and through him. "Work out your own salvation…for it is God which worketh in you both to will and to do of his good pleasure" (Philippians 2:12–13) clearly puts responsibility on man. In spite of God's sovereignty, Christians do not live perfect lives, which can only be attributed to their willful unbelief and disobedience, not to God's "failure."

Surely, "Thou shalt love the LORD thy God with all thine heart" expresses

God's will. Does the fact that most men do not so love God mean that those who fall short in this regard thereby "control God's gracious work" or cause God to fail? The entire Bible becomes meaningless by this reasoning. A rejection of love does not "control" the one who loves. Nor does a rejection of salvation put man in charge. God has conceived and accomplished full salvation for all mankind. That multitudes reject that salvation does not mean that man controls God.

1. Arthur W. Pink, *The Doctrine of Election and Justification* (Grand Rapids, Mich.: Baker, 1974),172.
2. John Calvin, *Institutes of the Christian Religion,* tr. Henry Beveridge (Grand Rapids, Mich.: Eerdmans, 1998), III: xxiii, 7.
3. John Piper and Pastoral Staff, *TULIP: What We Believe about the Five Points of Calvinism* (Minneapolis, Minn.: Desiring God Ministries, 1997), 22.
4. John MacArthur Jr., *Saved Without a Doubt* (Colorado Springs, Colo.: Chariot Victor, 1992), 59.
5. C. Samuel Storms, *Chosen for Life* (Grand Rapids, Mich.: Baker, 1987), 75.
6. Edwin H. Palmer, *The Five Points of Calvinism* (Grand Rapids, Mich.: Baker, 1999), 32.
7. Steven R. Houck, *God's Sovereignty in Salvation* (Lansing, Ill.: Peace Protestant Reformed Church, n. d.), 9.
8. John Murray, *The Epistle to the Romans* (Grand Rapids, Mich.: Eerdmans.1965), 1: 317.
9. James R. White, *The Potter's Freedom: A Defense of the Reformation* (Amityville, N.Y.: Calvary Press, 2000), 143

Defense, by James White

We read from the pen of Dave Hunt: "White's foundation is again an extreme view of sovereignty: 'His will is being accomplished in the world, all resulting in His glory and honor.'" I plead guilty as charged! If this is an extreme view, it is an extremely *biblical* view, as we proved in our first presentation. This is a truth that looks "extreme" only when contrasted with man's tradition of human autonomy, the lifeblood of human religion. Indeed, the pagan king Nebuchadnezzar understood this truth:

> "At the end of that period, I, Nebuchadnezzar, raised my eyes toward heaven and my reason returned to me, and I blessed the Most High and praised and honored Him who lives forever;
>> For His dominion is an everlasting dominion,
>> And His kingdom *endures* from generation to generation.
>> All the inhabitants of the earth are accounted as nothing,
>> But He does according to His will in the host of heaven
>> And among the inhabitants of earth;
>> And no one can ward off His hand
>> Or say to Him, 'What have You done?'" (Daniel 4:34–35)

Mr. Hunt's response is a study in misreading and misunderstanding. He says that the word *effectual* is not in Romans 8. No one said it was. But the fact remains that the term *calling* is used in more than one way in Scripture, and Hunt's refusal to allow it to be interpreted consistently does not add to our understanding of the biblical text. Likewise, it is obvious that when I say that all things are being accomplished according to God's will, I am not referring to His prescriptive will, but to His decree. These kinds of irrelevant comments are a hindrance to meaningful dialogue. Hunt publicly claims to have read "hundreds" of Calvinists, so why introduce these red herrings?

Hunt's traditions run aground on the golden chain of redemption. Refusing to recognize the different uses of *called* in Scripture, he says that "all" are called. This means that all will be justified and all will be glorified, resulting in universalism (*all* who are called are justified, *all* who are justified are glorified). Why Hunt does not see this is a mystery. Even in his own tradition it would be obvious that those who are called in Romans 8:30 are then justified (there is no way to escape this grammatically). Does Hunt believe that all will be justified? Surely not. Hence, his comments simply make no sense and have no connection at all to the text. By abandoning the text and ignoring context, Hunt creates a great deal of smoke but leaves the exegesis of Romans 8 unrefuted, and hence established.

Hunt eschews providing any meaningful exegesis. Again we hear only about what the text *does not mean*, not what it does mean. Given the nature of Hunt's response, I would like to use the short space I have to point out the key errors in his assertions.

Hunt ignores the lexical information in my presentation regarding *foreknown*, and in attempting to get around the established meaning and usage of this important term, he makes numerous simple errors. Ignoring such basic things as context and usage, he tries, and fails, to defend the idea that Paul is simply saying that God knew who was going to believe in Christ and on that basis elected them. He creates his own definition out of whole cloth, not even bothering to provide anything outside of his own authority as a basis, telling us that foreknowledge means "to know in advance what man will do of his free will." What Greek lexicon gives this as the meaning? It would be nice of Mr. Hunt to provide a positive presentation of his theology so we could test it for biblical consistency, but he has not done so. How God can know future events, for example, and yet not determine them, is an important point, but one Mr. Hunt does not address.

Hunt ignores the cited sources that substantiate the meaning of the verb *foreknow*. He then inexplicably completely misreads my presentation, in which I spoke of the use of the *verb* with God as the subject. I pointed out, correctly, that when the verb is used with God as the subject, the object in all four instances is personal. He writes, "Both statements are false. God has no knowledge of future events—only knowledge of people?" Hunt is confusing the verb with the noun. It is the verb that appears in Romans 8:30. Hunt has no response to the accurate information given and does not even seem to understand the important issue, which is the meaning of God's *action* of foreknowing and how that differs from the philosophical concept of divine foreknowledge.

Despite his ignorance of the background of and the scholarship relevant to the term, Hunt says, "Such attempts are completely without foundation." Simply declaring it to be so does not make it so. Indeed, one is truly amazed to read Hunt arguing that "John 2:24 declares that Jesus 'knew all men,' which, if *know* equals *love*, undermines the teaching that He only loves the elect." Such a statement violates almost every canon of sound interpretation and logic. No one has suggested that *know* means *love* in every instance; the term here is not *foreknow;* and, finally, the context is completely different from that of Romans 8. This is quite honestly one of the clearest examples of eisegesis in the service of tradition I have seen. The reader is strongly encouraged to compare the verse-by-verse, phrase-by-phrase exegesis offered initially with the scattergun, acontextual response to see what happens when tradition is placed in the position of ultimate authority.

The rest of Mr. Hunt's response has little to do with Romans 8 and consists of the constant repetition of mantralike phrases such as "man must be willing" and the like. As each of these claims has been tested by Scripture and no exegetically sound response has been offered, the reader can decide the issue.

J. WHITE

Final Remarks, by Dave Hunt

The quotation from Daniel 4:34 (that God "does according to His will in…heaven and…earth") does not mean that He wills *everything that happens.* Claiming that He does, Calvinism makes God the cause of evil: "God wills all things that come to pass[1]; God foreordains… all things[2]; God ordained…every evil thought, word, and deed in all of history[3]; Men do [only] what [God]…brings to pass."[4] White tries to disguise this libel against God by proposing a distinction between God's "prescriptive will [and] His decree." No dictionary knows such differentiation.

White says that I refuse "to recognize the different uses of *called* in Scripture" because I say that "'all' are called" by the gospel. But that is my point: the "called" in Romans 9:29 are those God foreknew would respond to the gospel; not so in Matthew 22:14.

I do provide an exegesis based on the correct meaning of *foreknew,* which White must reject or give up Calvinism. I give the usages in the context of *proginosko* and *prognosis,* showing that the meaning is *never* "foreordained" or "foreloved." And I refute White's claim that God's foreknowledge "is *always personal…never events.*"

Once again, White says that I don't explain how "God can know future events…yet not determine them." Apparently he hasn't read *What Love Is This,* for I discuss this on pages 143–162 and 219–234. God knows every thought, word, and deed beforehand because He is omniscient. That God foreknows all that will happen doesn't cause it to happen, because He exists outside of time.

White claims that "God's *action* of foreknowing…differs from the philosophical concept of divine foreknowledge." Such a distinction doesn't exist. There is no "*action* of foreknowing." That was Augustine's invention to turn foreknowledge into foreordination: "Consequently…predestination is signified also under the name of foreknowledge."[5] This is both irrational and unscriptural. I referenced the two times *prognosis* is used in the New Testament and the five times *proginosko* is used and showed that they always refer to knowing in advance. There is no *action* in knowing. Knowledge, whether of the past, present, or future, does not involve any activity.

That man must have a "willing heart" and a "willing mind" toward God is one of the most fundamental teachings in Scripture, from Genesis through Revelation. The Bible repeatedly requires men to willingly believe and obey God: "If ye be willing and obedient (Isaiah 1:19) and promises, "Whosoever will, let him take the water of life freely" (Revelation 22:17). Yet White rejects "man must be willing" as a "mantralike phrase" because it refutes Calvinism.

1. R. C. Sproul, *Almighty over All* (Grand Rapids, Mich.: Baker, 1999), 54.
2. Arthur W. Pink, *The Sovereignty of God* (Grand Rapids, Mich.: Baker, 1986), 240.
3. Edwin H. Palmer, *The Five Points of Calvinism* (Grand Rapids, Mich.: Baker, 1999), 24–5, 82, 97–100, 116.
4. John Calvin, *Institutes of the Christian Religion*, tr. Henry Beveridge (Grand Rapids, Mich.: Eerdmans, 1998), I: xviii, 1.
5. Augustine, *On the Gift of Perseverance*, 47.

D. HUNT

Final Remarks, by James White

———

M r. Hunt claims to have offered lexical and exegetical information regarding the verb *proginosko,* yet as was pointed out previously, he confused the verb with the noun, confused its use when it has God as its object, and in essence has never once touched the actual meaning of the term as we have documented it. In his final installment, Hunt again demonstrates that he has no concept of the issue at hand. He actually puts in print:

> White claims that "God's *action* of foreknowing...differs from the philosophical concept of divine foreknowledge." Such a distinction doesn't exist. There is no "*action* of foreknowing." That was Augustine's invention to turn foreknowledge into foreordination.... This is both irrational and unscriptural.

Unless Augustine wrote Romans 8:29, Mr. Hunt has made another major error of fact. Paul uses a verb, not a noun, in this verse. God *foreknows* as an action, just as all the other verbs in the golden chain are actions on God's part. Just as Mr. Hunt can turn *is not able* into *is not willing,* so too he can turn *foreknow* into *foreknowledge,* all because his tradition demands that it be so. Eisegesis proven, and documented, once again.

Mr. Hunt claims that God knows all future events because He exists outside of time. But merely making such a claim does not answer the question. Since Hunt specifically denies that God has knowledge of events in time due to God's decree, it must follow that events in time flow from something other than God's creative act. Is it fate? Man's free will? As a result, did things just "happen" to turn out right? Why should God be glorified for the end result if He just happened to "luck out" when He created? How can God know what these free creatures will do in the future, if they are truly free (the argument open theists are aggressively promoting today)? Hunt does not tell us. His tradition says that God knows, so, even if it is utterly inconsistent with his denial of God's decree, that is what he will believe.

Preaching on this passage on March 24, 1872, Spurgeon said:

> In Romans 11:2, we read, "God hath not cast away his people
> which he foreknew," where the sense evidently has the idea of fore-
> love; and it is so to be understood here. Those whom the Lord
> looked upon with favor as he foresaw them, he has predestinated
> to be conformed to the image of his Son.[1]

The divine truth has been vindicated: those whom God foreknows (a verb, not a noun, it is an action of God with the elect as the object) He predestines; those He predestines He calls; those He calls He justifies; those He justifies, He glorifies. Each is a divine act. Each is sovereign and free. None of the chain is dependent upon human cooperation. Which is why God, and God alone, is glorified by the perfect work of salvation. The more men struggle against this truth, the more clearly it shines!

---

1. Charles H. Spurgeon, "Glorious Predestination," sermon preached 24 March 1872.

J. WHITE

- Chapter Six -

PARTICULAR REDEMPTION:
TRUE ATONEMENT,
TRUE SUBSTITUTION

by James White

F ew topics reveal more clearly the role tradition plays in evangelical
theology than the commonly held views about the cross of Jesus
Christ. It is not that the Bible's teaching on the atonement is
unclear or confusing. Instead, the clear theology of Scripture is often
encrusted with the oft-repeated platitudes of tradition that, due to constant
repetition, become accepted as biblical axioms without the first shred of
meaningful biblical support. Emotion and sentimentality become attached
to these phrases of evangelical tradition so that any questioning of their
faithfulness to Scripture is met with accusations of heresy or worse.

The atonement has suffered greatly at the hands of the traditions of
men. At times during the history of the church, strange and grossly

unscriptural theories have held sway regarding just what God's purpose was in sending His Son to die upon Calvary's tree. But these traditions all have one thing in common: They are not derived from the consistent exegesis of *the entirety* of Scripture. They are at best patchwork quilts of biblical citations, divorced from context and standing in contradiction to those passages of Scripture that most fully enter into the purposes of God in the atonement. Those who truly follow the biblical mandate to "examine all things" in light of Scriptural teaching should be the first to place their own traditions under the microscope of God's Word.

Anti-Reformed writers and speakers love to hammer away at the doctrine of particular redemption, or limited atonement. Misrepresentations abound, and emotions run wild, but rarely is there a meaningful argument made against the *reality* of the belief that Christ died in the place of His elect people. It is easier, it seems, to attempt to inflame the emotions than to deal with the biblical evidence.

PARTICULAR REDEMPTION DEFINED

There are two questions that must be answered by anyone who would begin to seriously discuss the biblical doctrine of the atonement: What did the triune God *intend* to do at the very focal point of history, the cross of Calvary, and what was *accomplished* in that sacrifice? For some, *intention* and *accomplishment* are not necessarily the same. The Reformed answer to both questions is plain and clear: God the Father decreed the salvation of an elect people, Christ died with the intention of redeeming those people through their union with Him and accomplished that task, and without fail the Holy Spirit brings that accomplished work to fruition in the life of the elect at the time and in the manner determined by God. It was God's intention that the Son redeem His people by His death, and since salvation is of God and therefore not subject to failure, the Son accomplished that task.

The difference, then, between Hunt's view and the Reformed view of the atonement is simply this: Did Christ actually *save anyone* at the cross, or did He simply make people *savable?* Was His a truly substitutionary atonement, or was it merely theoretical, dependent upon the autonomous will of man for success? That is the question.

Evangelicals who speak of Christ dying "for them" often hold to clearly contradictory positions on the atonement. Most have never been challenged to see the inconsistencies in their beliefs. If Christ died in the place of every single individual human being, He was dying for many who had already died in rebellion against God and who will experience God's wrath for eternity.[1] One must either jettison the concept of substitution or accept the idea that Christ can die in the place of someone who will, despite that perfect work, be lost. The latter implies a limitation on the *effect* of the atonement, the *result* of the atonement, and it, rather than the Reformed doctrine of particular redemption, is probably more accurately called "limited atonement" (since it limits the *power* thereof).

Of course, it should be noted in passing that everyone who is not a Universalist limits the atonement. The evangelical who thinks he is honoring the atonement by making it universal in scope needs to realize the cost of his position. If Christ died in the place of every man and woman in all of history (universal scope and intention), the atonement must be limited in its power and efficacy, for it does not actually result in the salvation of many of those God intended it to save. Indeed, Spurgeon expressed it well:

If Christ on His cross intended to save every man, then He intended to save those who were lost before He died. If the doctrine be true, that He died for all men, then He died for some who were in hell before He came into this world, for doubtless there were even then myriads there who had been cast away because of their sins. Once again, if it was Christ's intention to save all men, how deplorably has He been disappointed, for we have His own testimony that there is a lake which burneth with fire and brimstone, and into that pit of woe have been cast some of the very persons who, according to the theory of universal redemption, were bought with His blood. That seems to me a conception a thousand times more repulsive than any of those consequences which are said to be associated with the Calvinistic and Christian doctrine of special and particular redemption. To think that my Savior died for men who were or are in hell, seems a supposition too horrible for me to entertain. To imagine for a moment that He was the Substitute for all the sons of men, and that God, having first punished the Substitute, afterwards punished the sinners themselves, seems to conflict with all my ideas of Divine justice. That Christ should offer an atonement and satisfaction for the sins of all men, and that afterwards some of those very men should be punished for the sins for which Christ had already atoned, appears to me to be the most monstrous iniquity that could ever have been imputed to Saturn, to Janus, to the goddess of the Thugs, or to the most diabolical heathen deities. God forbid that we should ever think thus of Jehovah, the just and wise and good![2]

How will the opponent of a fully substitutionary *and effective* atonement respond to this argument? Does God the Father actually place the sins of those He knows will spend eternity in hell upon His Son? Does He punish in Christ the sins of all of His enemies, knowing that He will punish them for the same sins for eternity? The only way out of the dilemma is to abandon the idea of truly penal substitution. Historically, this is what Arminians did. Today, any person who speaks of Christ "dying for me" is borrowing Calvinistic language, even if he does not know it.

The limitation placed upon the atonement by the insertion of the unbiblical concept of man's autonomous will strikes at the heart of the glorious work of God in uniting a people to Christ so that His death is their death. Indeed, the very truth of the imputation of our sins to Christ and His righteousness to us is inconsistent with libertarian free will. The intention of the Father in giving the Son must be consistent with the entirety of His work of salvation. We have already seen that it is His intention to save every single one of the elect by entrusting them to the Son, who raises them up on the last day (Ephesians 1:4–6; John 6:37–39). The scope of the atonement, then, is in perfect harmony with the scope of the electing grace of God. Christ atones for the sins of the elect from every tribe, tongue, and nation (Revelation 5:9).

BIBLICAL EVIDENCE

We have already noted in a previous chapter the remarkably clear testimony offered by Romans 8:31–34 with reference to particular redemption. The apostle Paul directly asserts that God the Father delivered up His Son for the elect and that He will, along with the Son, freely give that same group "all things." It is for these elect that the Son intercedes, guaranteeing their full and complete salvation.

The truth of the divine intercession of Jesus Christ for His people is without question the most compelling biblical proof of particular redemption. When we keep in mind the fact that, due to the nature of His work as High Priest, Christ intercedes for *all* of those for whom He died and *only* for those for whom He died, the intention and scope of His work becomes quite clear. The High Priest cannot intercede for those for whom no offering is made, of course. And it is His duty to intercede for those for whom the offering has been made. Hence, the question of the scope and intention of His work is answered by considering this question: "Can Christ fail to bring about the full salvation of any person for whom He dies and for whom He intercedes?" The Reformed response is a firm no. The non-Reformed response, when the question is pressed, must be "Yes, Christ can die for a person and intercede before the Father for that person, but since salvation is not a matter of what the Father or Son do but what the person allows them to do, Christ can and does intercede for multitudes of lost people, to no avail." One recoils from such an assertion, but it is nonetheless the conclusion of those who hold to universal atonement.

Consider the biblical teaching from Hebrews:

> Jesus, on the other hand, because He continues forever, holds His priesthood permanently. Therefore He is able also to save forever those who draw near to God through Him, since He always lives to make intercession for them. (Hebrews 7:24–25)

Why is Jesus able to save "forever" (other translations have "to the uttermost")? Because He *intercedes for them.* So if Jesus intercedes for those who are lost, this passage makes no sense. Obviously, the biblical truth is that if

Jesus intercedes for you, *you will be saved.* But since Christ intercedes for those for whom He dies, the group for which He dies must be as limited in number as those who are saved; that is, He dies for the elect. And the fact that His death does not merely make men savable but actually saves is also borne out in Hebrews:

> When Christ appeared as a high priest of the good things to come, He entered through the greater and more perfect tabernacle, not made with hands, that is to say, not of this creation; and not through the blood of goats and calves, but through His own blood, He entered the holy place once for all, having obtained eternal redemption. (Hebrews 9:11–12)

Did Christ enter the Holy Place having made salvation a possibility? Or had He actually *obtained eternal redemption?* The text is clear. That the Son's work is, in fact, complete and perfect and not dependent upon man's additions (even the addition of mere "faith") is also taught in Hebrews:

> By this will we have been sanctified through the offering of the body of Jesus Christ once for all.... For by one offering He has perfected for all time those who are sanctified. (Hebrews 10:10, 14)

If the offering of Christ perfects those for whom it is made, where is there room for an atonement that is universal in scope but ineffectual in result? Where is this hypothetical atonement of evangelical tradition? It finds no place in the theology of Hebrews, that is for certain.

Space does not allow a full development of the following texts, but each bears testimony to the truth of particular redemption. Note these words about the coming Messiah:

"She will bear a Son; and you shall call His name Jesus, for He will save His people from their sins. (Matthew 1:21)

Will He? Will He save His people, or only make salvation a theoretical possibility?

"For the Son of Man has come to seek and to save that which was lost." (Luke 19:10)

Does He accomplish His purpose? Does He actually save, or only make savable? If He actually saves, does this not limit the scope of the "lost"?

The Son of Man did not come to be served, but to serve, and to give His life a ransom for many. (Matthew 20:28)

As Dr. Pipa pointed out to Mr. Hunt in their debate, *all* in Scripture is often limited to kinds and classes, but *many* never means *all*.[3] Christ gave His life a ransom for many, and that ransom *is effective* in bringing redemption to those for whom it is made. That was likewise the point of Isaiah's prophecy long ago:

As a result of the anguish of His soul,
He will see it and be satisfied;
By His knowledge the Righteous One,

My Servant, will justify the many,

As He will bear their iniquities. (Isaiah 53:11)

How does the righteous servant justify "the many"? By substitutionally bearing their iniquities. That is particular redemption in bold prophetic announcement.

It is a trustworthy statement, deserving full acceptance, that Christ Jesus came into the world to save sinners, among whom I am foremost of all. (1 Timothy 1:15)

Did Christ come *to save* or *make savable?* Did He do what the Word says He did? The Lord Jesus said that He laid down His life for His sheep (John 10:11–15), but He likewise informed the Jews that they were not of His sheep (John 10:26).[4] So clear was the particularity of His work of redemption that in His High Priestly prayer the Lord says, "'I ask on their behalf; I do not ask on behalf of the world, but of those whom You have given Me; for they are Yours'" (John 17:9).[5] And are we truly to believe that in eternity the denizens of hell, while screaming out their hatred of God, will be able to say with the apostle Paul, "I have been crucified with Christ" (Galatians 2:20)? Surely not!

ALTERING REDEMPTION ITSELF

A most dangerous and troubling teaching that some have promoted is that Christ atoned for all the sins of all mankind except for the sin of unbelief, which alone can send a person to hell. Aside from the fact that there is not a shred of biblical basis for such a concept, are we to say that unbelief is not a sin? That Christ only atoned for *some* sins? Is there any believer who has per-fect faith and is not guilty of some level of unbelief? But the idea is wholly contradicted by the simple fact that men are *punished* for their sins. They are under the *wrath of God*, which throughout Scripture is directed against *sin*. Beyond this, we know that God's punishment is against sin (inclusive of, but not limited to, unbelief) because, as the Lord Jesus said, there will be some who receive a greater punishment. Chorazin and Bethsaida will face greater judgment than Sodom and Gomorrah. How can this be if punishment is for only unbelief? Are there "degrees" of rejection of Christ in this system? And did not the Lord Jesus say to the Jews that unless they believed He was the "I am," they would die not simply in unbelief but in their "sin"? Sadly, we must con-clude that the only reason this teaching is promoted is to give the proponents a way "out" of having to deal with the reality of the substitutionary *and particular* redemptive work of Christ.

THE TERRIBLE HORRIBLE "L"

Most of the arguments against the substitutionary, particular, perfect work of Christ on the cross are actually arguments against the unconditional electing grace of God, not particular redemption itself. Upon examination, the vast majority of those who call themselves "four point Calvinists" are actually not Reformed at all, for their objections are to God's freedom in electing men to salvation and to the total inability of man in his sin. Particular redemption flows inexorably from the truths of God's divine free-dom and man's enslavement to sin.

Arguments based upon assumed (but acontextual) meanings of *world* or *all* are hardly capable of standing up against the clear teaching of the Scriptures regarding the intention and accomplishment of Christ in His death. Christ, by His blood, redeemed men from every tribe, tongue, people, and nation (Revelation 5:9); that is, from the whole *world*, and this is the only consistent way of viewing His work. The biblical testimony is certain: The angel said that He would be called Jesus "for He will save His people from their sins" (Matthew 1:21). Reformed believers accept this plain testimony: Christ saves His people from their sins perfectly and fully in His death. His death does not bring about a theoretical redemption that requires man's actions to be effective. His words on the cross need to be accepted: "It is finished!" That is what particular redemption means, and that is why we gladly profess this truth today.

---

1. We do not here enter into the debate over hell. Both sides believe firmly in the eternal punishment of the wicked; hence, the many issues raised by those who deny this truth are not addressed here.
2. Charles H. Spurgeon, *Autobiography* (Ages Software, 1996), 1:189–90. Spurgeon's open and unequivocal proclamation of particular redemption flies directly in the face of Dave Hunt's assertions to the contrary (Dave Hunt, *What Love Is This?* [Sisters, Ore.: Loyal, 2002],19).
3. This debate took place in May 2002.
4. Should it be said that they were not of His sheep because they did not believe, note the actual order: Jesus said they did not believe because they were not of His sheep. So entrenched are our traditions that many automatically reverse the order the Lord Himself gave.
5. Note this passage likewise demonstrates yet another of the many uses of *world* in John's gospel.

Response, by Dave Hunt

White says that non-Calvinists use "emotion and sentimentality" and encrust Scripture "with oft-repeated platitudes of tradition." Yet he promotes Calvinist tradition. He asks, "What did the triune God *intend* to do [at] Calvary?" as though all would be saved if God *intended* to save all. If so, all the evil and sorrow on earth and the eternal suffering of billions in the lake of fire is exactly what God intended.

God desired "peace, and not...evil" for Israel (Jeremiah 29:11) and "would have healed" her (Hosea 7:1) and blessed her without limit (Psalm 81:13–16). Instead, reluctantly, He had to punish her. God's "will" is for "all men to be saved"(1 Timothy 2:4) and that not "one of these little ones should perish" (Matthew 18:14) but "that all should come to repentance" (2 Peter 3:9).

Calvinism explains away such Scriptures. White says, "God the Father decreed the salvation of an elect people, [and] Christ died with the intention of redeeming those people." He says that "four point Calvinists," who reject "particular redemption," are "not Reformed at all."

White corrupts a few Scriptures, avoids the numerous passages that clearly contradict Calvinism, and fails to produce one verse that plainly teaches particular redemption. From Hebrews 10:14 he says, "The offering of Christ perfects those for whom it is made." No, it perfects "those who are sanctified." Limiting the Cross to the latter is unwarranted.

White interprets "His people" in Matthew 1:21 as the elect. This is "consistent exegesis of *the entirety* of Scripture"? "His people" is found 150 times in the Old Testament. Most often the phrase means Israel or physically related; *never* does it mean Calvinism's elect. It occurs nine times in the New Testament; eight times it means Israel (Matthew 1:21; Luke 1:68, 77; Romans 11:1–2, 15:10; Hebrews 10:30) and one time the redeemed (Revelation 21:3). Yet White presents this as his closing proof.

Quoting "a ransom for many" (Matthew 20:28), he argues that "*many* never means *all.*" It *could* and sometimes does: "*Many*...that sleep in the dust...shall awake" (Daniel 12:2) means *all* the dead. One verse negates the *many* declarations that God wants all to be saved and that Christ died for all? He quotes, "[Jesus] came into the world to save sinners." *Some* sinners, but not *all?* Isaiah writes, "All we like sheep have gone astray...[and] the LORD hath laid on him the iniquity of us all" (Isaiah 53:6). As all Israel had gone astray, the sins of all Israel were laid upon Christ. "Ho, every one that thirsteth, come ye to the waters" (Isaiah 55:1). Since all men thirst, all are invited to drink.

Contrary to White's implication, we do not teach that unbelief is the one sin for which Christ did not atone but that it is the one sin for which there is no remedy. Nor do the arguments of John Owen and White follow; i.e., that because unbelief is a sin, all mankind would be saved if Christ died for the sins of all.[1]

White asks, "Did Christ actually *save anyone* at the cross, or did He simply make people *savable?*" God *provides* salvation; man must *believe* to be saved. Calvinism rejects faith as human "effort," so the elect must be saved the moment Christ paid the penalty for their sins. Yet if Christ actually saved all of the elect at Calvary, they could never have been lost and would not need to be saved later. Scripture doesn't say that a man is "saved already." It says that he is "condemned already," and not because Christ didn't die for him but *"because he hath not believed"* (John 3:18). Repeatedly we read that those who *believe* are saved and those who *believe not* "shall not see life" (John 3:36). If Christ's death in itself saved, the elect wouldn't need to believe.

White argues that without particular atonement, "the death of Christ must be only *potential*...[dependent upon] *the free choices of men in time."*[2] In fact, redemption is certain to all who believe—and God foreknew them all. Moreover, since the elect must be sovereignly regenerated and given faith to believe, they too are only "potentially" saved by the Cross. Lewis Sperry Chafer acknowledged: "Christ's death of itself forgives no sinner, nor does it render unnecessary the regenerating work of the Holy Spirit."[3]

Like White, Spurgeon argued that those who reject particular redemption must say that Christ didn't die "so as beyond a doubt to secure the salvation of anybody."[4] Did he forget God's foreknowledge? In fact, God infallibly knew the identity of those who would believe in Christ. Foreknowledge is declared to be the basis of predestination/election (Romans 8:29; 1 Peter 1:2). God knew from eternity past who would believe. Christ's death surely redeemed in "particular" those "he did foreknow." Calvinistic redemption is no more "particular" than that.

The blood of the Passover lamb, a type of Christ, saved only those who applied it to the doorposts. To deny "free will" (which White irresponsibly labels "libertarian") and to support "particular redemption," Calvinism must hold the unbiblical view that Christ's death saves without faith. Yet numerous Scriptures declare plainly that faith in Christ is essential to salvation; e.g., "Believe and be saved" (Luke 8:12); "Believing ye might have life" (John 20:31); "Believe...and thou shalt be saved" (Acts 16:31); "[The gospel is] salvation to every one that believeth" (Romans 1:16); "[If thou shalt] believe in thine heart...thou shalt be saved" (Romans 10:9); "By grace are ye saved through faith" (Ephesians 2:8). But Calvinism denies faith unto salvation in order to protect sovereign regeneration.

From Hebrews 7:25, White asserts that "Christ intercedes for those for whom He dies...[thus] He dies for the elect." On the contrary, the verse says that He saves "them...that come unto God by him." Christ interceded for all who crucified and mocked Him (Luke 23:34), which "undoubtedly included people who were not elect."[5] Attempting to refute Geisler, White quotes Calvin, who perversely turns Christ's prayer of forgiveness into confidence that the Father will punish His persecutors.[6]

White argues that those who deny particular atonement limit its "power and efficacy." Not so. The infinite power and efficacy of the Cross is not limited by the biblical truth that Christ died for all mankind and whosoever believes is saved. It is Calvinism that limits the power and efficacy of the Cross to a select group.

Christ's shed blood must pay for Adam's sin, which brought death upon the entire race; and it must pay for sin itself and thus for all sins of every person, making redemption available to all who believe. Owen admitted that Christ suffered "all the punishment that was due to sin."[7] Calvin contradicted "limited atonement" when he wrote: "With his own blood [Christ] expiated the sins which rendered [sinners] hateful to God.... Thus we perceive Christ representing the character of a sinner and a criminal...bearing, by substitution, the curse due to sin."[8]

White argues that without particular redemption, "[Christ] was dying for many...who will experience God's wrath for eternity." Spurgeon reasoned: "We dare not think that the blood of Christ was ever shed with the intention of saving those whom God foreknew never could be saved.[9] [This is] a thousand times more repulsive than particular redemption."[10] But all of Christ's blood had to be shed and the full penalty of sin paid to save one sinner. Old Testament sacrifices, a type of Christ, were offered for multitudes who are in hell.

Not the non-Calvinist but the Bible says that Christ died for all; e.g., "Behold the Lamb of God, who taketh away the sin of the world" (John 1:29); "God so loved the world, that he gave his only begotten Son...that the world through him might be saved" (John 3:16–17); "[The bread...is] my flesh, which I will give for the life of the world"(John 6:51); "I came...to save the world" (John 12:47); "He is the propitiation...for the sins of the whole world" (1 John 2:2).

Particular redemption flies in the face of scores of Scriptures for which Calvinism must adopt a peculiar definition of words. In *every* place where *world* doesn't fit their theory, Calvinists assign their own peculiar meaning. What a coincidence! Comparing Scripture with Scripture, however, reveals the un-Calvinistic truth that Christ died for all mankind.

The Old Testament is the foundation for the New. Paul declared that the "gospel of God" that he preached was the fulfillment of God's promises "by his prophets in the holy scriptures [i.e., the Old Testament]" (Romans 1:1–2). "The gospel...[is] that Christ died for our sins *according to the [Old Testament] scriptures;* and that he was buried, and...rose again...*according to the scriptures*" (1 Corinthians 15:1, 3–4, emphasis added). The word *redeemer* is found in the Old Testament all eighteen times it appears in the Bible, *atonement* is found there eighty of the eighty-one times it appears, and *redeemed* is found there fifty-five of sixty-two times.

Old Testament sacrifices faithfully pictured Christ's sacrifice upon the cross. Calvin himself admits that what "was represented figuratively in the Mosaic sacrifices is exhibited in Christ the archetype."[11] *Not one* of the Old Testament sacrifices fits "particular redemption." All were for all Israel.

God's promise ("When I see the blood, I will pass over you" [Exodus 12:13]) to spare the lives of all those sheltered in every house where the blood of the Passover lamb had been applied in faith to "the two side posts and on the upper door post" (v. 7) was clearly for "all the congregation of Israel" (v. 3). Paul declares: "Christ our passover is sacrificed for us" (1 Corinthians 5:7). Yet the fulfillment of the Passover in the sacrifice of "the Lamb of God, who taketh away the sin of the world" (John 1:29) is only for the elect?

Of the brass serpent lifted up on the pole it was promised, "every one that is bitten, when he looketh upon it, shall live" (Numbers 21:8). No "particular redemption" here! And so it is with *all* Old Testament types. Christ's application is clear: "As Moses lifted up the serpent in the wilderness, even so must the Son of man be lifted up: That whosoever believeth in him should not perish, but have eternal life" (John 3:14–15). Yet He was "lifted up" only for the elect?

Leviticus presents an entire system of offerings and sacrifices for sin, and not one is compatible with particular redemption. If the Levitical offerings were for all of Israel who would believe and obey God's Word, so the cross of Christ to which these sacrifices pointed must be to all of Israel, and thus to all the world.

According to White, non-Calvinists neglect "consistent exegesis of *the entirety* of Scripture." Yet he ignores Old Testament types. There is no reference to Leviticus in his entire book.

White argues that only the elect for whom Christ actually died can say with Paul, "I am crucified with Christ" and that the unregenerate man in hell can never say, "I was crucified with Christ." Of course. Paul's declaration expresses his faith in Christ. It is not true of those who rejected Christ's sacrifice on their behalf.

1. John Owen, ed. William H. Goold, *The Works of John Owen* (Edinburgh: Banner of Truth Trust, 1978), 10: 173–4.
2. James R. White, *The Potter's Freedom: A Defense of the Reformation* (Amityville, N.Y.: Calvary Press, 2000), 268.
3. Lewis Sperry Chafer, *Systematic Theology* (Dallas: Dallas Seminary Press, 1947), 3:93.
4. Charles H. Spurgeon, "Particular Redemption," *The C. H. Spurgeon Collection* (Ages Digital Library, 1998), a sermon preached 28 February 1858; cited in White, *Potter's Freedom*, 278.
5. Norman Geisler, *Chosen But Free* (Minneapolis, Minn.: Bethany House, 1999), 78; cited in White, *Potter's Freedom*, 263.
6. White, *Potter's Freedom*, 263–4.
7. Owen, *Works of John Owen*, 10:173.
8. John Calvin, *Institutes of the Christian Religion*, tr. Henry Beveridge (Grand Rapids, Mich.: Eerdmans, 1998), II: xvi, 2, 5–6.
9. http://www. Spurgeon.org/sermons/0181.htm.
10. Charles H. Spurgeon, "A Defense of Calvinism," in *The New Park Street Pulpit* (Pasadena, Tex.: Pilgrim Publications, 1978), 17–8.
11. Calvin, *Institutes*, II: xvi, 6.

Defense, by James White

L et us focus upon the key issues of the atonement. Is the atonement substitutionary? Did Jesus take the penalty of sin for every person who has ever lived, is living, and ever will live? If so, what was God's intention in laying the sin of every person on Christ? Was it His purpose to make men savable, or to actually atone for their sins? And if those sins have been borne by Christ and the punishment due them laid upon Him, upon what basis will those same sins be punished in those who reject Him? Did Jesus fail to accomplish His desire in His death? Does Jesus, as the faithful High Priest, intercede for those who will never be saved? And if so, what is the nature of this failed intercession? And is it not true that Mr. Hunt and those who follow his views limit the atonement's *effect and power,* while Reformed theologians limit its *scope and intention*? These are important questions for all concerned.

A meaningful response would have been focused upon these very issues, but as the reader can see, the response Mr. Hunt offered barely made mention of the key arguments presented. Instead, he presented a plethora of straw men and red herrings that leave the issue unengaged. Mr. Hunt accuses me of "corrupting a few Scriptures," though he is unwilling to even note that in his book, *What Love Is This?* he adopts (and defends!) the Jehovah's Witnesses translation of Acts 13:48 in their *New World Translation* (resulting in the repetition of his "better" translation of the passage by his followers all across the world). I can only assume that he means "White understands the application of Hebrews 10:10, 14 differently than I do," but such is hardly as forceful as accusing someone of corrupting God's Word!

And what clear and cogent reasoning does Hunt provide in support of such a serious charge? He quotes my statement that the sacrifice of Christ perfects those for whom it is made, and then says, "No, it perfects 'those who are sanctified.' Limiting the Cross to the latter is unwarranted." Really? Perhaps Hunt needs to reread Hebrews 10:10 and see that there is a connection here: "By this will we have been sanctified through the offering of the body of Jesus Christ once for all." According to this verse, the death of Christ sanctifies all those for whom it is made, so how is it a response, let alone a sufficient basis for the accusation of corrupting the Scriptures, to say that the death of Christ perfects those who are sanctified rather than those for whom it is made? Where is the difference?

Hunt spends much time discussing "His people" but never answers the question asked him. Jesus "will save His people from their sins" (Matthew 1:21). That is *not* the same thing as saying "Jesus will make a way for those who exercise their free will, despite being dead in sin and a slave, to be saved through theoretically bearing their sins." Either Jesus can, and will, *save His people from their sins* or He will not. Which is it, Mr. Hunt?

Hunt completely misunderstands how the perfect salvation wrought through the substitutionary and particular redemption of Christ on the cross is applied to the elect in time. He writes, "Yet if Christ actually saved all of the elect at Calvary, they could never have been lost and would not need to be saved later."

It becomes tiring to respond constantly to the repetition of such falsehoods as this one: "Calvinism must hold the unbiblical view that Christ's death saves without faith." No, God not only commands faith, *but He mercifully enables us to believe by freeing us from our sin*. The point is that faith is not the human "capacity" that makes man's will the ultimate decision maker in salvation. Christ's substitutionary death in behalf of His people is a real and finished work: It is not dependent upon the human act of faith for success or failure. When the time comes in God's sovereign providence to bring to spiritual life each of those for whom Christ died, the Spirit of God will not only effectively accomplish that work of regeneration but that new creature in Christ will, unfailingly, believe in Jesus Christ ("all that the Father gives Me *will come to Me*"). Hence, we are not saved "without" faith, but at the same time, Christ's atonement is not rendered useless and vain without the addition of libertarian free will.

In the first words he wrote in response to this chapter, Dave Hunt let us know his real problem with having a perfect atonement, wherein Christ actually *accomplishes* the intention of the Father, Son, and Spirit:

[White] asks, "What did the triune God *intend* to do [at] Calvary?" as though all would be saved if God *intended* to save all. If so, all the evil and sorrow on earth and the eternal suffering of billions in the lake of fire is exactly what God intended."

Consider well what this means. Yes, if God intended to save all, all would be saved. God intended to save His elect people (Matthew 1:21), and He did that through the union of those elect with Christ on Calvary. Hunt's real objection is to the sovereignty of God over the creature, man. Hunt refuses to believe Proverbs 16:4: "The LORD has made everything for its own purpose, even the wicked for the day of evil."

For some unknown reason, Hunt prefers a God who created without a purpose and decree—even though He fully knew that His creation would be filled with senseless, purposeless, gratuitous evil and suffering! This is the price of libertarian freedom, and it is a price Mr. Hunt seems willing to pay. The result? A theoretical atonement at best; an impersonal, failed one at worst. Behold the power of human tradition!

Final Remarks, by Dave Hunt

White claims that non-Calvinists neglect "consistent exegesis of *the entirety* of Scripture," yet he neglects the Old Testament offerings and other types of Christ. "Will save His people from their sins" promises the fulfillment in the Messiah of these sacrifices, which were offered for all Israel but were efficacious only for believers.

Spurgeon says, "I could not conceive of my Saviour bearing the punishment for Judas."[1] White agrees that if Christ died for all, God exacts double payment from those in the lake of fire. No, God does not exact it; the Christ-rejecters themselves insist upon eternally paying for their own sins.

Calvinists are driven to such reasoning because *no Scripture* clearly says that Christ died only for the elect. It is, however, stated plainly many times that Christ died for the sins of the world. White never refutes my response that Christ's shed blood must pay in full for Adam's sin and thus for the penalty hanging over all of mankind. All of Christ's blood had to be shed to redeem even one sinner, as John Owen admitted in the quote I gave.

White insists that "world" in "propitiation for...the sins of the whole world" (1 John 2:2) can't mean everyone; otherwise, many for whom Christ is the propitiation would spend eternity in the lake of fire. Again faith is the key: "[It is] a propitiation through faith in his blood." Clearly, propitiation is only for those who believe that Christ shed His blood for their sin.

White refers to God's *intention* for Calvary. The Bible doesn't know this idea. If White is right, that only and whatever God *intends* is always done, the rampant evil and suffering in this world are what God intended.

He asks what was *accomplished* on the cross. The answer is: Full payment of sin's penalty. "Believe...and...be saved" can't be true, says White, or salvation depends upon man's acceptance, giving man the last word. Rejecting free will as "libertarian" eliminates loving and obeying God from the heart.

White says that non-Calvinists don't believe that Christ's death saved anyone. I pointed out that if Christ's death automatically saved, the elect were never lost and didn't need to believe the gospel. White ridicules this idea but doesn't refute it. He admits that faith is required, and then says, "Christ's substitutionary death...is not dependent upon the human act of faith" Scores of Scriptures clearly state that only those who believe are saved.

There is no way that Christ could pay the penalty for only a select group of sinners. Calvin says, "Wherefore, in order to accomplish a full expiation...'he made him to be sin for us'" (2 Corinthians 5:21).[2] It was not the *sins* of the elect, but sin itself, for which Christ paid the full penalty. This is no "theoretical atonement" based upon tradition, as White charges, but solidly upon the entire Word of God!

---

1. Charles H. Spurgeon, "Plenteous Redemption," a sermon preached at Exeter Hall, Strand, London, 23 December 1860.
2. John Calvin, *Institutes of the Christian Religion*, tr. Henry Beveridge (Grand Rapids, Mich.: Eerdmans, 1998), II: xvi, 6.

D. Hunt

Final Remarks, by James White

I n this section on the atonement I have tried, more than once, to invite Mr. Hunt to engage the real issues, but so far he has not done so. In his closing comments, he says that God does not exact punishment from sinners who reject Christ; instead, they insist upon paying it themselves. So the punishment of hell is voluntary? It is hard to make sense of such a statement.

Then Mr. Hunt attempts, briefly anyway, to interact with the *intention* of Christ in dying on Calvary. He says, "The Bible doesn't know this idea." Really? The Bible does not tell us what God intended to do in sending His Son to the cross? Paul did not say that the purpose was so that we might be made the righteousness of God in Him (2 Corinthians 5:21)? Hebrews 10:10 does not say that through the offering of the body of Jesus Christ once for all we have been sanctified, set apart, made holy? Again, one is simply left in a state of amazement at such assertions.

Of course, we are again given the *world* arguments, the *all men* arguments, and the like, despite the clear documentation of uses of these terms that refute Hunt's assertions.

In *What Love Is This?* Dave Hunt actually asserted that Spurgeon "unequivocally" denied limited atonement.[1] So it seems fitting to allow Spurgeon to conclude our discussion on this topic:

The Arminians say, Christ died for all men. Ask them what they mean by it. Did Christ die so as to secure the salvation of all men? They say, "No, certainly not." We ask them the next question—Did Christ die so as to secure the salvation of any man in particular? They answer "No." They are obliged to admit this if they are consistent. They say "No, Christ has died that any man may be saved if"—and then follow certain conditions of salvation. We say, then, we will just go back to the old statement—Christ did not die so as beyond a doubt to secure the salvation of anybody, did he? You must say "No"; you are obliged to say so, for you believe that even after a man has been pardoned, he may yet fall from grace, and perish. Now, who is it that limits the death of Christ? Why, you. You say that Christ did not die so as to infallibly secure the salvation of anybody, We beg your pardon, when you say we limit Christ's death; we say, "No, my dear sir, it is you that do it. We say Christ so died that he infallibly secured the salvation of a multitude that no man can number, who through Christ's death not only may be saved, but are saved, must be saved, and cannot by any possibility run the hazard of being anything but saved. You are welcome to your atonement; you may keep it. We will never renounce ours for the sake of it.[2]

---

1. Dave Hunt, *What Love Is This?* (Sisters, Ore.: Loyal, 2002), 19.
2. Charles H. Spurgeon, "Particular Redemption," sermon preached 28 February 1858.

J. WHITE

Chapter Seven

IRRESISTIBLE GRACE: GOD SAVES WITHOUT FAIL

by James White

The doctrine of "irresistible grace" is easily understood. It is simply the belief that when God chooses to move in the lives of His elect and bring them from spiritual death to spiritual life, no power in heaven or on earth can stop Him from so doing. It is really nothing more than saying that it is God who regenerates sinners, and that freely. The doctrine has nothing to do with the fact that sinners "resist" the common grace of God and the Holy Spirit every day (they do)[1] or that Christians do not live perfectly in the light of God's grace. It is simply the confession that when God chooses to raise His people to spiritual life, He does so without the fulfillment of any conditions on the part of the sinner. Just as Christ had the power and authority to raise Lazarus to life without obtaining his "permission" to do so, He is able to raise His elect to spiritual life with just as certain a result.

Objections to irresistible grace are, by and large, actually objections to the previously established truths of the doctrines of grace. Obviously, if God is sovereign and freely and unconditionally elects a people unto salvation, and if man is dead in sin and enslaved to its power, God must be able to free those elect people in time and bring them to faith in Jesus Christ, and that by a grace that does not falter or depend upon human cooperation. Those who disbelieve God's right to kingship over His creation or the deadness of man in sin and put forward the tradition of man's autonomous will can hardly confess that God's grace *actually saves* without the freewill cooperation of man. From their perspective, the autonomous act of human faith must determine God's actions. That act of faith becomes the "foreseen" act that controls God's very decree of predestination, and, of course, that act of faith becomes the "trigger" that results in one being born again.

Neither side in the debate will deny that God is the one who raises men to spiritual life. The question is: Does He do so because men fulfill certain conditions, or does He do so freely, at His own time, and in the lives of those He chooses to bring into relationship with Himself through Jesus Christ? This question is normally framed in the context of the relationship of faith and regeneration. Do we believe to become born again, or must we first be born again before we can exercise true, saving faith? Can the natural man do what is pleasing to God? Can the dead choose to allow themselves to be raised to life? This is the issue at hand.

EXEGESIS PROVIDES SOLID FOUNDATION

The need to do solid exegesis of texts, rather than allowing our traditions to determine the meaning, is demonstrated by looking closely at what the apostle John says in 1 John 5:1:

Whoever believes that Jesus is the Christ is born of God, and whoever loves the Father loves the child born of Him.

Dave Hunt, upon citing this passage, renders it as follows:

"Whosoever believeth that Jesus is the Christ is [as a result of believing] born of God."[2]

Is this what the text says? Let's find out. In 1 John we find two other passages that in the original language use the exact same construction we find in 5:1.[3] Let us apply Mr. Hunt's understanding and interpolation to these passages and see the result:

If you know that He is righteous, you know that everyone also who practices righteousness is [as a result of practicing righteousness] born of Him. (1 John 2:29)

Beloved, let us love one another, for love is from God; and everyone who loves is [as a result of loving] born of God and knows God. (1 John 4:7)

The disastrous result of interpreting the Bible by tradition is clearly seen here. In 1 John 2:29 the one "who practices righteousness" is directly parallel to "the one believing" in 1 John 5:1; in 4:7 "the one loving" is the parallel phrase. Mr. Hunt would not say that we can become born of God by practicing righteousness or by loving God. Yet he is forced to say so if, in fact, 1 John 5:1 says that by believing we become born again. In reality, in each of these instances, the tense of *born* points us to a preceding, determining, divine action that then *results in* the ongoing actions noted. That is, Christians *practice righteousness, love God, and believe* because they have been born of God. That divine act of regeneration is the ground, the condition that *results in* the acts of doing good, loving God, and exercising ongoing faith, the only faith that truly saves. Therefore, careful and accurate exegesis of the text in its own context reveals that John taught that God's act of regeneration *resulted in* the ongoing faith of believers. Only man's traditions can turn this testimony on its head.

The same truth is brought out in probably the most famous passage on this subject, famous due only to the tremendous amount of errant commentary offered upon it. When Paul wrote to the Ephesians, he spoke of God's work of gracious salvation:

> For by grace you have been saved through faith; and that not of yourselves, it is the gift of God; not as a result of works, so that no one may boast. (Ephesians 2:8–9)

The relevance of Paul's testimony here is based on the meaning of *that* in the phrase "that not of yourselves." What in the preceding clause is not of ourselves but is the gift of God? Again, careful exegesis shines the light upon both traditional readings and those offered on the basis of less-than-thorough study of the Greek language. It is obvious that one cannot simply say that "faith is the gift" and leave it at that. [4] The word *that* is a neuter gender in the Greek language, *faith* is a feminine term, and *have been saved* is a masculine participle. There is nothing in the first phrase that matches *that* in gender. Instead, the neuter demonstrative pronoun *that* refers to the

entirety of the preceding clause. There is *nothing* in the first clause of
Ephesians 2:8 that finds its origin in man, and that includes faith.

MORE BIBLICAL EVIDENCE

That faith is *of necessity* a divine enablement and dependent upon God's
grace is the teaching not only of Paul but of all the inspired writers. Note just
a few examples:

> For to you it has been granted for Christ's sake, not only to believe
> in Him, but also to suffer for His sake. (Philippians 1:29)

While our eyes are immediately drawn to suffering for Christ, note that
the first thing that is "granted" to the believers at Philippi for Christ's sake
is "to believe in Him." It has been *granted* to them, given to them as a gift.
Here faith itself is described as a gift given by God *to believers*. Surely no one
will suggest that it has been "given" to unbelievers to suffer for Christ! So
has the general ability "to believe" been given to all? Surely not. Saving faith,
the faith that is focused upon Christ and is ongoing and lasting, is the work
of the Spirit in the heart of the elect. As Paul expressed elsewhere: "The fruit
of the Spirit is love, joy, peace, patience, kindness, goodness, faithfulness,
gentleness, [and] self-control" (Galatians 5:22–23).

The word *faithfulness* can be translated as "faith" as well, and just as no
believer would ever say that the love he has in his heart comes from himself;
none would say that his patience or goodness came from his flesh. So why
insist that faith is a capacity available to all, including the natural man? The
answer is simple: Because without that assertion, God must be sovereign in
salvation and man utterly dependent upon Him. This is the only reason.

Fixing our eyes on Jesus, the author and perfecter of faith, who for the
joy set before Him endured the cross, despising the shame, and has
sat down at the right hand of the throne of God. (Hebrews 12:2)

The redeemed heart rejoices to consider the truth that Jesus is the author
and perfecter of faith. The term "author" refers to the origin, the source, and
"perfecter" means one who completes and finishes. While Jesus is surely the
origin and source of "the faith" as in the Christian faith as a whole, in this
passage, following right after the "faith hall of fame" in Hebrews 11, our
steadfast faith in God is in view. Christ is the origin of that faith, and He will
likewise perfect it.

That true and saving faith is one vital aspect of the work of the Holy
Spirit in the work of regeneration comes out over and over again in the text
of the New Testament. Note Paul's words to the church at Colosse:

We give thanks to God, the Father of our Lord Jesus Christ, praying always for you, since we heard of your faith in Christ Jesus and
the love which you have for all the saints. (Colossians 1:3–4)

Why should we give thanks to God upon hearing of the faith of fellow
believers, if in fact having faith in Christ is something that every person is
capable of having without any gracious enablement by God? Paul gives
thanks for their faith in Christ and their love for the saints. Is not the love
that disciples have for the saints the result of the work of the Spirit within
their lives? Of course. Then how can the faith they have in Jesus Christ be
anything less?

Peace be to the brethren, and love with faith, from God the Father and the Lord Jesus Christ. (Ephesians 6:23)

Here again we have a passage that combines things (peace and love) with faith that no Christian would ever argue come from our flesh. The consistent way of interpreting all of these passages is to see that divine and saving faith is a gift of God, just as love and peace are gifts from His Spirit. Simple consistency demands it.

The Scriptures also refer to faith as something that is "received." Peter wrote:

Simon Peter, a bond-servant and apostle of Jesus Christ, to those who have received a faith of the same kind as ours, by the righteousness of our God and Savior, Jesus Christ. (2 Peter 1:1)

Christians can even be described as those who have "received" faith! Are these the words we would expect if in fact faith is something we generate from ourselves, the function of an autonomous will free of the slavery of sin? Surely not. Instead, we must believe what the Word says: Faith is found *in* Christ Jesus: "The grace of our Lord was more than abundant, with the faith and love which are found in Christ Jesus (1 Timothy 1:14).

Grace, faith, and love—all divine in origin. Christian faith endures and perseveres because it is divine. Without this vital truth, there is no meaningful basis for believing in the permanence of Christian salvation.

GOD'S GRACE BRINGS SALVATION
WITHOUT DEPENDENCE UPON MAN

The supernatural power of God's grace to save is illustrated many ways in the text of Scripture. Space prohibits a full listing, but the following texts are more than sufficient to demonstrate the biblical teaching.

> A woman named Lydia, from the city of Thyatira, a seller of purple fabrics, a worshiper of God, was listening; and the Lord opened her heart to respond to the things spoken by Paul. (Acts 16:14)

If we have libertarian free will, why would God have to open Lydia's heart to respond to the things spoken by Paul? Is that not a violation of "free will"? And if God can open Lydia's heart, why does He not open *every* person's heart in the same way? Shouldn't the text say that she opened her own heart? Isn't that the way it is normally presented? Yes, but that is not the biblical perspective.

> By His doing you are in Christ Jesus, who became to us wisdom from God, and righteousness and sanctification, and redemption, so that, just as it is written, "LET HIM WHO BOASTS, BOAST IN THE LORD" (1 Corinthians 1:30–31).

By whose doing is anyone in Christ Jesus? Every evangelical will say, "Oh, it is God's doing, surely," but if such a person denies that God's grace saves powerfully and without the addition of human actions, even the autonomous action of faith, does that person truly believe it is by God's doing that they are in Christ?[5] Did not God do the same for every lost person, and yet for some reason they are still lost, but that person, due to some difference, some goodness, on his part, accepted God's "offer," while others did not? Surely that was not the view of the apostle Paul. He knew God's sovereign grace firsthand: It had stopped him in his tracks and knocked him off of his horse. God's grace paid no heed to Paul's "free will"; it overwhelmed him, changed him, resurrected him, and gave him a new heart—without Paul's assistance. As Paul said to the Galatians:

> When God, who had set me apart even from my mother's womb and called me through His grace, was pleased to reveal His Son in me so that I might preach Him among the Gentiles, I did not immediately consult with flesh and blood. (Galatians 1:15–16)

When did Paul come into relationship with Jesus Christ? Was it when he "chose" to "accept Jesus"? No, it was when *God* was pleased to reveal His Son in Paul. Not before, not after. God chose the time and the place and the method, and when that time came, no power in heaven or on earth could stop Him from accomplishing His purpose in Paul's life. Indeed, how could it be otherwise? What if Paul had continued in his rebellion, despite being struck blind? Are we to imagine God wringing His hands, wondering what He was going to do now, since the very missionary He was going to use to bring the message to a major portion of the world just refused to "cooperate"? Surely this is not the God we saw in our opening presentation! No, God was working out all things, even the persecution of the church itself, for His own purposes and glory. And so at the appointed time He drew Saul of Tarsus, who had surely not "disposed himself" to eternal life, into union with Jesus

Christ. He took out the heart of stone and gave him a heart of flesh. Paul could no more stop this divine resurrection than Lazarus could have stopped the Messiah from commanding Him to come forth. This is the testimony of the redeemed:

> He saved us, not on the basis of deeds which we have done in righteousness, but according to His mercy, by the washing of regeneration and renewing by the Holy Spirit, whom He poured out upon us richly through Jesus Christ our Savior. (Titus 3:5–6)

CONCLUSION

And so we see that the Bible speaks clearly to the necessity of divine regeneration as the free and sovereign work of God, resulting in faith and repentance on the part of the new creature in Christ. And while this truth is plainly taught in the text of Scripture, we recognize that the traditions of men say otherwise. We have seen (as in our examination of 1 John 5:1) how assuming a tradition and reading it into the text of Scripture can lead us into error, even to the point of completely reversing the actual meaning of the text. But as long as people continue to look to their traditions rather than the exegesis of the text, they will not see this divine truth. There is really no way to make people see the truth when they are looking the other direction. We can, however, trust God to turn the eyes of His elect to the truth and to give them the divine ability to see and to obey that makes us humbly cry out with the psalmist, "Open my eyes, that I may behold wonderful things from Your law" (Psalm 119:18).

1. Hence the irrelevance of citing passages such as Acts 7:51.

2. Dave Hunt, *What Love Is This?* (Sisters, Ore.: Loyal, 2002), 315.

3. That is, in 1 John 5:1 we have a present tense participle, "the one believing," and a perfect tense verb, "has been born of God." Perfect tense verbs refer to completed actions in the past, with abiding results in the present. Present participles in conjunction with perfect tense verbs can refer to contemporaneous or antecedent action.

4. Calvin is often misquoted on this point, for he decried those who said faith alone was the "gift" in Ephesians 2:9, when the gift is obviously broader than faith alone. Calvin did, however, affirm that faith is the gift of God (see James R. White, *The Potter's Freedom: A Defense of the Reformation* [Amityville, N.Y.: Calvary Press, 2000], 316–9, 326–7). Mr. Hunt is in error in *What Love Is This?* when he says "White and others" limit the "gift" to "faith" (p. 362). Hunt has misread both Calvin and myself on this matter.

5. Theologians use the terms "monergism" and "synergism" to describe these very different positions. Monergists (such as Calvinists) believe there is one power involved in bringing about salvation (God's), while synergists (Arminians, Roman Catholics, and most of man's religions) believe it to be a cooperative effort, with the majority, of course, being done by God, but, in the final analysis, with control remaining in the hands of man.

Response, by Dave Hunt

I n *The Potter's Freedom,* White states that "'irresistible grace' is a reference to God's sovereign regeneration of His elect: any other use of this phrase is in error."[1] It's amazing how precise he can be about a phrase that isn't even found in Scripture! We need Calvinism's explanation because those inspired to write Scripture didn't know this concept.

Irresistible grace is an oxymoron. Grace is the opposite of irresistible. Moreover, if God's grace can irresistibly cause every sinner to believe on Christ, the fact that it is limited to the elect disparages His love. And why is irresistible grace no longer irresistible once a person is saved, so that Christians can so often be carnal?

White's arguments are based upon reasoning from a few arguable Scriptures while avoiding the multitude of passages that plainly contradict Calvinism. He cannot produce even one verse that clearly states any of Calvinism's five points. He says that "it is God who regenerates sinners... freely." Of course, sinners can't regenerate themselves. But only the sinners who "received him...them that believe on his name" (John 1:12) become the sons of God.

When Nicodemus asked how a man could be regenerated, Christ said that it could only be through faith in Him and His death for sin. Just as the Israelites, in order to be saved from God's judgment, had to apply the blood of the Passover lamb to their houses and remain inside (Exodus 12:22), and just as only those bitten by "fiery serpents" who "beheld the serpent of brass…lived" (Numbers 21:8–9), so the gospel of "Christ our passover… sacrificed for us" (1 Corinthians 5:7) and "lifted up" on the cross to be "made…sin for us" (2 Corinthians 5: 21) is "the power of God unto salvation [only] to every one that *believeth*" (Romans 1:16, emphasis added).

Yet White says, "God chooses to raise His people to spiritual life…without the fulfillment of any conditions on the part of the sinner." But he can't offer *one* verse that says so. He offers nothing that can nullify the numerous Scriptures that say there is a condition: believing the gospel. He continues to mistakenly equate spiritual death with physical death and reasons that because Lazarus didn't give "permission" to Jesus to raise him from the dead, sinners don't have to believe the gospel to be sovereignly regenerated.

Yes, the physically dead can't believe, but that doesn't mean the spiritually dead can't believe. This false analogy is foundational to Calvinism, yet it fails miserably. The physically dead don't do *anything*. They don't disbelieve, or sin, or displease God, and they are certainly not "enslaved to [sin's] power," as White claims. Nor can the physical resurrection of Lazarus, who died again, be equated with spiritual resurrection to eternal life. White must rely on this false and unbiblical comparison because he can neither produce a Scripture that presents irresistible grace, nor refute the numerous Scriptures that clearly declare that no one is saved or regenerated without believing the gospel.

Yes, we declare on the authority of Scripture that God's grace alone cannot save anyone without Christ's full payment for sin and that the gospel is effective for salvation only to those who believe (Romans 1:16). This clear biblical teaching we have substantiated by quoting *many* Scriptures, none of which White has even addressed.

White persists in the Calvinist claim that regeneration precedes faith in Christ unto salvation. He "proves" this by stating that "whoever believes that Jesus is the Christ is born of God" (1 John 5:1) really means "whoever is born of God believes that Jesus is the Christ." I won't object. The verse can be taken both ways. Of course every truly born-again person believes that Jesus is the Christ.

Nor do I need this verse, for there are *many* others that declare in language that cannot be reversed that faith precedes regeneration. White claims that I interpret the Bible by tradition. On the contrary, I interpret 1 John 5:1 by the scores of verses, some of which I have already quoted, that state in unequivocal language that believing the gospel is essential to salvation and regeneration.

Surely there is no "regeneration" without eternal life from God and no eternal life without regeneration by God. Both in his book and this debate, White avoids Peter's clear statement that we are "born again…by the word of God…which by the gospel is preached" (1 Peter 1:23, 25).

Does White dare to turn "that believing ye might have life through his name" (John 20:31) into "that having life through his name, ye might believe," or "believe…and thou shalt be saved" (Acts 16:31) into "be saved and thou shalt believe," or "come unto me…and I will give you rest" (Matthew 11:28) into "all who are at rest come unto me," or "he that believeth is not condemned" (John 3:18) into "he that is not condemned believeth," or "he that believeth…shall never die" (John 11:25–26) into "he that shall never die believeth"? The biblical teaching is too clear to corrupt.

From Ephesians 2:8–9 he tells us that faith is "the gift of God." He calls upon the Greek but can't make his case. Salvation is the subject of this entire section, and that is clearly the gift. We are told plainly that "the gift of God is eternal life" (Romans 6:23). The same is declared in many other Scriptures in slightly different words. Salvation, or eternal life, as a gift from God, is called "living water" in John 4:10, an "unspeakable gift" in 2 Corinthians 9:15, and the "promise by faith of Jesus Christ" in Galatians 3:22. We read of the gifts of the Holy Spirit (Acts 11:17; 1 Corinthians 13:2; 2 Timothy 1:6) and of the gift of grace to preach the gospel (Ephesians 3:7), but never do we read of saving faith as God's gift to a sinner.

The Bible speaks continually of faith as something for which the individual is responsible; e.g. "According to your faith be it unto you (Matthew 9:29); "Where is your faith?" (Luke 8:25); "Your faith is spoken of" (Romans 1:8); "Your faith is increased" (2 Corinthians 10:15); "We heard of your faith" (Colossians 1:4); "[I am beholding the] steadfastness of your faith" (Colossians 2:5); "[Timothy has brought us] good tidings of your faith" (1 Thessalonians 3:6); "Your faith groweth exceedingly" (2 Thessalonians 1:3), and fifteen other similar verses. We read that our faith is to be tested (James 1:3; 1 Peter 1:7). What is the meaning of "*your faith*" and "ye of little faith" (Matthew 6:30; 8:26; 14:31; 16:8, etc.) if faith is God's gift requiring nothing from man?

Even if faith were a gift, a gift must be received and used. The recipient must actively believe. My faith is not passive, something that God does to me. Yet, we are told that "God hath dealt to every man [Christian] the measure of faith" (Romans 12:3), but "every man" contradicts Calvinism. Indeed, "faith cometh by hearing...the word of God" (Romans 10:17), again showing human participation.

There is not one verse that says faith comes by regeneration. Both saint and sinner are commanded to believe, to have faith. Hebrews 11, the great faith chapter, is a tribute to the faith of many under trial. Never once does it say that faith is a gift. Indeed, no one can even approach God without faith

(Hebrews 11:6). If faith is a gift, why don't the elect all live lives of perfect faith? Clearly there is responsibility on the part of the person exercising the faith.

White attempts to use other Scriptures to support his contention that saving faith is a gift, but none directly says what he wants it to say, and all but one of his examples are about faith for believers, not faith unto salvation. That "it has been granted...to believe in Him" (Philippians 1:29) does not say that faith to believe is a gift without responsibility on man's part, but that the privilege to believe on Christ has been granted. Yes, one of the fruits of the Spirit is faith, but this is faith given to believers for living the Christian life, not faith given to the unsaved for believing the gospel. Hebrews 12:2 is also speaking to Christians and says nothing about saving faith given to sinners for believing the gospel. Colossians 1:3–4 refer to the faithfulness of those believers, not to saving faith. And so it is with the other Scriptures he offers. Not one clearly states that faith to believe unto salvation is a gift of God that causes sinners to believe the gospel.

Never do we suggest that "faith in Christ is something that every person is capable of having without any gracious enablement by God." In fact, we believe that *enablement* from God is essential. But what could White mean by that word? Enablement implies a responsibility on the part of the one who is being enabled to do something—a complete refutation of Calvinism. The faith that is "*found* in Christ Jesus" refers to the ongoing faith to live the Christian life; Christians aren't free of the responsibility to "live by faith." As Paul said, "I also labour, striving according to his working, which worketh in me mightily" (Colossians 1:29).

White is never quite able to escape the non-Calvinist expressions that disprove his point. He asks, "Why would God have to open Lydia's heart...to respond to the things spoken by Paul?" *Respond?* So Lydia was *responsible* after all to *respond* from her heart to the gospel? This is the antithesis of Calvinism! How does *respond* fit with White's declaration that "God saves powerfully… without…human actions, even…faith"? What is this "response," if not faith from the heart?

As for Paul's conversion, the Lord says to him, "I am Jesus whom thou persecutest: It is hard for thee to kick against the pricks" (Acts 9:5). Clearly convicted in his conscience, Paul responds, "Lord, what wilt thou have me to do" (v. 6). This is saving faith as a gift from God without any responsibility on Paul's part? Hardly, but it is the best White can offer. Talk of "God wringing His hands, wondering" is nonsense. Has White forgotten biblical foreknowledge?

White says that Paul's "relationship with Jesus Christ" began "when *God* was pleased to reveal His Son in [him]." Surely he can't mean that God just came to that decision during Paul's lifetime. Paul's salvation had been God's pleasure before the world began. If Paul had had a relationship with Christ since then, why did he persecute Christians and need to get saved?

White's closing statement is "the Bible speaks clearly to the necessity of divine regeneration as the free and sovereign work of God, resulting in faith and repentance on the part of the new creature in Christ." This is a bluff. He hasn't given us *any* Scripture that speaks with such clarity. And that Calvinism has the cart before the horse is seen once again in his assertion that "faith and repentance" unto salvation are needed by "the new creature in Christ." It is only by faith and repentance that one *becomes* a new creature in Christ.

White has given us further proof that, for Calvinists, God's sovereignty is everything and God's love for the lost is nothing. Calvinists are without compassion for the lost, but how could they have compassion on those for whom God has no compassion and whom He has predestined to eternal tor-

RESPONSE, BY DAVE HUNT

ment for His good pleasure? All is to the glory of God's limited grace, Christ's limited atonement, and God's limited love, attributing to God lower standards of each than He expects of us.

White's last word is the same false accusation that, for non-Calvinists, "in the final analysis, the control remain[s] in the hands of man." God is in control. He makes the rules. No one enters heaven except on His terms. That man can reject the gospel and go to hell no more puts the sinner "in control" than a criminal "controls" those who established the laws and the police who arrest him.

---

1. James R. White, *The Potter's Freedom: A Defense of the Reformation* (Amityville, N.Y.: Calvary Press, 2000), 137.

D. Hunt   215

Defense, by James White

I n *What Love Is This?* Dave Hunt lists 1 John 5:1 as one of the "scores of Scriptures" that teach that faith precedes regeneration.[1] He then gives us a modified translation that, as we saw previously, violates the text as John wrote it. We have seen Hunt repeat the assertion that "scores" and "hundreds" of verses support his position, and yet when we begin looking carefully at his cited texts, we find that he is in error. And when faced with the refutation of his published words, does Mr. Hunt admit error? No. Instead, he says he simply does not "need this verse." Why? Because "scores" of verses say that "believing the gospel is essential to salvation and regeneration."

The careful reader knows that we have already corrected his misapprehensions and documented that faith in the gospel is indeed part and parcel of God's work of salvation. No Calvinist says otherwise. We simply acknowledge the fact that God must free us from the slavery of sin and spiritual death before we can believe. Hunt again confuses *salvation* and *regeneration*, the first being a subset of the second. All those God regenerates will believe (John 6:37).

Despite the presentation of clear evidence that saving faith is indeed a gift of God (Philippians 1:29), Hunt claims "never do we read of saving faith as God's gift to a sinner." Even while ignoring the material presented to him, Hunt lists passages that, upon examination, refute his position. He claims that faith is something for which the individual is responsible (something no

Calvinist would ever deny, of course, showing again how completely cursory Mr. Hunt's recent study of Reformed theology has been), and to support this, he cites Colossians 1:4. But note what Paul said:

> We give thanks to God, the Father of our Lord Jesus Christ, praying always for you, since we heard of your faith in Christ Jesus and the love which you have for all the saints. (Colossians 1:3–4)

Notice that the apostle has been giving thanks to God for the Colossians ever since he heard of their faith and love. Why thank God for the Colossians' faith if that faith is not divine in origin? This is a good example of how often Mr. Hunt's long lists of passages do not, in fact, carry any meaning.

One of the many passages he presents comes from Luke's narrative of the conversion of Lydia and has to do with the fact that the Lord opened her heart to respond to the preaching of Paul. Amazingly, despite claiming to have read "hundreds" of Calvinists, Mr. Hunt writes:

> Respond? So Lydia was responsible after all to respond from her heart to the gospel? This is the antithesis of Calvinism! How does respond fit with White's declaration that "God saves perfectly... without...human actions, even...faith?"

Please note two things: First, Hunt did not respond to the verse. The passage speaks of God's opening Lydia's heart. How is this "fair"? How is this in harmony with libertarian free will? How is it consistent with everything Hunt has asserted is "plain" biblical teaching supported by "hundreds" of texts? We are not told.

J. WHITE

Second, since we have already shown that all those the Father gives the Son *will come to the Son* in faith, what is so shocking about the fact that Lydia responded to this divine work in faith? This is Calvinism 101, and yet Dave Hunt *refuses* to recognize the most basic, elementary assertions of Reformed faith. His tradition functions as a lens that filters out anything that does not fit into the "mold" he has created for "Calvinism." This explains how, in responding to a presentation that contains numerous verses that do, in fact, teach that faith is a gift of God, Hunt can glibly deny they exist.

Hunt failed to respond to the exegesis offered of Ephesians 2:8–9. No one argues that salvation is not a gift. The point was the identity of the "gift" in Ephesians 2:8, and this Hunt ignored.

Hunt writes, "My faith is not passive, something that God does to me." Most assuredly. No one has argued otherwise. He continues, "Yet we are told that 'God hath dealt to every man [Christian] the measure of faith' (Romans 12:3), but 'every man' contradicts Calvinism." If, as Hunt has rendered it, the passage is about Christians (as it is), then how can this be considered contradictory to Calvinism? We are not told.

Hunt briefly addresses Philippians 1:29: "That 'it is granted…to believe in Him'…does not say that faith to believe is a gift without responsibility on man's part but that the privilege to believe on Christ has been granted." What does this mean? He has built another straw man to say that man has "no responsibility."

This misconception on Hunt's part comes from his rejection of compatibilism and the biblical texts that teach it. Hunt's libertarian position cannot allow him to accept the fact that God can work in the heart so that without fail the regenerated person will naturally, fully, consciously cling in faith to Jesus Christ. Calvinists believe, firmly, in believing in Christ, embracing the gospel, and *continuing* to do so throughout one's life. The issue is whether enemies of God, slaves of sin, spiritually dead men, can by the exercise of their own enslaved, corrupted will, do what is right and good in God's eyes and respond in faith *so that* God can then cause them to be born again. The biblical data has been clearly presented. Mr. Hunt's responses have relied upon his own misunderstandings of the Reformed position, nothing more. As a result, the position, as presented, stands unrefuted.

What a glorious truth it is that there is no power in heaven or earth that can stop the sovereign, triune God from saving the objects of His mercy. This is the confidence that the Word of God gives us in the proclamation of the Gospel of Jesus Christ. *Soli Deo Gloria!*

---

1. Dave Hunt, *What Love Is This?* (Sisters, Ore.: Loyal, 2002), 315.

J. WHITE

Final Remarks, by Dave Hunt

White claims that "looking carefully at his cited texts, we find [Hunt] is in error." Yet he ignores almost all of them. Instead, he rehashes arguable verses, devoting an entire page to 1 John 5:1, which isn't crucial. He turns faith for living the Christian life (Galatians 5:22; Hebrews 12:2) into saving faith as a gift to the elect and goes into detailed analysis of the Greek in verses where Greek scholars disagree.

White accuses me of denying the eternal security of the regenerated. Preposterous! Without Scripture to support his position, he distinguishes salvation from regeneration simply by saying so. Insisting that regeneration *precedes* faith unto salvation, he avoids conclusive verses to the contrary; e.g., "[These are written] that believing ye might have life" (John 20:31); "[Ye have been] born again…by the gospel" (1 Peter 1:23–25). Why the gospel, if the nonelect can't believe it and the elect are regenerated without it? Scripture repeatedly says that salvation comes by believing the gospel. Thus, Calvinism's sovereignly regenerated elect are still unsaved until given faith! Where is that in Scripture?

White argues that if saving faith is not a gift to the elect alone, those who believe could boast of "some goodness on their part." It takes no "goodness" to accept a pardon, and faith eliminates boasting (Romans 3:27).

He charges me with "misunderstandings of the Reformed position." Yet he avoids scores of Old Testament texts that express God's desire to bless all

Israel and state that the Israelites' future depended upon their free choice; e.g., "My people have forsaken me" (Jeremiah 2:13); "I am pained at my very heart" (Jeremiah 4:19–22), "I called you.... Obey my voice...that it may be well unto you. But they hearkened not" (Jeremiah 7:13, 23–24); "[Therefore] I will bring evil upon them" (Jeremiah 11:11).

Calvinism says that God's pleading was insincere; He had predestined their eternal doom because it "pleased" him, and He deliberately withheld the "irresistible grace" they needed to be able to repent. Then why, if one's destiny depends only upon whether God sovereignly regenerates and applies irresistible grace, did Paul *persuade* men (2 Corinthians 5:11)? Why did Peter exhort us to have a ready answer for those who ask a *reason*? Why did Paul reason "of righteousness...and judgment" (Acts 24:25), causing Felix to tremble?

The will is mentioned *thousands* of times in Scripture. The unregenerate are repeatedly called upon to choose to obey God. Yet Calvinism denies this God-given prerogative, and White dodges these many Scriptures.

The phrase "whosoever will" is found thirteen times in the Bible, and never would the ordinary reader imagine Calvinism's special meaning. "If any man thirst, let him come unto me, and drink" (John 7:37) is not a sincere call from Christ to the thirsty but only to the elect, whom God by *irresistible* grace will *cause* to drink? Calvinism's callousness toward the lost is appalling! God's final appeal in the Bible, "Whosoever will, let him take the water of life freely" (Revelation 22:17), is not addressed to *whosoever will*, but to the elect whom alone the Father will draw to Christ?

Whosoever will — 13 times

Final Remarks, by James White

On March 7, 1858, in a sermon entitled "Human Inability," Spurgeon taught:

Coming to Christ is just the one essential thing for a sinner's salvation. He that cometh not to Christ, do what he may, or think what he may is yet in "the gall of bitterness and in the bonds of iniquity." Coming to Christ is the very first effect of regeneration. No sooner is the soul quickened than it at once discovers its lost estate, is horrified thereat, looks out for a refuge, and believing Christ to be a suitable one, flies to him and reposes in him. Where there is not this coming to Christ, it is certain that there is as yet no quickening; where there is no quickening, the soul is dead in trespasses and sins, and being dead it cannot enter into the kingdom of heaven.[1]

I am truly thankful to have the privilege to write in defense of the sovereignty, freedom, and power of God's grace to save dead sinners. This was the key issue that separated the Reformers from Rome in those vital early decades of the Reformation, and it remains a vital issue today. Synergism and grace are antithetical, and despite the great inroads the extrabiblical concept of libertarian free will has made in "evangelicalism" as a whole, I gladly stand in defense of the power and ability of God's grace to *actually save*.

I believe that the careful reader will note that Mr. Hunt's last section consisted primarily of the repetition of objections that have been fully addressed, interspersed with continued misunderstandings and misrepresentations of the issue at hand. 1 John 5:1, a passage that teaches the very doctrine Hunt's tradition denies, though improperly cited in his book, "isn't crucial." He again confuses all of salvation with regeneration, again ignores the fact that God ordains the ends as well as the means, and despite repeated correction, ignores the role of the gospel in God's drawing His elect to Himself. By this point, the reader has surely begun to see the consistency of Mr. Hunt's replies: He consistently ignores the exegesis that refutes his position, while repeating the same mantralike phrases. He piles groundless accusations one upon the other, all in an effort to provide some semblance of argumentation. The result should be clear to all who seek consistency in interpretation of the text of Scripture.

This should be especially important to those who seek to vindicate God's truth over the errors of false teaching in our day. Reformed theology offers the consistent interpretation of the Word that is the only solid foundation of apologetic ministry. It is impossible to point to the exegetical errors of false teachers while allowing your own tradition to override the plain meaning of the text of Scripture itself. One cannot claim to practice *sola scriptura* and allow tradition to rule over the text of Scripture, as we have seen Mr. Hunt do in his writings.

---

1. Charles H. Spurgeon, "Human Inability," sermon preached 7 March 1858.

J. WHITE

Part II
{ Calvinism Denied }

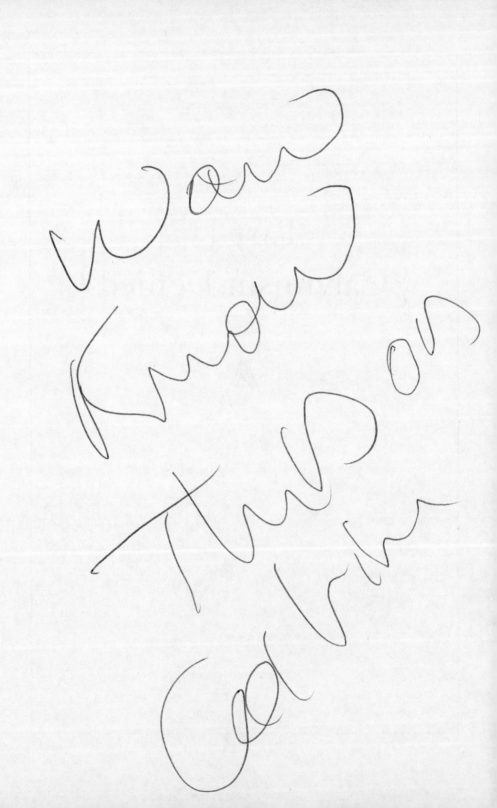

Chapter Eight

CALVIN AND AUGUSTINE: TWO JONAHS WHO SINK THE SHIP

by Dave Hunt

How can anyone call Calvin a great exegete, considering his faulty reasoning and false doctrines? How can his unchristian conduct at Geneva be defended? And what about Augustine, the source of so much of Roman Catholicism (including the advocacy of force to impose religion), being the admitted source of Calvinism?

In an otherwise extremely sympathetic and supportive biography of Calvin, Bernard Cottret admits that "Calvinism was not rationalism. Its stress on education...its determination to eradicate idolatry and superstition did not prevent the support in broad daylight of behavior all the more shocking...indeed, barbarous...imprisonment, torture, the stake."[1] Theology inevitably affects behavior. And to understand

Wow — Bad

Calvin's theology, we must turn to the question of his conversion.

Calvin's one brief account contains nothing about receiving Christ as his Savior. It simply relates his deliverance from some of Rome's false doctrines and practices in favor of Luther's complaints against Rome. This account was not written until 1557 (twenty-four years after the fact), and then probably to bolster his doctrine of predestination:

> My father had destined me for the study of [Roman Catholic] theology. [Later] I was…put to the study of law…. But God, by the secret guidance of his providence…[when] I was too obstinately devoted to the superstitions of Popery to be easily extricated…by a sudden conversion subdued and brought my mind to a teachable frame.[2]

This "sudden conversion"—not to salvation but to deliverance from certain Roman Catholic doctrines—apparently occurred early in 1534. On August 23, 1533, while visiting his hometown of Noyon, Calvin participated in organizing a religious procession against the plague. Back in Paris, he was present on November 1 when the new rector of the University, Nicolas Cop, in his All Saints Day address, expressed sympathy for the Reformation. Calvin's flight to Angoulême the next day, for fear of arrest, is no proof that he had already embraced Luther's ideas but was more likely because of his close friendship with Cop, who fled to Basel.

In Angoulême, sheltered by the du Tillet family, Calvin "first wove…the fabric of his *Institutes*,"[3] though he was still attending church and even "gave an occasional sermon or prayer."[4] Not until May 1534 did Calvin formally break with Rome by returning to Noyon to surrender the church benefices that had given him considerable income for more than a dozen years.[5]

The first edition of the *Institutes* in Latin must have been finished sometime in 1535 in order to have been published in Basel in March 1536. It comprised 516 pages in six chapters "devoted to the Law, the Creed, the Lord's Prayer, and the sacraments of Baptism and the Lord's Supper…the classic order of Luther's *Catechisms*."[6]

Thus a recent convert to Luther's Reformation wrote the *Institutes* while he was still struggling to break free from Roman Catholicism. Calvin admits that at this time he was "a mere novice and tyro."[7] Moreover, like Luther, Calvin continued under the spell of Augustine, one of Rome's most admired "saints," having become a serious student of Augustine while in residence at the Collège de Montaigu.[8]

Later, expanded editions of the *Institutes* did not change Calvin's basic doctrines but elaborated upon them. His reliance upon Augustine continued to grow, and he frequently used such phrases as "by the authority of Augustine," "Augustine ably expounds in these words," and "This cavil I prefer refuting in the words of Augustine."[9]

White calls Calvinism "Calvin's doctrine,"[10] but Spurgeon suggested that "perhaps Calvin himself derived it mainly from the writings of Augustine."[11] Warfield acknowledged that "The system of doctrine taught by Calvin is just the Augustinianism common to the whole body of the Reformers…. It is Augustine who gave us the Reformation."[12] Sproul says, "Augustinianism is presently called Calvinism or Reformed Theology."[13] Calvin himself admitted that "Augustine is so wholly with me, that if I wished to write a confession of my faith, I could do so…out of his writings."[14] Yet Warfield also declared that Augustine was "in a true sense the founder of Roman Catholicism,"[15] and "the creator of the Holy Roman Empire."[16] No wonder so much Catholicism remains in Calvinism.

Augustinian teachings found in the *Institutes* include infant baptism for salvation; the overemphasis upon sovereignty that makes God the cause of all, including sin; predestination/election of some to salvation and others to damnation/reprobation; faith as an irresistible gift from God; and imposition of Christianity by force. He advocated figurative interpretation of the early chapters of Genesis, reliance upon the decisions of church councils for the true interpretation of all of Scripture, [17] and a vital role for Mary in salvation.[18] He taught that Mary was sinless, promoted her worship, and with Jerome and Ambrose supported the decree of Pope Siricius in 387 ordering the unfrocking of any priest who married or continued to live with his wife.[19]

While Calvin did not accept all of Augustine's heresies, he did not warn against them but hailed Augustine as the one "whom we quote most frequently as being the best and most faithful witness of all antiquity."[20] François Wendell concedes: "Upon points of doctrine he borrows from St. Augustine with both hands."[21]

Augustine was one of the first to place the authority of tradition on a level with the Bible. Embracing apostolic succession from Peter as one of the marks of the true church, he declared, "I should not believe the gospel unless I were moved to do so by the authority of the Catholic Church"[22] ...[which] alone is the body of Christ.... Outside this body the Holy Spirit giveth life to no one."[23] Though Calvin meant the church universal, not the Roman Catholic Church, in echoing Augustine, he sounds like a practicing Catholic:

> I believe in the Holy Catholic Church...whence flow perpetual remission of sins, and full restoration to eternal life.[24]... Let us learn, from her single title of Mother...[that] there is no other means of

230

entering into life unless she conceive us in the womb and give us birth, unless she nourish us at her breasts.... [Outside her] no forgiveness of sins, no salvation, can be hoped for...hence the abandonment of the Church is always fatal.[25]

That's Catholicism, which most Calvinists would surely reject. Yet, White declares, "Even Calvin's detractors are forced to admit the value of his commentaries on the Bible even to this day."[26] One is dumfounded at the acclaim heaped upon both Calvin and Augustine by many otherwise sound Christian leaders, without a word of caution concerning anything Calvin said or did. To admit Calvin's many errors would open the door to questioning the key doctrines of Calvinism itself.

The Eucharist had held Calvin to Rome and was the last and most difficult tie for him to break. Nor was he ever able fully to renounce its mystical power and to accept the bread and wine as only symbols:

As I began to emerge a little from the shadows of the papacy...when I read in Luther that Oecolampadius and Zwingli left nothing of the sacraments but naked figures and symbols without reality, I confess that this turned me away from their books.[27]

Luther rejected transubstantiation but kept the "real presence of Christ" in the bread and wine through "consubstantiation." Calvin retreated a bit further from Rome, denying the physical presence of Christ, but retaining his own brand of sacramentalism, which made the ingesting of these physical elements a powerful source of spiritual life:

As bread nourishes, sustains, and protects our bodily life, so the body of Christ is the only food to invigorate and keep alive the soul…[and] the same is spiritually bestowed by the blood of Christ…to foster, refresh, strengthen, and exhilarate…by the sacred Supper, where Christ offers himself to us with all his blessings, and we receive him in faith….

I maintain that the flesh of Christ is eaten by believing, because it is made ours by faith…. Now…the knowledge of this great mystery is most necessary…. Bread and wine…represent the invisible food which we receive from the body and blood of Christ….

We say that Christ descends to us…that he may truly quicken our souls by the substance of his flesh and blood.[28]

Calvin also retained from Roman Catholicism and practiced at Geneva an unbiblical partnership between state and church. He said that the job of the civil authorities was to see to it "that no idolatry, no blasphemy against the name of God, no calumnies against his truth, nor other offences to religion, break out and be disseminated among the people…to prevent the true religion…from being with impunity openly violated and polluted by public blasphemy."[29]

From 1555 to 1564, Calvin's "control of the city continued without weakening. It became the symbol and incarnation of that 'other' Reformation."[30] He was determined to make Geneva the base for building Augustine's City of God everywhere. Spurgeon rejected this adulterous partnership with the severest language:

The union of the church with the state renders persecution possible; and hitherto churches have not been slow to avail themselves of the secular arm that they might confound all dissent with arguments which come home to the bone and the flesh. All churches, who lose the spirit of Christ are very prone to persecute.... Had true church principles prevailed, the crimes which make us shudder would have been impossible.... Put forward the doctrine that a state should propagate or maintain religion, and you have uncaged the lion; no one knows how much he may devour.[31]

Had Calvin's religion in Geneva lost the spirit of Christ? Calvinists boast that Calvin's control made Geneva a city of exemplary morals. The facts do not agree: "In the years 1558–59 there were 414 prosecutions for moral offenses; between 1542 and 1564 there were 76 banishments and 58 executions [among] 20,000 [people]."[32]

Anti-French outbreaks did not cease, nor did rowdiness, even during sermons: "In September 1558 it became necessary to remind people again that all games should cease during preaching...[especially] on days of the Lord's Supper because of 'the scandal the papists could make of it.'"[33] Calvin protested in a sermon: "'When there is a whore in prison, pies have to be brought to feast her.'" There was even licentiousness during sermons, with offenders displayed in the 'collar,' a pillory, the following Wednesday".[34] "In December 1556 several people complained of the rigor of the measures taken against fornication" as too rigid 'under grace' and that adulterers should not be condemned to death."[35]

In defense of what he practiced in Geneva, Calvin wrote: "Nothing is done here by the rashness of man, but all in obedience to the authority of

God."[36] Augustine had declared that heretics could be treated "the same way as other criminals...including poisoners and pagans."[37] Augustine supported the death penalty for those who were baptized as believers after conversion to Christ (later known as Anabaptists) and for other alleged heretics. For Calvin the greatest heretics were the Anabaptists.[38] In an incredible abuse of Luke 14:23, Augustine insisted:

> Why therefore should not the Church use force in compelling her lost sons to return?... The Lord Himself said, "Go out into the highways and hedges and compel them to come in."... Wherefore is the power which the Church has received...through the religious character and faith of kings...the instrument by which those who are found...in heresies and schisms—are compelled to come in, and let them not find fault with being compelled.[39]

Calvin followed the principles of punishment, coercion, and death that Augustine advocated. Concerning just one period of panic in the face of plague and famine, Cottret describes "an irrational determination to punish the fomenters of the evil." He tells of a man who "died under torture in February 1545 without admitting his crime":

> The body was dragged to the middle of town, in order not to deprive the inhabitants of the fine burning they had a right to. Sorcerers, like heretics...were characterized by their combustible qualities.... The executions continued. Yet those detained refused to confess; the tortures were combined skillfully to avoid killing the guilty foolishly.... [Some] were decapitated.... Some committed

suicide in their cells to avoid torture.... One of the arrested women threw herself from a window.... Seven men and twenty-four women died in the affair; others fled.[40]

In a letter Calvin advised a friend:

The Lord tests us in a surprising manner. A conspiracy has just been discovered of men and women who for three years employed themselves in spreading the plague in the city by means of sorcery.... Fifteen women have already been burned, and the men have been punished still more rigorously. Twenty-five of these criminals are still shut up in the prisons.... So far God has preserved our house.

Cottret continues:

Calvin therefore shared in all respects the fantasies of his entourage. He found occasion to exhort his contemporaries to pursue sorcerers in order to "extirpate such a race," as he proclaimed.... A pair of these henchmen of Satan had just been burned the previous month.[41]

Calvin even believed that the devil, at least on one occasion, helped rid Geneva of evil, "for in October 1546 he [the devil] bore away through the air (so Calvin himself testifies) a man who was ill with the plague, and who was known for his misconduct and impiety."[42]

Calvin justified his actions by Augustine's false interpretation of Luke 14:23. In his *Defence of the Orthodox Faith Concerning the Holy Trinity,* Calvin "defended not only his own attitude at the trial of Servetus but, more generally, the ancient Augustinian principle of repressing heresy by the secular sword."[43] Henry H. Milman wrote, "Augustinianism was worked up into a still more rigid and uncompromising system by the severe intellect of Calvin."[44]

Calvin's supporters claim that he only reflected his times, but a Christian must live as Christ: "He that saith he abideth in him ought himself also so to walk, even as he walked" (1 John 2:6). Yes, Calvin preached earnestly, visited the sick, cared for his flock. But his reviling of and vengeful behavior against those who disagreed with him were a reproach to Christ and cannot be ignored in evaluating his theology.

Many living in Calvin's time recognized the wickedness of using force to promote "Christianity." Full approval was lacking even among Calvin's closest friends.[45] Rebuking Calvin for the burning of Servetus, Chancellor Nicholas Zurkinden, a magistrate, said that the sword was inappropriate for enforcing faith.[46] In spite of many such rebukes, Calvin insisted that the civil sword must keep the faith pure. His conduct was in line with his rejection of God's love to all and his denial of human choice to believe the gospel.

1. Bernard Cottret, *Calvin: A Biography* (Grand Rapids, Mich.: Eerdmans, 2000), 180–1.
2. John Calvin, trans. James Anderson, *Commentary on the Book of Psalms* (Grand Rapids, Mich.: Eerdmans, 1948), preface xl–xli.
3. Florimond de Raemond, *L'histoire de la naissance de l'heresie* (Rouen: La Motte, 1629), 7: 883–4.
4. Cottret, *Calvin*, 77.
5. Abel Lefranc, *La Jeunesse de Calvin* (Paris: Fischbacher, 1888), 112.
6. François Wendel, trans. Philip Mairet, *Calvin: Origin and Development of His Religious Thought* (Grand Rapids, Mich.: Baker, 2000), 112.
7. Calvin, *Commentary on the Book of Psalms,* I: xl–xli.

8. Wendel, *Calvin*, 18–9.

9. John Calvin, *Institutes of the Christian Religion*, tr. Henry Beveridge (Grand Rapids, Mich.: Eerdmans, 1998), III: xxiv, 1.

10. James R. White, *The Potter's Freedom: A Defense of the Reformation* (Amityville, N.Y.: Calvary Press, 2000), 20.

11. Charles H. Spurgeon, ed., *Exposition of the Doctrine of Grace* (Pasadena, Tex.: Pilgrim Publications, 1978), 298.

12. Benjamin B. Warfield, *Calvin and Augustine*, ed. Samuel G. Craig (Phillipsburg, N.J.: Presbyterian & Reformed, 1956), 22, 322.

13. R. C. Sproul, *The Holiness of God* (Chicago: Tyndale 1993), 273.

14. John Calvin, trans. Henry Cole, "A Treatise on the Eternal Predestination of God," in John Calvin, *Calvin's Calvinism* (Grandville, Mich.: Reformed Free Publishing, 1987), 38, cited in Laurence M. Vance, *The Other Side of Calvinism* (Pensacola, Fla.: Vance Publications, 1999), 38.

15. Warfield, *Calvin and Augustine*, 318.

16. Ibid., 318.

17. Augustine, *De vera religione*, xxiv, 45.

18. Augustine, Sermon 289 cited in Durant, IV, 69.

19. Will Durant, *The Story of Civilization: The Age of Faith* (New York: Simon & Schuster, 1950), IV: 45.

20. Calvin, *Institutes*, IV: xiv, 26.

21. Wendel, *Calvin*, 124.

22. John Paul II, *Augustineum Hyponensem* (Apostolic Letter, 28 August 1986; www.cin.org/jp2.ency/augustin.html.

23. Augustine, *On the Correction of the Donatists*, www.newadvent.org/fathers/1410.htm, 11:50.

24. Calvin, *Institutes*, "Method and Arrangement," 28.

25. Ibid., IV: 1, 4.

26. White, *Potter's Freedom*, 28.

27. John Calvin, *Secunda defensio... De sacramentis fidei, contra J. Wesphali calumnias* (1556), cited in Cottret, *Calvin*, 66.

28. Calvin, *Institutes*, IV: xvii, 1, 3, 5, 9, 19, 24.

29. Ibid., IV: xx, 3, 9.

30. Cottret, *Calvin*, 250.

31. Charles H. Spurgeon, *The Sword and the Trowel* (London: Passmore & Alabaster), 2:113–4, 116.

32. Will Durant, *Caesar and Christ*, (New York: Simon & Schuster, 1950), 474.

33. Cottret, *Calvin*, 250–1.

34. Ibid., 250, 252.

35. Ibid., 252–3.

36. Calvin, *Institutes*, IV: xx, 10.

37. W. H. C. Frend, *The Rise of Christianity* (Philadelphia, Pa.: Fortress Press, 1984), 671.

38. Cottret, *Calvin*, 208.

39. Cited in E. H. Broadbent, *The Pilgrim Church: Tracing the Pathway of the Forgotten Saints from Pentecost to the Twentieth Century* (Grand Rapids, Mich.: Gospel Folio, 1999), 49.

40. Cottret, *Calvin*, 180–1.

41. Ibid.

42. Wendel, *Calvin*, 85.

43. Ibid, 98.

44. Henry H. Milman, *History of Latin Christianity* (London, England: A. C. Armstrong & Son, 1886), 3:176.

45. Ferdinand Buisson, *Sebastien Castellion: Sa vie et son oeuvre,(1515–1563)* (Paris: Hachette, 1892), I:354.

46. Letter from N. Zurkinden to Calvin, 10 February 1554, cited in Cottret, *Calvin*, 227.

Response, by James White

When engaging in a debate, it is best to respond to the strongest case your opponents can make and to do so with a full understanding of their particular position. In this exchange it would help Dave Hunt to realize that the Reformed position is being defended by an elder in a Reformed Baptist church who, by definition, would never claim Calvin's blessings upon the entirety of his theology. I believe what I believe not because John Calvin taught it but because the consistent exegesis of the text of Scripture leads me inevitably to the truths of the doctrines of grace. Trying to respond to my position by engaging in an attack upon the character and teachings of Augustine or Calvin shows a fundamental misunderstanding of my position. As my positive presentations of the doctrines of grace prove, I believe what I do because of the text of Scripture, not because I follow a particular individual's teachings.

We can, however, learn from Mr. Hunt's presentation something concerning his use of sources and the sort of argumentation that makes up his recent campaign against Reformed theology. The most amazing element of his presentation is the assertion of "crypto-Catholicism." While Hunt defends a system that stands shoulder to shoulder with Rome on the issue of the will of man and the idea that grace, while necessary, is not sufficient without the cooperation of man (i.e., Mr. Hunt is an avowed synergist who opposes the monergism of Luther and Calvin), he asserts that it is Calvinism that in fact contains "so much Catholicism."[1] How Mr. Hunt substantiates this assertion tells us much about why he opposes "Calvinism."

WAS CALVIN A CHRISTIAN?

It seems to be Mr. Hunt's purpose, both in *What Love Is This?* and in this work, to question whether men like John Calvin or Augustine were believers. By ignoring the vast differences in culture, context, and time, and by choosing his materials very selectively, he gives a horrifically biased and unfair presentation meant to poison the minds of modern evangelicals who have never given any thought to the history of the church and the lives of believers in the past. While in a single sentence Hunt admits that, in fact, Calvin did display an attitude of Christlike humility and godliness in certain situations ("Yes, Calvin preached earnestly, visited the sick, cared for his flock."), the thrust of his writing is clear: He questions whether Calvin was even *saved*, and, on that basis, seeks to cast doubt upon Calvinism, as if the system stands or falls upon the personal standing of Calvin himself.[2] For example, Hunt writes:

> To understand Calvin's theology, we must turn again to the question
> of his conversion.... This "sudden conversion"—not to salvation but
> to deliverance from certain Roman Catholic doctrines—apparently
> occurred early in 1534.

Did Calvin say that this conversion was merely a deliverance from Catholic doctrines? Hardly. Hunt has missed a basic element of context. Calvin actually stated:

First, since I was too obstinately devoted to the superstitions of Popery to be easily extricated from so profound an abyss of mire, God by a sudden conversion subdued and brought my mind to a teachable frame, which was more hardened in such matters than might have been expected from one at my early period of life. Having thus received some taste and knowledge of true godliness I was immediately inflamed with so intense a desire to make progress therein, that although I did not altogether leave off other studies, I yet pursued them with less ardor.[3]

Calvin speaks of tasting "true godliness" and being inflamed with an "intense" desire to make progress therein. Any fair-minded reading of his own words would lead one to believe that he is, indeed, speaking of his conversion *to Christ*. But this would not serve Hunt's purpose, for he wishes to inculcate the idea of incipient Romanism in Calvin's theology.[4] He states,

Calvin continued under the spell of Augustine, one of Rome's most admired "saints."... Yet Warfield also declared that Augustine was "in a true sense the founder of Roman Catholicism," and "the creator of the Holy Roman Empire." No wonder so much Catholicism remains in Calvinism.

For those unfamiliar with the writings of Augustine and his historical context, such assertions might raise emotional barriers to any fair examination of Calvin's writings or theology. But anyone familiar with history in general, and with Augustine in particular, finds such argumentation utterly without merit. Throughout his recent attacks upon Reformed theology Mr.

Hunt ignores the reality Warfield expressed when he noted that the Reformation, inwardly considered, was just the victory of Augustine's doctrine of grace over Augustine's doctrine of the church. The reason Augustine could be cited, properly and in context, by both sides in the Reformation is well known. Augustine encountered two major battles in his life, both of which indelibly marked his theology, and, in hindsight, created the contradiction that Hunt seems to ignore.

The first, the Donatist controversy, created Augustine's doctrine of the church that did indeed lay the foundations upon which later medieval theology would create the Roman Church. The latter, the Pelagian controversy, created his doctrine of grace from which the Reformers quoted with regularity. From a biblical perspective, the two theologies are contradictory. The Reformers, examining everything in the light of Scripture, rejected many aspects of Augustine's view of the church and claimed that his view of grace had been shrouded by tradition over the centuries. Obviously, if Hunt is going to make a meaningful connection between the elements of Augustine's theology that eventually created elements of Roman Catholicism and influenced Calvin, and hence Calvinism, he must show that the Reformers were drawing from those particular beliefs and not from Augustine's view of grace. This Hunt fails to do, for he does not even seem aware of the dichotomy in Augustine's teaching.

Further, Hunt seems to grant to Rome an antiquity that plays directly into the hands of modern Roman Catholic apologists. The "Roman Catholic" church did not exist in Augustine's day, and he would never have understood the term "Roman Catholic." Augustine's rejection of the authoritarian letters of Zosimus, the bishop of Rome, for example, shows how far he was from the modern "faithful son of Rome."[5] It seems to me that Hunt is willing to grant much to Rome if only to attempt, wrongly, to sully the name of John Calvin.

Hunt's misrepresentation of men of the past, which is part and parcel of his polemic, is truly troubling. His comments on Augustine's beliefs are obviously meant to paint him as a heretical, false teacher whose beliefs continue on in "Calvinism" today. Why else even discuss it in a debate on this topic? Yet Hunt not only fails to demonstrate that any of these beliefs have, in fact, influenced "Calvinism" but also propagates errors regarding Augustine's beliefs. The most troubling to me, as one who engages in refuting Rome's claims to authority, is his assertion that Augustine taught "reliance upon the decisions of Church councils for the true interpretation of all of Scripture." Such a statement flies directly in the face of mountains of citations from Augustine. William Webster and David King have produced a three-volume defense of *sola scriptura* that contains extensive direct citations of Augustine based upon primary research of his writings.[6] Just one such quotation, which illustrates the fallacy of handing Augustine over to the Roman system, comes from Augustine's response to Maximin the Arian. We read:

> I should not press the authority of (the Council of) Nicea against you, nor should you press the authority of (the Council of) Ariminum against me. I do not acknowledge the one just as you do not acknowledge the other. Instead, let us both come to common ground, the testimony of the Holy Scriptures (ii, 14).

These are hardly the words of the "founder" of Roman Catholicism! It is truly a shame to see the bright testimony that Augustine offered to the perspicuity and authority of Scripture sacrificed in an effort to discredit

Reformed theology. What is worse is the use of a citation from Augustine that even Calvin refuted, but which Roman Catholic apologetic works cite constantly to this day. Hunt writes:

> Augustine was one of the first to place the authority of tradition on a level with the Bible. Embracing apostolic succession from Peter as one of the marks of the true church, he declared, "I should not believe the gospel unless I were moved to do so by the authority of the Catholic Church."

Calvin refuted this very passage in the *Institutes*,[7] and any fair reading of Augustine's own writings disproves this misrepresentation by Hunt.[8] Anyone familiar with the *real* Augustine realizes that Hunt has created a caricature that has little resemblance to the historical reality.

HUNT'S ARGUMENT

Hunt's entire presentation is a blatant attempt to poison the well through poor argumentation. He is saying:

1. Augustine was a Roman Catholic.
2. Calvin cited from Augustine heavily and respected him.
3. Therefore, Calvinism is suspect by association with Catholicism through Augustine.

The first premise is manifestly false. Even if one replaces the first statement with, "Augustine held to doctrines modern evangelicals do not hold to," the argument does not follow, for it assumes that Calvin exercised no discernment in reading Augustine and that Calvinism as a system is dependent upon Calvin's use of Augustine. Neither of these things is true. Hunt adds to the confusion by attacking the character of Calvin and citing the fact that the Reformers were involved with a state church, all in the hope, it seems, of evoking an emotional response that will cause the readers to question the theological system that has been associated with the name "Calvin." I could argue, and I think far more convincingly, in the same way. For example:

1. Rome affirms free will and the necessity of human cooperation.
2. Dave Hunt affirms free will and the necessity of human cooperation.
3. Rome engaged in the Inquisitions and Crusades.

Therefore…what? Does the argument prove something? No, it does not. Nor do Hunt's (unfair and inaccurate) attacks upon Calvin's character. Calvinism is genetically related to Augustinianism; Dave Hunt's Arminianism is genetically related to Rome's semi-Pelagianism. These are facts.

I hope the reader will see that in the opening statements I have presented a positive, exegetically based position, while Mr. Hunt has focused upon negatively attacking Calvin and "Calvinism" without providing any kind of substantive defense of the position he *assumes* to be true. To the word and to the testimony (Isaiah 8:20)! Let us reject this kind of false argumentation and return to the sound exegesis of Scripture, which is the marrow of Reformed theology.

1. It is interesting to note the comment of Roman Catholic apologist Dave Armstrong regarding this issue. He writes, "Most Protestants today, it must be noted, espouse free will.... When Protestant denominations reject Calvinism, they are taking a step back in the direction of Catholicism." *A Biblical Defense of Catholicism* (no pub., 2001), 20.
2. For a fair and scholarly review of Calvin and his theology, see John T. McNeill, *The History and Character of Calvinism* (London: Oxford, 1967).
3. John Calvin, *Calvin's Commentaries* (Garland, Tex.: Galaxie Software) 1999.
4. The reader is encouraged to check the context of the citations of *both* sides thoroughly throughout this work.
5. See for example the formal debates against Roman Catholic apologists Tim Staples and Robert Sungenis, available electronically at www.aomin.org.
6. See William Webster and David King, *Holy Scripture* (Christian Resources, 2001), I: 80–5, III: 95–119, 250–3, 295–7.
7. John Calvin, *Institutes of the Christian Religion*, tr. Henry Beveridge (Grand Rapids, Mich.: Eerdmans, 1998), I: VII:3.
8. For a scholarly discussion of how Calvin refuted this misuse of Augustine, see David T. King, *Holy Scripture*, I: 80–1, and Heiko Oberman, "*Quo Vadis?* Tradition from Irenaeus to Humani Generis," *Scottish Journal of Theology*, 16 (1963): 234–5.

Defense, by Dave Hunt

White dismisses my careful documentation as "a horrifically biased and unfair presentation...and inaccurate attacks upon Calvin's character...and teachings of Augustine." The historical evidence, however, is impeccable for Calvin's use of the state to enforce godliness, his abusive language, and his endorsement of the death penalty for heretics ("One should...burn them cruelly."[1]), "barbarous... imprisonment, torture, the stake,"[2] and floggings, quartering and hanging body parts in strategic sites as a warning.[3]

Not only has White failed in the past to report the sordid truth about Calvin's conduct in Geneva but, when confronted with the facts, excuses it as "differences in culture, context, and time." Christians are to conform to their culture and times? Does the life of Christ living in those crucified with Him (Galatians 2:20), who "walk in the Spirit" (Romans 8:1; Galatians 5:16) "as he walked" (1 John 2:6), conform to this world? Even in Calvin's day, many rejected using the sword to compel faith,[4] saying, "Better to let...a thousand heretics live than to put a decent man to death."[5]

True, Calvin didn't use the exact phrase, "deliverance from Catholic doctrines." He said, "extricated [from] the superstitions of Popery." What is the difference? Nor does "some taste and knowledge of true godliness [and] intense desire to make progress therein" constitute conversion to Christ. In fact, Calvin's conversion as an adult would have denied his belief that he had become a child of God at his Roman Catholic infant baptism.[6] Like Luther, he fiercely opposed those baptized as babies who "got saved" and were baptized as believers, as do many Calvinists today. He insisted that anyone baptized as a baby, though by a godless Catholic priest, was one of the elect.[7] Does White believe this? Calvin's errors were serious.

Hunt, says White, "shows a fundamental misunderstanding of my position." *My position*? Please, this debate is not about White's position or Hunt's position but about Calvinism, which he defends and I oppose. And now, claiming not to "follow a particular individual's teachings," he disavows any influence from Calvin!

Yet in *The Potter's Freedom*, he refers to Calvin's "exegetical insight [and] profoundly biblical works"[8] and praises him as "a tremendous exegete of Scripture…fair and insightful."[9] He spends thirteen pages defending Calvin as a Calvinist[10] and quotes him as authoritative numerous times.[11] Calvinists such as White admire Calvin as their theology's founder and leading commentator. This is why I begin with Calvin's life and conduct. Life reflects doctrine (2 Timothy 3:10).

White denies that "Calvinism as a system is dependent upon Calvin's use of Augustine." Yet leading Calvinists and historians say that Calvin's theology came largely from Augustine. Sproul says, "Augustinianism is presently called Calvinism or Reformed Theology."[12] White claims that I make no "meaningful connection" between Augustinian doctrines foundational to Roman Catholicism and Calvin's theology. What about infant baptism, amillennialism, substitution of the Church for Israel, allegorical interpretation of the Bible, a state Church, persecution of "heretics," and clergy with special powers? Calvin credits Augustine with originating the doctrines that he expounds in his *Institutes*.[13]

D. HUNT

White produces an unconvincing quote to deny what I said about Augustine's "reliance upon Church councils for the true interpretation of all of Scripture." I could produce other quotes on my side. Of course he looked to Scripture, but when opinions differed on theological matters, he held that the councils were the final authority.[14] *Dichotomy?* Yes, I recognize that Augustine, like Calvin, often contradicted himself. Nor was everything that Augustine taught Roman Catholic and false. White blames *me* for "argumentation utterly without merit," but I am simply quoting leading Calvinists. Let him quarrel with Warfield, who called Augustine "the founder of Roman Catholicism."[15] That "Roman Catholicism" was unknown in Augustine's day does not negate the fact that his teachings became its foundation.

The quotes White gives to defend Calvin and Augustine are unconvincing. Luther said, "In the beginning, I devoured Augustine, but when...I knew what justification by faith really was, then it was out with him."[16] Yet Calvin quoted Augustine more than four hundred times without any reservation as "the best and most faithful witness of all antiquity"[17] and called him by such titles as "holy man" and "holy father."[18]

Why won't Calvinists acknowledge Calvin's false doctrines and reprehensible behavior at Geneva? To their shame, Calvinists either ignore Calvin's un-Christian conduct at Geneva (as White has in the past), or attempt to whitewash it (as White does now). But there is no escaping the fact that the doctrine that God, "for His good pleasure" predestines to eternal torment multitudes He *could save*, continues today to influence attitudes toward the nonelect.

1. Ronald H. Bainton, *Michel Servet, hérétique et martyr* (Geneva: Droz, 1953), 152–3; letter of 26 February 1533, now lost.

2. Bernard Cottret, *Calvin: A Biography* (Grand Rapids, Mich.: Eerdmans, 2000), 180–1.

3. François Wendel, trans. Philip Mairet, *Calvin: Origin and Development of His Religious Thought* (Grand Rapids, Mich.: Baker, 2000), 100; Cottret, *Calvin*, 198–200.

4. Letter from N. Zurkinden to Calvin, 10 February 1554, cited in Cottret, *Calvin,* 227.

5. Sebastien Castellion, cited in Ferdinand Buisson, *Sebastien Castellion* (Paris, Hachette, 1892) I: 374.

6. John Calvin, *Institutes of the Christian Religion*, tr. Henry Beveridge (Grand Rapids, Mich.: Eerdmans, 1998), IV: i, 7; xv, 1–2; xvi, 22, 31; xvii, 1, passim.

7. Ibid., IV: xv, 16–7.

8. James R. White, *The Potter's Freedom: A Defense of the Reformation* (Amityville, N.Y.: Calvary Press, 2000),19, 93, 119, passim.

9. Ibid., 19, 161.

10. Ibid., 253–65.

11. Ibid., 76–7, 161, 182–3, 193, 256–7, 259–60, 263–4, 317–9, 326–7.

12. R. C. Sproul, *The Holiness of God* (Chicago: Tyndale 1993), 273.

13. Calvin, *Institutes*, III: xxi, 2, 4; xxiii, 1, 5, 8, 11, 13–4; IV: xiii, 9, 11, 13–4, passim.

14. Augustine, *De vera religione*, xxiv, 45; Augustine, *On Baptism* VII: 101, passim.

15. Benjamin B. Warfield, *Calvin and Augustine*, ed. Samuel G. Craig (Phillipsburg, N.J.: Presbyterian & Reformed, 1956), 313.

16. Timothy George, *Theology of the Reformers* (Nashville, Tenn.: Broadman, 1988), 68.

17. Calvin, *Institutes*, IV: xiv, 26.

18. John Calvin, "Eternal Predestination," 39, 146, 148–9, cited in Laurence M. Vance, *The Other Side of Calvinism* (Pensacola, Fla.: Vance Publications, 1999), 104.

Final Remarks by James White

I t is a shame that Dave Hunt chooses to use the kind of argumentation that he does regarding Calvin and Augustine, both here and in *What Love Is This?* This kind of argumentation is called "poisoning the well." It is an appeal to the emotions of those who are easily prejudiced. If you can paint someone as horrible from the start, you can inculcate bias, even if there is no logical reason to do so. Hence, even though there are complexities in the contexts and resultant theologies of both Augustine and Calvin that explain, in large part, the differences they would have with modern evangelicals, Hunt dismisses these issues as irrelevant and accuses anyone who would seek to point them out of not only "whitewashing" but seeking to "relativize" the faith. One can only imagine how such argumentation could be used against almost *any* Christian of the past. Sadly, many will take Hunt's one-sided, biased presentation and think it is accurate, never taking the time to go to scholarly sources and read the whole story for themselves. As a result, many will not know the truth of the matter until eternity itself.

Because of its importance in other areas, I strongly encourage all readers to take the time to read the references to King and Webster's *Holy Scripture*, which I noted in my rebuttal, and see for themselves the truth concerning Augustine's views of biblical authority. Mr. Hunt is simply in error on this point, but, sadly, his errors will be taken as gospel truth by many who will then be subject to the authority claims made by Roman Catholic apologists.

As a consistent adherent to *sola scriptura*, I test all things, including the teachings of Augustine, John Calvin, Martin Luther, and even the words of the London Baptist Confession of 1689 (used by my church as its statement of faith), by the consistent teaching of the God-breathed Scriptures. This is central to what it means to be Reformed, as the motto *semper reformanda* means "always reforming." We are always concerned to test even our traditions by the higher standard of Scripture. And this I do with John Calvin. I can appreciate his tremendous insights, his vitally important writings, and the dedication he showed to the cause of Christ, even in the face of constant opposition and hatred. At the same time, I reject his sacramentalism, inherited from those who came before him, and his views of infant baptism (as I noted, I am a Reformed Baptist). Mr. Hunt at one point asks why I have not "warned" people about these things before. Ironically, Mr. Hunt is the one who admitted he had never read the Reformers before the summer of 2000, and hence must have missed my teachings, and even debates, on those subjects in the preceding years. In any case, I exhort the reader to read the sources that provide a fair and balanced view of Calvin and his life and ministry.

J. WHITE

Final Remarks, by Dave Hunt

White refutes neither my facts concerning Augustine and Calvin nor their relevance to Calvinism today. Instead, he vaguely declares that "the kind of argumentation" I use is "an appeal to the emotions of those who are easily prejudiced." Yet his appeal is without evidence. He alludes to "complexities" that allegedly justify "the differences [Augustine and Calvin] would have with modern evangelicals" but neither explains them nor their relevance to this debate.

I connected Calvinism with Catholicism not only through Augustine but through Calvin himself. White cannot rebut what I say, so he diverts attention with the absurd claim that I stand "shoulder to shoulder with Rome" because I believe that God has given man the power to choose to love Him and others. That Rome also believes this only shows that no one is wrong about everything.

He protests that he consistently adheres to "*sola scriptura*" and tests all things by that rule. This commendable claim contributes nothing to the issues at hand. He even faults my ignorance of his own "teachings… [and]debates…in the preceding years." What about this debate? White evades the issue.

Saying that I "sully the name of John Calvin," he claims that Calvin relied upon Augustine only selectively and with discernment. Citing just a few of Calvin's more than four hundred quotations of Augustine proves the contrary. Calvin relied upon Augustine completely, with no mention of his errors. For example: "It is wisely observed by Augustine, that [Christ] did not become the Son of God by living righteously, but was freely presented with this great honour [proving God's] free right of electing and reprobating."[1] Here Calvin denies Christ's eternal Sonship and uses the heresy of "election to Sonship" to justify election to salvation.

Calvin denied the biblical descent of Christ into Hades to deliver "the spirits in prison" (1 Peter 3:19) and declared it to be "nothing but a fable. To conclude...that the souls of the dead are in prison is childish."[2] His errors are many and serious.

White says I "poison the minds of...evangelicals" and raise "emotional barriers" with a "horrifically biased and unfair presentation." Again he gives no proof. He merely suggests "scholarly sources" that agree with him.

Praising Calvin's "tremendous insights...[and] vitally important writings," White says that he rejects Calvin's "sacramentalism...and his views of infant baptism"—a small admission considering Calvin's many unbiblical beliefs. He praises "the dedication [Calvin] showed to the cause of Christ" but won't denounce Calvin's torture and execution of heretics.

White claims that "Calvin refuted" Augustine's declaration: "I should not believe the gospel [but] by the authority of the Catholic Church." In fact, Calvin admitted the statement and tried to justify it.[3] As for Calvin's own assertions that "The Holy Catholic Church" gives us birth, with no forgiveness of sin or salvation outside of her,[4] White avoids them.

---

1. John Calvin, *Institutes of the Christian Religion*, tr. Henry Beveridge (Grand Rapids, Mich.: Eerdmans, 1998), III: xxii, 1.
2. Ibid., II: xvi, 9.
3. Ibid., I: vii, 3.
4. Ibid., II: xvi, 12.

D. HUNT

Chapter Nine

THE CENTRAL ISSUE: GOD'S LOVE AND CHARACTER

by Dave Hunt

H ow could God, who *is* love, predestine *anyone* to eternal torment, much less take pleasure in doing so? How could God who *is* love, not love all mankind when He commands us to do so? How could God love those He has predestined to eternal damnation and from whom He withholds the gift of grace and eternal life?

Surely love is the most important and most thrilling subject of all—and nothing is so beautiful as God's love manifest in Jesus Christ. Tragically, Calvinism robs us of what ought to be "the greatest story ever told." It reduces God's love to a form of favoritism without passion, and it denies man the capability of responding from his heart, thereby robbing God of the joy of a genuine response from man and the glory that it alone can bring.

John MacArthur Jr. writes that "God has designed for some of us to ful-fill the redemptive purpose and purely on that basis alone we are redeemed."[1] Only because God has so *designed* it, *some* of mankind are redeemed? Where is love's wooing and winning? Didn't God *"so love the world"* that He sent Christ to die for our sins? That *"God is love"* (1 John 4:8) can only mean that love is the very essence of God's nature. This is the only attribute of which it is said that God *is*. Of nothing else—not His justice, holiness, truth, goodness, grace, or purity—is this said. All of God's attrib-utes must be understood in relation to the fact that He *is* love.

There is a huge difference between believing that God loves everyone and that He loves only the elect. Between believing that Christ's love caused Him to die for everyone and that He died only for an exclusive few. Between believing that God desires to save all, has provided salvation for all in Christ (though men must believe to receive) and that He is pleased to damn mul-titudes He *could* save but instead has predestined to eternal torment. Between believing that God has "no pleasure in the death of the wicked; but that the wicked turn from his way and live" (Ezekiel 33:11) and that He takes pleasure in predestining multitudes to destruction. It is quite clear which is the God of the Bible!

While many Calvinists are fervent in preaching the gospel, why should they be concerned for the salvation of those who God Himself never intended to save and for whom Christ didn't die? The elect rejoice in *their* salvation. But what is there for those predestined to eternal torment? White says that many have been "left to eternal destruction…'according to the kind intention of [God's] will.'"[2] So it is God's kindness that damns so many!

One of the most disturbing things about Calvinists is their lack of con-cern for the lost. They *dare not* be concerned! To be concerned for those

God has predestined to salvation would be to doubt Him. And to be concerned for those God has predestined to eternal doom would be to rebel against Him. Edwin Palmer writes, "By the decree of God, for the manifestation of His glory, some men and angels are...foreordained to everlasting death...to the praise of His glorious justice."[3] Where is God's love in this scheme?

John MacArthur Jr. says, "God has that complex of motives which in the end must manifest justice; not in every case but in some, at His own discretion." God who is perfect in justice doesn't manifest justice in *every* case? God requires us "to do justly, and to love mercy (Micah 6:8) but God is not just "in every case"? We are to be merciful to all, but God Himself is not? Yet the psalmist said, "The LORD is good to all; and his tender mercies are over all his works" (Psalm 145:9).

Spurgeon himself recognized the importance of understanding what Scripture reveals about the character of God.[4] He said that what Calvin, White, and some others we quote stand for uncompromisingly is "ultra-Calvinism" and that:

> [It] goes vastly beyond the teaching of Christ [and] gets some of its support from a wrong view of God. To the ultra-Calvinist His absolute sovereignty is delightfully conspicuous.... He...too much forgets that God is love. He does not make prominent enough the benevolent character of the Divine Being."[5]

White calls sovereignty "The Vital Issue,"[6] and many Calvinists emphasize sovereignty to the exclusion of God's love.

The Calvinist claims that everything, even sin, is God's doing. So the love that we are to manifest to one another must come from God. With the love that God gives us we are to love everyone, including our enemies, and we are to forgive everyone who trespasses against us—yet God Himself doesn't love all and won't forgive all? Calvinism libels God in its denial of the very essence of His nature, which is love.

Christ commands, "Be ye therefore merciful, as your Father also is merciful" (Luke 6:36). Those who believe that "He who selects those whom he is to visit in mercy does not impart it to all"[7] need only be merciful to a select few. Those who believe that God has "mercy upon all" (Romans 11:32) will be moved by His love to be merciful to all. What a difference!

Our view of God affects both our theology and behavior, and it either brings glory to Him or denies Him the glory He ought to have from our hearts. Sproul writes that "How we understand the person and character of God the Father affects every aspect of our lives."[8] He is called "the God of love" (2 Corinthians 13:11). We are to "walk in love" (Ephesians 5:2) and to "follow after...love" (1 Timothy 6:11). God has "given us the spirit of...love." (2 Timothy 1:7). Would He not love all? How could He do otherwise?

The very first of the Ten Commandments is, "Thou shalt love the LORD thy God with all thine heart, and with all thy soul, and with all thy might" (Deuteronomy 6:5). The person God has predestined to eternal hell is to love Him with all his heart? Mankind is repeatedly reminded to love God. Four times we are told to love God with our whole heart and mind (Deuteronomy 6:5; Matthew 22:37; Mark 12:30; Luke 10:27). Clearly "love" must come as a voluntary response from the heart, and that requires the power of choice, but Calvinism denies that man has this capacity.

God summarized the remainder of the Law like this: "Thou shalt love thy neighbour as thyself: I am the LORD" (Leviticus 19:18). Six times this command is repeated: Matthew 19:19; 22:39; Mark 12:31; Romans 13:9; Galatians 5:14; James 2:8. After explaining that without love we have missed everything (1 Corinthians 13:1–3), Paul describes the love we are to have for God and man: "Love suffereth long, and is kind...believeth all things, hopeth all things, endureth all things. Love never faileth" (1 Corinthians 13:4, 7–8).

That this perfect selflessness characterizes the love of God for each individual is clear from John's admonition: "Beloved, let us love one another; for love is of God.... He that loveth not knoweth not God; for God is love.... If we love one another, God dwelleth in us, and his love is perfected in us" (1 John 4:7–8, 12). In other words, loving others is the very essence of God's nature, and those who truly know Him and in whom His love dwells cannot but love as He loves. Yet, God does not love billions?

Stanley Gower, a member of the Westminster Assembly, said that there is no greater heresy than suggesting that "God loveth all alike."[9] Loraine Boettner is very firm: "We believe that from all eternity God has intended to leave some of Adam's posterity in their sins, and that the decisive factor...is to be found only in God's will."[10] When we ask, "What about God's love?" the Calvinist tries to show that God loves those He has predestined to eternal doom, but it can't be done.

There is much scholarly rationalization and resorting to "original languages" to "explain" how God who *is* love could predestine billions to eternal torment in the lake of fire. Calvinists insist that although God loves everyone, He doesn't love everyone enough to provide a way for all to be forgiven of their sins and welcomed into heaven. They justify this apparent contradiction by the fact that in the Greek there are three words for love and say that God simply has a "different kind of love" for those He damns.

J. I. Packer writes, "God loves some in all ways (that is…He brings them to faith, to new life and to glory according to his predestinating purpose)." Then in defense of Calvinism he declares that God "loves all in some ways (everyone whom he creates…receives many undeserved good gifts).[11] After all, He gives them sunshine and rain through so-called "common grace." It is not love at all for God to predestine people to eternal torment, no matter what temporal "kindness" He shows them!

MacArthur declares that "God's love to the world is unlimited in extent (common grace). He loves them enough that the gospel should be preached to all of them, but God's love to the world is limited in degree."[12] Piper agrees: "Every time the gospel is preached to unbelievers it is the mercy of God that gives this opportunity for salvation."[13] Is this reasonable?

It is a manifestation of God's love and grace for the gospel to be preached to those to whom it offers no hope because He has predestined them not to believe it and to be eternally doomed? *What love is this*? Calvin argues that God "takes care of the whole human race."[14] What comfort is His care in this brief life to those He has predestined to eternal doom?

Surely it is not any "kind" or "degree" of love to preach the gospel to those God has predestined to destruction and from whom He withholds the grace and faith to believe. Sproul writes that "God is not at all that loving toward [those] not elected unto salvation…. It would have been more loving of God not to have allowed them to be born."[15] "*That* loving" toward some and "*more* loving" toward others are meaningless phrases in the context of 1 Corinthians 13. It is not loving—period—for God to damn for eternity *anyone* He *could* save.

Foundational to all MacArthur says in his series "The Love of God" is his premise that God doesn't love everyone equally.[16] *Love* predestines to hell those it could save? Zane Hodges notes that "The non-elect are both unloved and doomed. The cruelty implicit in such a view is obvious to any observer outside of those who have been brought up in [Calvinism], or have bought into, this kind of theology."[17]

"Love" that only "loves…in some ways" is not love at all! Man is not allowed by the Law and conscience to "love in some ways" but understands that love that does not go all the way is not true love. Incredibly, Calvinism portrays the God who "*is* love" and "the God of all grace" (1 Peter 5:10) as less loving and gracious than He requires man to be.

When Jesus was asked, "Master, which is the great commandment in the law?" He replied:

> Thou shalt love the Lord, thy God with all thy heart, and with all thy soul, and with all thy mind. This is the first and great commandment. And the second is like unto it, Thou shalt love thy neighbour as thyself. (Matthew 22:36–39)

Attempting to justify himself, the questioner asked, "And who is my neighbor?" Jesus responded with the well-known story of the Good Samaritan to show that everyone in need is our neighbor. Israel was commanded: "The stranger that dwelleth with you…thou shalt love him as thyself" (Leviticus 19:34). Yet God himself neglects to love multitudes in the greatest need of all?

Solomon warned: "If thou forbear to deliver them that are drawn unto death, and…sayest, Behold, we knew it not…doth not…he that keepeth thy soul…know it?" (Proverbs 24:11) Yet the God who requires us to deliver those in danger of death not only doesn't deliver those heading for eternal doom but predestines them to that fate—and does so for His good pleasure? Is this believable? Is it biblical?

Christ told hypocrites, "Ye have not the love of God in you" (John 5:42). If the "love of God" dwelling in man causes him selflessly to care for those in need, surely that same love flowing from God Himself would provide an escape from hell for everyone who would receive it on His just terms.

There is no question that the commands to love God with one's whole heart and one's neighbor as oneself are written in every conscience. Thus, James speaks to all when he says: "If a brother or sister be naked, and destitute of daily food, And one of you say unto them, Depart in peace, be ye warmed and filled; notwithstanding, ye give them not those things which are needful to the body, what doth it profit?" (James 2:15–16) Surely Christ's explanation of "neighbor" tells us that "brother" and "sister" means everyone. John elaborates: "Whoso hath this world's good, and seeth his brother have need, and shutteth up his bowels of compassion from him, how dwelleth the love of God in him?" (1 John 3:17). And yet God himself shuts up His compassion upon billions on the brink of eternal doom?

John writes, "My little children, let us not love in word, neither in tongue, but in deed and in truth" (1 John 3:18). The God who gives us this command sees billions on their way to hell and withholds from them the grace they need to be saved yet condemns us if we neglect one person in need? God is not as kind as the Samaritan? He tells us to do good to all, but He won't? Are we required to be more forgiving and loving than God? The Calvinist argues that it is not a contradiction but a mystery that God loves those He predestines to eternal doom. When we object that such a theory offends the conscience, the Calvinist parrots Calvin, who declared: "Truly does Augustine maintain that it is perverse to measure divine by the standard of human justice."[18] On the contrary, God calls to all men, "Come now, and let us reason together" (Isaiah 1:18). How could God reason with man except on the basis of the conscience He has given him?

Yes, God is perfect and infinite in love and justice, so we cannot fully comprehend Him. Yet the very standards of love and kindness by which our conscience bears witnesses, our "thoughts the mean while accusing or else excusing one another" (Romans 2:15) are given to us by God. Surely His standards are not lower than those to which He holds us.

Piper goes to great lengths to "show from Scripture that the simultaneous existence of God's will for 'all men to be saved' (1 Timothy 2:4) and his will to elect unconditionally those who will actually be saved...is not a sign of divine schizophrenia."[19] He writes an entire book "to defend the claim that God is not unrighteous in unconditionally predestining some [of all mankind] to salvation and some to condemnation."[20] God's righteousness is not the question. To my thinking, God would be righteous in sending all mankind to hell. But God *is* love and has offered salvation to all and desires all to be saved.

1. John MacArthur Jr., "The Love of God," Audiotape, part 4, 1995.
2. James R. White, *The Potter's Freedom: A Defense of the Reformation* (Amityville, N.Y.: Calvary Press, 2000), 177.
3. Edwin H. Palmer, *The Five Points of Calvinism* (Grand Rapids, Mich.: Baker, 1999), 124–5.
4. Iain H. Murray, *Spurgeon versus Hyper-Calvinism: The Battle for Gospel Preaching* (Edinburgh: Banner of Truth Trust, 1997), 88–9.
5. Charles H. Spurgeon, "Even So Father," in *Metropolitan Tabernacle Pulpit*, (London: Passmore & Alabaster), 7: 370.
6. White, *Potter's Freedom*, chapter 1, 33–52.

7. John Calvin, *Institutes of the Christian Religion*, tr. Henry Beveridge (Grand Rapids, Mich.: Eerdmans, 1998), 16.

8. R. C. Sproul, *The Holiness of God* (Chicago: Tyndale 1993), 20.

9. Stanley Gower, in the first of "Two Attestations" to John Owen, book 1 of *The Death of Death in the Death of Christ* (no pub., 1647), in Owen, ed. William H. Goold, *The Works of John Owen* (Edinburgh: Banner of Truth Trust, 1978), X:147.

10. Loraine Boettner, *The Reformed Doctrine of Predestination* (Phillipsburg, N.J.: Presbyterian & Reformed, 1932), 104.

11. J. I. Packer, "The Love of God: Universal and Particular," in *Still Sovereign*, ed. Thomas R. Schreiner and Bruce A. Ware (Grand Rapids, Mich.: Baker Books, 2000), 283–4.

12. MacArthur, "The Love of God," part 4.

13. John Piper and Pastoral Staff, *TULIP: What We Believe about the Five Points of Calvinism* (Minneapolis, Minn.: Desiring God Ministries, 1997), 14.

14. Calvin, *Institutes*, I: xvii, 1.

15. R. C. Sproul, *Chosen by God* (Chicago: Tyndale, 1986), 32.

16. MacArthur, "The Love of God," part 4.

17. Zane C. Hodges, "The New Puritanism, part 3: Michael S. Horton, 'Holy War with Unholy Weapons,'" *Journal of the Grace Evangelical Society* 7 (Spring 1994): 12, 17–29.

18. Calvin, *Institutes*, III: xxiv, 17.

19. John Piper, "Are There Two Wills In God?" in *Still Sovereign*, ed. Thomas R. Schreiner and Bruce A. Ware (Grand Rapids, Mich.: Baker Books, 2000), 107.

20. John Piper, *The Justification of God: An Exegetical and Theological Study of Romans 9:1–23* (Grand Rapids, Mich.: Baker, 2000), 179.

Response, by James White

The central thesis of Dave Hunt's new attack upon Reformed theology is simple: God loves all equally, without distinction or difference, and hence could never decree election but would try to save each and every person equally. This concept is assumed throughout *What Love Is This?* and forms the substance of the presentation to which I now respond. Surely it is a part of modern evangelical tradition to say, "God loves you and has a wonderful plan for your life," but providing a meaningful biblical basis for this assertion is significantly more difficult. Unfortunately, most are never challenged to think through their traditions, and Hunt's work is an important example of how this leads to an unintended, but nonetheless real, denial of biblical truth.

The question that Dave Hunt and those who repeat his allegations against Reformed theology do not address is one that has a very clear and firm biblical answer: Does the Bible teach that God lacks the ability to discriminate in the kind and nature of the love He exercises toward His creation? That is, does God have at least the same level of ability and freedom to exercise different *kinds* of love that man obviously possesses? Or is man superior to God in being able to discriminate in the matter of how he loves?

Human beings are made in the image of God. Our capacity to love, to adore, to worship, and even to dislike or hate, comes from the fact that we are made to have the freedom and ability to express that image in how we relate to others. The Bible commands us to love God, showing that love is not merely an emotion, but an action of the will, an attitude, a decision. Of course, the ability to love comes from our Maker, God, who is described as love (1 John 4:8).

But it is self-evident that man has the ability to love in different ways and that it is proper for him to do so. Think about it. The love a mother has for her children is rightly different in nature and extent than the love she has for someone else's children. There is a special nature to the love she has for the fruit of her own body. Likewise, men are commanded to love their wives as Christ loved the church. Surely a man is not to love anyone else's wife the way he loves his own. He is to *discriminate* in the *kind* of love he shows to his wife. This is right and proper.

A man who cannot defend his wife and family from an attacker because he can only "love" the attacker is hardly a man. We do not respect such a person. There is a time to love and a time to hate just as there is a time for war and a time for peace (Ecclesiastes 3:8). An inability to discriminate in such matters is a sign of sickness in a man. We confine in prisons those who act warlike in times of peace. We despise and shun those who are cowards in times of war. We have no respect for the man who cannot make sound and proper decisions in these matters.

Scripture recognizes this basic fact. Paul confesses a special, specific love that he has for the Corinthians (2 Corinthians 2:4) that he does not have for anyone else. Why would this be? Surely the love we have for a fellowship, for friends and fellow saints, grows and changes as we experience life with them. The love we have for fellow believers grows and deepens as we serve with them, cry with them, rejoice with them. I have close friends in Christ who are closer to me than family members who are unbelievers. We all understand this, so that when we read Paul saying that we are to do good to all men, "especially to those who are of the household of the faith" (Galatians 6:10), we understand perfectly what he is saying. It is part of our capacity to exercise freedom in how we love.

GOD'S LOVE

It should hardly be surprising, then, to discover that the Bible plainly teaches that God's love is surely not *less* than man's. He is not *less free* than His creature in the matter of how He loves His creation. There is no basis in the Bible for asserting that God's love knows no levels, kinds, or types. Just the opposite is true.

The love of God for plants and animals obviously differs from His love for human beings. God "loves" nonhuman creatures in the sense of providing them food and life itself. In the human realm, God's love is manifest in many ways. Psalm 5:5 tells us that God hates all who do iniquity. Psalm 11:5 tells us that He hates those who love violence. Obviously, if God's love is to have any reality, it must, as it is in His creature man, be joined with a hatred of anything that harms the objects of His love. The reality of His freedom to love in different ways and with different *kinds* of love is so obviously taught in Scripture that it is impossible to deny. Is anyone going to seriously argue that God loved the Egyptian foot soldier crushed under the falling waters of the Red Sea in the same way He loved Moses, who passed safely through the sea? That He loved the pagan Canaanite priest wiped out by the Israelites as they moved into the Promised Land to the same degree He loved Joshua? That He loved the captain in the Assyrian army He used to chasten Israel in the same fashion He loved the prophet Isaiah? Indeed, did not Jesus Christ, God incarnate, have a special love for His apostles, and even then, a special and unique love for John, who is called the apostle "Jesus loved"? (John 21:20). And is not Christ's love for the church utterly unique in its character? Will someone actually suggest that Christ loves any other organization, such as the United Nations, in the same way and to the same extent He loves the church? Surely not! And yet it is just this kind of differentiation in God's love that Hunt denies.

How can *any* of these things be true if God's love is undifferentiated and equal in all aspects? To claim otherwise is a glaring misunderstanding of what "omnibenevolence" means when applied to God. If we derive our beliefs *from* the Bible (rather than assuming them as a tradition and then reading them back into Scripture), we will conclude that the phrase "God is love" does *not* mean that "God has the same kind and level of love for all things, including for each and every single individual human being." No matter how one understands "JACOB I LOVED, BUT ESAU I HATED" (Romans 9:13), this verse alone should be enough to refute such an errant view of God's love.[1]

No matter how often Arminian tradition repeats its mantralike chant that God is *not* free to love a particular people redemptively, the Bible is plain on the matter. God loved Israel with an undeserved love that He did not show to any other people. And the love God has for His own people, the elect, is different than the love He shows to the creation in general or to rebel sinners outside of His grace in particular.

Dave Hunt calls it "irrational" to believe that every moment of extended mercy given to rebel sinners is properly styled "love." And yet this only shows the unbiblical nature of the tradition he is importing into this discussion. He asks how a loving God could eternally choose to send anyone to hell. Such a question completely misses the point. The proper biblical question is: How could a *holy God* give of Himself in sacrificial love to rebel sinners so as to bring them into a completely undeserved relationship with Himself? The biblical teaching is that God brings His elect to Himself in love while showing much patience toward those who deserve to be cut off *immediately* under His wrath (Romans 9:22–23). The underlying assumption in Hunt's position is that God *cannot be free* in the matter of *how* He loves or *how* He shows His grace. But this is merely a human tradition he is pressing, not a biblical teaching. Indeed, Hunt even inaccurately represents my own writings in trying to press this idea. We read: "White says that many have been "left to eternal destruction…'according to the kind intention of [God's] will.' So it is God's kindness that damns so many!"

In reality, I was exegeting Ephesians 1:5, and in the process I asked:

Why is one man raised to eternal life and another left to eternal destruction? The Scriptures offer an answer that is satisfying to the believer, but insufficient for the person unwilling to trust in God's goodness. What is the basis of God's act of predestination? It is "according to the kind intention of His will." [2]

The *positive* choice of a people in Christ Jesus is according to the kind intention of His will. The punishment of deserving sinners glorifies Him in the demonstration of His holiness and righteousness.

Let the reader understand: The heart of Dave Hunt's argument denies to God the freedom to love in different forms and fashions. Given the centrality of this concept to the *entirety of his argument,* he must explain how his view is biblically defensible in light of these considerations. Failing to do so results in the collapse of his position.

THE UNSTATED CONCLUSION

Dave Hunt presents us with a view of God loving those in hell with the same kind of love with which He loves the saints in heaven. Since he has not chosen to state his beliefs in a positive fashion, his theological conclusions cannot be examined on the same basis as my own. Nevertheless, denying God's freedom to love redemptively, as he does repeatedly, leads to an unavoidable, if unstated, conclusion to his position: If God loves without differentiation, His love fails to bring about the redemption of a large portion of those upon whom it rests, just as His grace tries but fails to save autonomous sinners without their aid.

Indeed, it must be remembered that the tradition Hunt proposes so exalts the autonomous will of man that the very work and intention of the triune God is left subject to abject failure. Not only can God's love fail, but the attempts of the Father, Son, and Spirit to save each and every individual person on earth also fail on behalf of those who enter into eternal punishment. Only an unbiblical commitment to libertarian free will can explain why anyone would think that this view of God and His love is superior to the confident promise of Scripture in the naming of Jesus: "You shall call His name Jesus, for He will save His people from their sins" (Matthew 1:21). The text does not say that "He will try, but often fail, to save" but that He *will* save *His people* from their sins. Redemptive love in Jesus Christ fulfills to the uttermost the saying, "Love never fails." This is powerful and effective love, powerful and effective grace, and why anyone would wish to diminish that power is truly beyond my comprehension.

1. Other passages demonstrating the error of an undifferentiated, nonspecific "love of God" include Isaiah 43:4, Jeremiah 31:3, Romans 8:35, 1 John 2:15 (we are *not* to love the "world," showing yet another of the many meanings of *world* in John's writings), and Revelation 3:19.
2. James R. White, *The Potter's Freedom: A Defense of the Reformation* (Amityville, N.Y.: Calvary Press, 2000), 177.

Defense, by Dave Hunt

White makes the point that God and man are "free" to love different people in different ways. True. But different ways to love different people (e.g., wife, child, friend, neighbor) cannot include predestinating to eternal torment *anyone* who *could* be saved. That's not love at all.

Calvinists say that God loves those He predestines to hell, but with a "different kind of love." To provide sunshine and rain in this brief life for those predestined to eternal suffering is a manifestation of God's *love*? What madness is this? The very idea is offensive to our God-given conscience! The God who *is love* will not act toward anyone inconsistently with the essence of His being. Of course, God's love cannot and will not override His justice. But neither will the fact that all men deserve eternal judgment prevent God from redeeming all who are willing. There is no possible explanation for a "love" that rescues some and leaves multitudes of others *who could be saved* to suffer eternally.

I've never said that "God lacks the ability to discriminate in the kind and nature of the love He exercises" or that He is "*less free* than His creature in the matter of how He loves." But "freedom" *to love* can't justify *not loving at all*. No one can say that God loves those He *could* save but instead damns eternally for His "good pleasure."

White ridicules the idea that "God loved the Egyptian foot soldier crushed under the falling waters of the Red Sea in the same way He loved Moses, who passed safely through the sea." God loves all, but love does not force itself; it can be received or rejected. Nor will God act unjustly. That a judge pronounces the sentence demanded by the law upon his own son does not mean that he doesn't love him. However, it would not be love if he *could* justly pardon him but doesn't.

No one goes to the lake of fire who has not rejected the witness of creation and conscience, whether it be an Egyptian soldier, an Israelite, or anyone else at any time or anywhere. We leave that decision to Him who *is love* and who "is good to all...[whose] tender mercies are over all his work" (Psalm 145:9), confident that "the Judge of all the earth [will] do right" (Genesis 18:25).

White admits that the "all men" to whom we are to "do good" includes those not of "the household of faith" (Galatians 6:10). But to "do good" doesn't mean temporarily and then to torture or kill. Nor would God be "good to all" if He gave temporary blessings while withholding eternal salvation.

Spurgeon said, "We win hearts for Jesus by love, by pleading with God for them with all our hearts that they would not be left to die unsaved."[1] But how can we love those God doesn't love, and plead with Him to save those He has already damned? And what is this about *winning* hearts for Jesus if all are predestined either to heaven or hell? But Spurgeon was biblical: "He that winneth souls is wise" (Proverbs 11:30). White quotes Calvin: "We ought to pray that...every man may be saved...the whole human race."[2] Why would Calvin pray for the salvation of those he says "it was [God's] pleasure to doom to destruction"?[3]

White falsely claims that "it is just this kind of differentiation in God's love that Hunt denies." No. It is rather Calvinism that perverts God's love.

"Love" is not without reason. It does not excuse sin or set aside discipline: "As many as I love, I rebuke and chasten" (Revelation 3:19). But to predestine to eternal damnation those who could be rescued is not "differentiation in God's love"—it is the opposite of love!

Never have I heard, much less uttered, the alleged "mantralike chant that God is *not* free to love a particular people redemptively." God is free to love anyone in any way He pleases. But love *is* loving.

Justifying the predestination of billions to damnation, White says that the real question is how God could "give of Himself in sacrificial love to rebel sinners so as to bring them into a completely undeserved relationship with Himself." No, the question is why God's self-sacrificial love wouldn't save all. Would we praise a man for saving from certain death one person and letting others he *could* save die?

White's final argument is that "If God loves without differentiation, His love fails to bring about the redemption of a large portion of those upon whom it rests." Love that is rejected has not "failed." Did God fail because Israel rebelled or because Adam and Eve sinned or because the entire world routinely breaks His commandments? Calvinism's denial of God's sovereign gift of free will to man, reflects a failure to understand that love can't force a heart response.

Spurgeon said, "If anything can call faith into exercise, it is the knowledge that Christ is willing to receive thee."[4] But how can anyone have that confidence if he cannot be sure Christ died for *him* because, as Jay Adams says, only God knows whom He has elected?[5]

Christ commanded, "Love your enemies, bless them that curse you, do good to them that hate you...that ye may be the children of your Father who is in heaven" (Matthew 5:44–45). Why would loving and blessing everyone prove that we belong to our heavenly Father if He doesn't do the same? What White calls "powerful and effective love," which refuses to save those whom it *could* save, is not love.

1. Iain H. Murray, *Spurgeon versus Hyper-Calvinism: The Battle for Gospel Preaching* (Edinburgh: Banner of Truth Trust, 1997), 4.
2. James R. White, *The Potter's Freedom: A Defense of the Reformation* (Amityville, N.Y.: Calvary Press, 2000), 256.
3. John Calvin, *Institutes of the Christian Religion*, tr. Henry Beveridge (Grand Rapids, Mich.: Eerdmans, 1998), III: xxi, 7.
4. Charles H. Spurgeon, "An Appeal to Sinners," *New Park Street Pulpit* (London: Passmore & Alabaster, 1858), 4: 437.
5. Jay E. Adams, *Competent to Counsel* (Grand Rapids, Mich.: Baker, 1970), 70.

D. HUNT

Final Remarks, by James White

n oft-repeated assertion of Mr. Hunt during our brief exchange is that I "ignore" or "forget" literally "hundreds" of Scriptures that support his view. I think it should be noted that when in fact I have taken some of my very limited space to address his lists of verses, I have consistently shown him to be in error in his application or interpretation. But most of the time I have passed over these lists because they are based upon a misunderstanding on Hunt's part and hence are irrelevant. The careful reader will see this.

Dave Hunt often speaks of Calvinism's "extreme" view of sovereignty, and yet he presents an "extreme" view of God's love. To what do I refer? Well, any view of God that is imbalanced is "extreme." I reject his assertion that Reformed theology is imbalanced regarding God's sovereignty, given its constant appearance in the biblical text, its centrality to creation itself, and God's character. It is the ground upon which stands the very purpose of God in Christ, and it gives richness and fullness to the grace, mercy, and love of God displayed at Calvary. But Mr. Hunt flattens out the attributes of God, especially His justice, the freedom of His grace and power, by making omnibenevolence the *articulus omnium fundamentalissimum*, the central, all-defining attribute of God. Based on this theory about God's love, Hunt then determines what God would or would not do.

I am thankful, at the very least, that I have had the opportunity of pointing out the error of the constantly repeated claim that "God loves everyone" means "God's love for each and every person is identical in form, content, intention, and purpose." And while Mr. Hunt is forced to admit the weight of my argument, he does not seem to see how fatal that admission is to his entire position. The emphasis in Scripture is upon the positive election of a people unto salvation as a demonstration of God's love and mercy, a fact Mr. Hunt constantly reverses, even to the point of misrepresenting my writings on the matter.

Hunt's repeated argument is that God cannot love those who are not saved since, in his mistaken (and seemingly unshakeable) view of Calvinism, they are unfairly condemned without any "chance." Mr. Hunt is scandalized by the idea of God being *able* to save everyone but not doing so. In other words, Mr. Hunt believes that if God is loving, *as he understands it,* God's grace cannot truly be free. That is, God's omnibenevolence will leave no room for the demonstration of His justice or holiness, for it will force Him to save everyone. Whether he admits it or not, Hunt's theory is that God loves each person equally, which means that there can be no redeeming love. It is just here that I have shown his fundamental error, for to say this is to deny to God the personal characteristics that mark us, His creatures.

Final Remarks, by Dave Hunt

White says that he has consistently shown me to be in error in my application or interpretation of the many verses I've cited. Not in this debate. Nor in *The Potter's Freedom* does White refer to *any* of the passages concerning the Passover, the Levitical sacrifices, or the serpent lifted up in the wilderness. He avoids them there, as he does here, because since they are for *all* Israel, they refute Calvinism. He shuns as "irrelevant" Old Testament Scriptures foundational to biblical salvation/redemption.

White says that I flatten out "the attributes of God, especially His justice," and that for God's grace to "truly be free," God must be free to damn those He *could save*. God is not "free" to act contrary to His character or to His Word, which explicitly states that His will is for all to be saved. White claims that it would undercut God's justice for Him to love and save all. Not so! If God can justly pardon one, He can justly pardon all on the same basis. God's love has provided pardon for all who will receive it. Calvinism undercuts both God's justice and love by limiting salvation to a select group and excluding multitudes who are no more guilty than those saved. Christ said, "Love your enemies, bless them that curse you, do good to them that hate you.... Be ye therefore perfect...as your Father...in heaven" (Matthew 5:44, 48). The heavenly love and mercy we are to reflect would never predestine to eternal torment any who could be saved!

I've been "forced to admit the weight of [his] argument"? Hardly. That love shows differentiation (love cannot exonerate the guilty) is obvious, but Calvinism limits God's love.

I've *never* said that the lost "are unfairly condemned without any 'chance.'" We all deserve condemnation. The dispute is over God's love and character. God expects us to love even our enemies. Paul was willing to be damned forever if that would save his brethren, the Jews. Surely any humane person would rescue from hell everyone he possibly could. Scripture repeatedly declares that God loves all mankind, wants all to be saved, and does not want anyone to perish. Yet Calvinism insists that God doesn't love everyone, that He doesn't want everyone in heaven, and that He even takes pleasure in predestinating multitudes to eternal suffering.

If a doctor had a cure for a plague decimating mankind, yet gave it only to a select group, he would be justly condemned. Sadly, Calvinism presents God as less loving, kind, and compassionate than our God-given conscience, biblical commands, and example tell us we ought to be.

Calvinists rejoice that God *could* save everyone but chooses not to. This should shock every conscience as blaspheming the character of God, who desires all men to be saved but has given each the power to choose in order that man may genuinely love and obey Him from his heart. It is a libel against God to suggest that He would act toward anyone with less kindness, compassion, and love than He expects of us, His creatures.

- Chapter Ten -

REGENERATION BEFORE FAITH AND SALVATION?

by Dave Hunt

Why do Calvinists insist that men must be sovereignly regenerated *before* they can believe the gospel, when the Bible repeatedly says that regeneration comes through believing it? Would three of TULIP'S five points collapse if Paul's "Believe...and thou shalt be saved" (Acts 16:31) were true?

We have seen that Calvin, despite declaring that "We are justified by faith alone,"[1] insisted that God regenerates and justifies infants without faith. He then declared that God *must* sovereignly regenerate all who would be saved, even though Scripture clearly requires faith in the gospel for regeneration to take place: "Being born again...by the word of God, which liveth and abideth for ever.... And this is the word which by the gospel is preached unto you" (1 Peter 1:23, 25). Convinced by Calvin, many evangelicals who reject the error of infants being regenerated by baptism nevertheless accept the idea that the elect must be sovereignly regenerated before they can believe the gospel.

Indeed, the idea that regeneration *must precede* faith is essential to Calvinism. The Synod of Dort declared: "Therefore all men…without the regenerating grace of the Holy Spirit…are neither able nor willing to return to God."[2] White declares that "The Reformed assertion is that man cannot understand *and embrace* the gospel nor respond in *faith and repentance* [emphasis his] toward Christ without God first freeing him from sin and giving him spiritual life (regeneration)."[3] Sproul affirms that "The Reformed view of predestination teaches that before a person can choose Christ…he must be born again… One does not first believe, then become reborn.[4] A cardinal point of Reformed theology is the maxim, 'Regeneration precedes faith.'"[5] Likewise, Palmer insists that "only when the Holy Spirit regenerates man and makes him alive spiritually can man have faith in Christ and be saved."[6] Agreeing with this basic tennet of Calvinism, Piper states, "We do not think that faith precedes and causes new birth. Faith is the evidence that God has begotten us anew."[7]

But doesn't Scripture say that the new birth comes as a result of faith? Paul reminded the Galatians that they were "all the children of God *by faith* in Christ Jesus" (Galatians 3:26, emphasis added). Yet White insists that "regeneration must take place first."[8] Here are yet more statements from Calvinists that directly contradict God's Word: "A man is not saved because he believes in Christ; he believes in Christ because he is saved"[9]; "A man is not regenerated because he has first believed in Christ, but he believes in Christ because he has been regenerated"[10]; "We do not believe in order to be born again; we are born again in order that we may believe"[11]; "No man can believe, unless he be begotten of God."[12]

Scripture repeatedly says the opposite: "Believe on the Lord Jesus Christ, and thou shalt be saved" (Acts 16:31); "If thou shalt...believe in thine heart...thou shalt be saved" (Romans 10:9). Here are a few more of the many Scriptures that state unequivocally that faith precedes and is the sine qua non of receiving salvation/eternal life through regeneration: "[The devil takes away the seed] lest they should believe and be saved" (Luke 8:12); "Whosoever believeth in him should...have eternal life" (John 3:15); "He that...believeth...is passed from death unto life" (John 5:24); "Every one who...believeth on him, may have everlasting life" (John 6:40); "'He that believeth on me hath everlasting life'" (John 6:47); "He that believeth in me, though he were dead, yet shall he live" (John 11:25); "[These are written] that believing ye might have life through his name" (John 20:31); "If thou shalt...believe... thou shalt be saved" (Romans 10:9); "It pleased God...to save them that believe" (1 Corinthians 1:21); For by grace are ye saved through faith" (Ephesians 2:8); "[Christ's longsuffering is a pattern for those who] should hereafter believe on him to life everlasting (1 Timothy 1:16); "[We are of] them that believe to the saving of the soul (Hebrews 10:39).

That the gospel must specifically be believed for the new birth to take place is clear: "The gospel...is the power of God unto salvation to every one that believeth" (Romans 1:16); "In Christ Jesus I have begotten you through the gospel" (1 Corinthians 4:15); "[He] begat he us with the word of truth" (James 1:18); "Whosoever believeth that Jesus is the Christ is born of God" (1 John 5:1).

Calvinists at times betray the falseness of their position by inadvertently making biblical statements, as when Sproul writes, "Once Luther grasped the teaching of Paul in Romans, he was reborn."[13] If God must sovereignly regenerate the elect *before* they can believe the gospel, what rebirth was this that Luther received *after* he believed the gospel?

White asks, "If a person can have saving faith without the new birth, then what does the new birth accomplish?"[14] It makes those who believe in Christ "sons of God," as John said: "To them gave he power to *become* [through the new birth] the sons of God, even to them that believe on his name; which were born...of God." (John 1:12–13, emphasis added).

Why do Calvinists, in spite of so many Scriptures to the contrary, insist that God must sovereignly regenerate sinners *before* they know and believe the gospel? The answer is simple: If this were not the case, three of TULIP's five points would collapse: total depravity, unconditional election, and irresistible grace. The totally depraved are *unable* to believe and therefore *must* be regenerated without faith. Nor would unconditional election or irresistible grace be necessary if the unregenerate could believe the gospel.

White spends an entire chapter ("The Inabilities of Man") attempting to prove that "totally depraved" man lacks the "ability" to believe the gospel and must therefore be sovereignly regenerated in order to be given the faith to believe.[15] What ability is required to believe in and receive Christ? None, of course. The "gift of God is eternal life" (Romans 6:23). White fails to show that any special ability is needed to believe in Christ and thereby receive God's free gift of eternal life.

God's gift of eternal life is in Christ and is given to all who receive Him. Never is there a hint that some special ability is needed to believe on Him. Believing anything depends upon two abilities every normal person has: an understanding of the facts and the willingness to believe. The Bible never says that believing the gospel is the one act of believing that requires a special ability for which one must first be regenerated—an ability God withholds from all except a select group. The smallest child with any understanding is able to believe in Christ and in childish faith receive the gift of pardon and eternal life, which God graciously offers as a gift to all. Paul reminded Timothy that "from a child thou hast known the holy scriptures, which are able to make thee wise unto salvation through faith which is in Christ Jesus" (2 Timothy 3:15).

How can the Calvinist ignore the clear teaching of Scripture that salvation is by faith and conclude that faith comes as a result of being saved? This theory is arrived at by deduction from a few Scriptures while ignoring scores of others, as, for example, Christ's statement that "No man can come to me, except the Father who hath sent me draw him" (John 6:44). From that Scripture, White reasons that the Father must regenerate a person before he can have the faith to believe in Christ. But Christ does not say that no man can come to Him except the Father regenerate him, and there is no basis to conclude that the Father's *drawing* means *regeneration.*

Furthermore, inasmuch as Scripture never says that coming to Christ requires any special ability, Christ's statement cannot signify inability. It is rather like saying, "No one can enter the museum without a ticket." This has nothing to do with one's ability to walk through a door; it has to do with the fact that access is restricted to ticket holders. It is a simple statement to the effect that the Father must draw men to Christ. He does not say that the Father draws only some and not others.

In support of the Calvinistic assertion concerning the alleged inability of natural man to believe the gospel, White quotes the declaration of the *London Baptist Confession* that "man has lost all ability to will the performance of any of those works, spiritually good, that accompany salvation."[16]

But what works and what spiritual good are required for salvation? None whatsoever. The good works follow salvation, as Ephesians 2:10 clearly says: "We are his workmanship, created in Christ Jesus unto good works."

White argues that while "unregenerate man" can understand the gospel, he cannot "submit himself to that gospel."[17] In fact, he is not called upon to submit but simply to believe. Nor can White produce a single verse that states in plain language that the unsaved person is incapable of believing the gospel.

White works hard to support "the Reformed doctrine of the total depravity of man and the bondage of man to sin."[18] He argues that an unregenerate man "can choose not to commit a particular act of sin: what he cannot do is choose to do that which is spiritually pleasing to God.... One cannot choose to do what is holy and righteous before God unless he or she is given a new nature in regeneration."[19] Of course. He seems to forget that salvation is offered to sinners, not to doers of good works "spiritually pleasing to God." Even if the unregenerate could do works pleasing to God, it would not help, because salvation is "not of works" (Ephesians 2:9). Faith, not works, is the essential ingredient: "He that cometh to God must believe that he is" (Hebrews 11:6). Faith must precede even coming to God.

In *The Potter's Freedom*, White quotes Christ's words to the Jews: "Ye cannot hear my voice" (John 8:43) and paraphrases Paul's declaration that "the natural man...cannot understand...the things of the Spirit of God"(1 Corinthians 2:14) as further proof of unregenerate man's natural *inability* to believe the gospel. [20] He then argues that "something must happen *before* [his emphasis] a person can 'hear' or believe in Christ: and that is the work of God in regenerating the natural man and bringing him to spiritual life."[21] This is a deduction that, as I have shown, not only has no clear biblical support but is repeatedly contradicted by Scripture.

Cannot is often used in God's Word to signify something other than inability. For example, it is often used in the sense of moral restraint; e.g., Genesis 34:14; 44:22; Numbers 22:18; Judges 11:35; Isaiah 59:1. It is also often used, as is the case in White's examples, to denote not inability but unwillingness, not an impossibility but a choice: e.g., Joshua 24:19; Psalm 77:4; Jeremiah 24:3, 8; Mark 11:33; Luke 11:7; 14:20; 16:3; Hebrews 9:5. Furthermore, as we point out in chapter 12, in 1 Corinthians 2:14, Paul is referring not to the gospel but to "the deep things of God" (1 Corinthians 2:10), which Peter says "the unlearned and unstable" twist to their own destruction (2 Peter 3:16).

The Calvinist fails (in fact he doesn't even attempt) to support from Scripture the idea that even the most depraved sinner is unable to believe the gospel, much less that to do so requires any special "ability" that the natural man lacks. There are many passages in the Bible declaring that man is a sinful, wicked rebel alienated from God. But there is *not one* to support the assertion that depraved sinners, no matter how evil, lack some special ability required to believe in Christ. *Not one!*

There is no hint anywhere in Scripture that any special ability is required to keep any command, from not eating of the fruit of the tree of knowledge to not committing murder or adultery. There is no suggestion that any special ability was ever required to offer any sacrifice, to keep the Passover, to cry out to God for mercy, to "return unto the LORD" (Isaiah 55:7). There is no Scripture that says anyone needs a special ability to seek the Lord with all his heart and find Him (Jeremiah 29:13–14). The requirement of special ability was invented to support Calvinism.

The Passover (to which we will return) is acknowledged even by Calvinists to be a beautiful picture of Christ's sacrifice and the redemption offered to all through His blood shed for the sins of the world. Unquestionably the offer of deliverance from God's judgment that night in Egypt was made to all without exception—even to the Egyptians who were willing to join themselves to Israel.[22] All that was required—and it was required of all—was to believe God's pronouncement of judgment and promise of deliverance and in faith to slay the lamb, apply the blood to the door posts, and eat the Passover inside the house while the destroying angel passed through the land.[23] This was apparently carried out by all of Israel without any special ability required. Nor is there any suggestion that God had to regenerate them in order to give them the faith to believe and obey this command.

Certainly neither the Israelites nor Egyptians had been regenerated to enable them to believe God's promise and keep the Passover. Nicodemus was a godly rabbi who kept the Law to the best of his ability, yet he had not been born again or even heard the term, because that concept is not in the Old Testament. Yet there were many men and women in the Old Testament, from Enoch and Noah to David and the prophets, who sought, knew, and obeyed God. Then how can it be said that in order to seek God and believe Him one must first be sovereignly regenerated? It isn't biblical.

Most Israelites were ungodly, as their subsequent rebellion and idolatry proved. Though "totally depraved"—and *without* being "regenerated" and supernaturally given faith—they believed the Passover promise and fulfilled the required works, "pleasing to God," of applying the blood of the lamb. Perhaps two million believed, obeyed, and were delivered from Egypt. Yet the great majority of those who journeyed with Moses through the wilderness for forty years proved that they were not the Lord's by their idolatry and continual rebellion against Him.[24]

Unquestionably, God's promise was for all Israel, and it was His good intention to bless them all with its fulfillment.[25] Every Israelite (not just some "elect" among them) was expected to believe God's promises and to enter the Promised Land by faith. Yet out of that entire generation who kept the Passover and left Egypt together, only Caleb and Joshua entered Canaan.

God's dealings with Israel don't even suggest that regeneration had to occur before the Israelites could hear His voice and obey Him. His commandments, promises, and warnings were not for a certain elect among them, but for all:

Now, Israel, what doth the LORD thy God require of thee, but to fear the LORD thy God, to walk in all his ways, and to love him, and to serve the LORD thy God with all thy heart and with all thy soul, to keep the commandments of the LORD, and his statutes, which I command thee this day for thy good? (Deuteronomy 10:12–13)

There is not a hint that God needed to sovereignly regenerate any of them before they could submit to Him totally. But the Calvinist argues that the natural man, being "dead in trespasses and sins" (Ephesians 2:1) is "no more able to respond to God than a cadaver." MacArthur reiterates: "How can a person who is dead in sin, blinded by Satan…exercise saving faith? A corpse could no sooner come out of a grave and walk."[26] Then why are we commanded to preach the gospel to those who can neither hear nor believe?

There is not one Scripture to support that view. In fact, as we have seen, the Bible teaches the opposite. The error is in equating spiritual and physical death. Of course, a corpse can't walk—but neither can it sin. And that the spiritually dead can believe in Christ is clear: "The hour…now is, when the dead shall hear the voice of the Son of God; and they that hear [i.e., heed and believe] shall live" (John 5:25; see also Ephesians 5:14). Clearly the spiritually dead, far from needing first to be sovereignly regenerated, hear the gospel, believe it, and as a result of believing, receive by faith eternal life, i.e., regeneration. Yet because TULIP would otherwise collapse, the Calvinist continues to teach regeneration before faith.

1. John Calvin, *The Epistles of Paul the Apostle to the Romans and to the Thessalonians* (Grand Rapids, Mich.: Eerdmans, 1961), 28–9.
2. Canons of Dort (Dordrecht, Holland: 1619), III, IV: 3.
3. James R. White, *The Potter's Freedom: A Defense of the Reformation* (Amityville, N.Y.: Calvary Press, 2000), 101.
4. R. C. Sproul, *Chosen by God* (Chicago: Tyndale, 1986), 72.
5. Ibid., 10.
6. Edwin H. Palmer, *The Five Points of Calvinism* (Grand Rapids, Mich.: Baker, 1999), 27.
7. John Piper and Pastoral Staff, *TULIP: What We Believe about the Five Points of Calvinism* (Minneapolis, Minn.: Desiring God Ministries, 1997), 11.
8. White, *Potter's Freedom,* 84.
9. Loraine Boettner, *The Reformed Doctrine of Predestination* (Phillipsburg, N.J.: Presbyterian & Reformed,1932), 101.
10. Arthur W. Pink, *The Holy Spirit* (Grand Rapids, Mich.: Baker, 1978), 55.
11. Grover E. Gunn, *The Doctrines of Grace* (Memphis, Tenn.: Footstool, 1987), 8.
12. John Calvin, *Commentary on the Gospel According to John* (Grand Rapids, Mich.: Baker, 1984), 43; cited in White, *Potter's Freedom,* 183.
13. R. C. Sproul, *The Holiness of God* (Chicago: Tyndale, 1993), 144.
14. White, *Potter's Freedom,* 185.
15. Ibid., 75–89.
16. Cited in ibid., 78.
17. Ibid, 101.
18. Ibid., 79.
19. Ibid., 113, 115.
20. Ibid., 109.
21. Ibid., 112–3.

22. "The children of Israel journeyed...about six hundred thousand on foot...beside children. And a mixt multitude went up also with them" (Exodus 12:37–38). "The mixed multitude that was among them fell to lusting" (Numbers 11:4).

23. Exodus 12:6–13.

24. Acts 7:40–43.

25. e.g., Psalm 81.

26. John MacArthur Jr., *Saved Without a Doubt* (Colorado Springs, Colo.: Chariot Victor, 1992), 58.

Response, by James White

Dave Hunt's third presentation unfortunately engages in a tremendous amount of rhetorical argumentation aimed at straw men. It is difficult to respond concisely to such a presentation, for it takes only a few words to present an error but many more to correct it. I will focus on the primary errors and trust the reader to examine the sources Hunt cites to detect the rest.

CONFUSING TERMS

The most fundamental error Mr. Hunt makes in this section is confusing *regeneration* with the entirety of *salvation*. Salvation includes regeneration, forgiveness, adoption, and sanctification. He actually goes so far as to ask: "How can the Calvinist ignore the clear teaching of Scripture that salvation is by faith and conclude that faith comes as a result of being saved?"

Such a statement means that Mr. Hunt is either ignorant of Reformed writing or unwilling to accurately represent it. I have long defended *sola fide* against those who deny it. I simply recognize the totality of biblical revelation and see that saving faith is a gift of God given to His elect as part of the Spirit's work of regeneration. To confuse *regenerated* with *saved* and then quote dozens of Scriptures about being saved by faith is to engage in empty rhetoric that has nothing to do with the question under debate, which remains very clear: Can dead rebel sinners exercise saving faith to cause their own spiritual birth? Hunt's confusion of terms renders the first third of his argument against the Reformed position irrelevant, despite his claim that "Such teaching is the very antithesis of Scripture." In reality, it is Hunt's misunderstanding of the basic issues that creates the false contradiction.

Hunt is likewise in error in asserting that in my chapter on man's inabilities I taught that man needs a "special ability" to believe.[1] Surely no one reading my work with an open mind would come to such a conclusion. My point was that unregenerate men are incapable of exercising saving faith because they are spiritually dead, enslaved to sin. They lack *all ability to do what is pleasing to God*, and I demonstrated this by exegeting the relevant texts. Hunt does not even attempt to deal with that exegesis but instead dismisses the argumentation by redefining terms.

EXEGESIS VERSUS TRADITION

The reader will note that Mr. Hunt either ignores or passes over very lightly the primary passages I discussed in my positive presentation of the inabilities of man. He utterly ignores key passages, such as Romans 8:7–8, and dismisses entire chapters of exegetical argumentation with short sentences. And when Hunt does attempt to engage some relevant passages, he errs gravely, as he did in his book *What Love Is This?*

It is instructive to see how Hunt's tradition drives him to turn a passage on its head and give the opposite meaning than that conveyed by the text. I refer to John 6:44. Here we have the assertion of inability in the strongest terms. Jesus says, "No man is able." If those words do not indicate inability, how could any language ever communicate such an idea? I have presented a positive exegesis of the passage in another section. Briefly, this is indeed speaking of coming to Christ in faith. The drawing of the Father is in fact limited to the elect, those who are given by the Father to the Son. The drawing results in their coming to Christ and being raised to eternal life.

Though I have presented these facts to Hunt in other venues, he has yet to provide a meaningful, exegetical response. Instead, he tells us that drawing does not mean regenerate. Then what does it mean, since those who are drawn come to Christ in faith and are raised up on the last day? Why does Jesus parallel drawing with hearing and learning from the Father in John 6:45? Hunt believes that "drawing" does not infallibly result in salvation, contrary to Jesus' own words in 6:44, where He says that the one drawn is raised up, and in 6:45, where He says that all who learn from the Father come to Christ. Hunt says there is "no basis" for believing that the drawing of the Father involves regeneration, yet he ignores the arguments that have been presented on the topic. Why not say, "I disagree with the arguments," instead of just denying that the arguments exist?

Hunt's presentation gives an excellent example of how misrepresentation can be joined with tradition to result in *eisegesis*. His tradition, based upon libertarian free will and a denial of God's eternal decree of election, cannot deal with Jesus' teaching that no man is able to come to Him outside of the sovereign work of the Father. So he writes: "Furthermore, inasmuch as Scripture never says that coming to Christ requires any special ability, Christ's statement cannot signify inability."

As we have already noted, the phrase *special ability* is a red herring. Combine this false conclusion with one's tradition and the result is eisegesis on the highest level: The text says "no man is able," but Dave Hunt reads it to mean "every man is able." How can one read "no man is able" and then say that "Christ's statement cannot signify inability"? If saying "no man is able to come to Me unless the Father...draws him" does not mean that men lack the ability to come to Christ outside of the Father's work, language itself is incapable of communicating even the most basic meaning. Hunt tries to dismiss this passage without telling us what it really means: "It is a simple statement to the effect that the Father must draw men to Christ. He does not say that the Father draws only some and not others."

Why must the Father draw men to Christ if they are *able* in and of themselves to come to Him? And given the context of John 6:37–45, how can Hunt assert that the one raised up on the last day *isn't the same as* the one who is drawn? As we have pointed out elsewhere, Dave Hunt must explain to us upon what basis he makes the one drawn different from the one raised up in John 6:44. Further, if this is just a "simple statement" about the Father needing to draw men, is He not drawing *these* men as well? The explanation muddles the passage. Hunt's tradition, not exegesis, is driving his response.

COMPLETE MISUNDERSTANDING

Hunt writes:

> White argues that while "unregenerate man" can understand the gospel, he cannot "submit himself to that gospel." In fact, he is not called upon to submit but simply to believe. Nor can White produce a single verse that states in plain language that the unsaved person is incapable of believing the gospel.

Any person familiar with the debate knows that the last assertion is simply without merit: John 6:44 is very clear, as is Romans 8:7–8. Hunt's refusal to see these texts outside of his Arminian tradition does not render

J. WHITE

them unclear. And as for the citation given, it would be good to read it in its original context, since it responds to an error Hunt repeats:

> It must immediately be said that it is *not* the Reformed position that spiritual death means "the elimination of all human ability to understand or respond to God." Unregenerate man is fully capable of understanding the facts of the gospel: he is simply incapable, due to his corruption and enmity, to submit himself to that gospel. And he surely responds to God every day: negatively, in rebellion and self-serving sinfulness. The Reformed assertion is that man cannot understand *and embrace* the gospel nor respond *in faith and repentance* toward Christ without God first freeing him from sin and giving him spiritual life (regeneration).[2]

It is a facile argument to say that we are not called to submit to the gospel but rather to believe in it. True belief involves submission; true submission involves faith. My point was clear: While unregenerate men may know the facts of the gospel, they have no desire to believe in the Lord Jesus Christ and cast themselves solely upon Him. It requires the work of the Spirit to take out their stony hearts and give them hearts of flesh (Ezekiel 36:26). Dave Hunt is actually defending the idea that a man with a heart of stone can choose to remove that heart and implant a heart of flesh in its place and that he possesses the capacity to perform this operation on himself. The contrast between the God-centeredness of the doctrines of grace and the man-centered emphasis of human tradition could hardly be stronger!

Quoting my statement that "one cannot choose to do what is holy and righteous before God unless he or she is given a new nature in regeneration," he says, "of course." However, he does not seem to realize that saving faith is a holy and righteous thing, something pleasing to God, so he follows this up by stating, "He seems to forget that salvation is offered to sinners, not to doers of good works 'spiritually pleasing to God.'" This is a canard. Anyone even remotely familiar with my position knows I am not talking about "good works." There is no need to engage in such rhetorical straw-man argumentation. If there is an answer for what I have said, why not offer it?

LIGHTING UP THE STRAW MAN

It is hard to know which is most disappointing: Mr. Hunt's failure to interact with the key texts on an exegetical level, his dogged dedication to an extrabiblical tradition, or the constant misrepresentation of the position he seeks to attack in his new campaign against Calvinism. Note the following words:

> The Calvinist fails (in fact he doesn't even attempt) to support from Scripture the idea that even the most depraved sinner is unable to believe the gospel, much less that to do so requires any special "ability" the natural man lacks.... But there is *not one* to support the assertion that depraved sinners, no matter how evil, lack some special ability required to believe in Christ. *Not one!*

Mr. Hunt references entire chapters in my book relating to this subject (the vast majority of the material in those chapters he does not even *attempt* to rebut). He well knows of the extensive discussions in Sproul, Piper, Calvin, and so many others. How then can he make a statement such as this? It is self-evidently false, so what is the value in making it, outside of rallying the troops through emotional grandstanding? Just because he rejects the teaching of the many passages that have been carefully exegeted and honestly presented does not mean they do not exist, so how can he make such a statement? Would it not be far more honest to say, "I disagree with all the exegetical interpretations Reformed theologians present"? This kind of response does not help anyone better understand the issues, nor does it direct us to the real basis for answering these questions, the God-inspired Scriptures.

REFOCUSING

Mr. Hunt's confusion of terms aside, we can see that even taking an entire positive section of presentation to attack the truth of God's divine work of regeneration has failed to accomplish his desired goal. Fair and sound exegesis of the Scriptures plainly reveals man's slavery to sin and his resulting inability to come to Christ outside of the work of the Father in regeneration. As Paul had expressed it, it is "by His doing you are in Christ Jesus" (1 Corinthians 1:30). Man's traditions would have us hear that as saying "He made it possible for you to join yourself to Christ Jesus," but that is not what it says. First John 5:1 says that all those who have been born of God are believing. Salvation is all of God, all to His glory alone. *Soli Deo Gloria!*

---

1. James R. White, *The Potter's Freedom: A Defense of the Reformation* (Amityville, N.Y.: Calvary Press, 2000), 75–120..

2. Ibid., 101.

Defense, by Dave Hunt

White says I engage in "rhetorical argumentation aimed at straw men" because I "confuse *regenerated* with *saved.*" Yet Spurgeon said: "A man who is regenerated...is saved."[1] MacArthur also equates being saved with being regenerated.[2] White is a consistent Calvinist: If God gives the faith to be saved only *after* regeneration, regeneration can't equal salvation. Yet the biblical evidence that we are saved by faith is overwhelming. So Calvin's newly regenerated elect are unsaved! Such is the consequence of this key Calvinist doctrine. Is this why White objects to my quoting "dozens of Scriptures about being saved by faith" and responds to *none*?

Instead of explaining to Nicodemus the "difference" between "born again" and being "saved," Christ equates being born again with receiving "everlasting life" through believing on Him. Was Christ misinformed? If regeneration and salvation are not the same, the "life" received in "regeneration" *without faith* is different from the "everlasting life" received *through faith* in Christ. What could this Calvinist "life" be?

Calvin declared that "every man, from the commencement of his faith, becomes a Christian."[3] But if the elect must be regenerated before they have faith, their regeneration leaves them still non-Christians. What "regeneration" is this that doesn't save? Spurgeon said it was "ridiculous" to preach Christ to the regenerate,[4] yet White says only those regenerated can believe.

Contradicting White and himself, Calvin titled a chapter, "Regeneration by Faith."[5]

White repeatedly misuses John 6:44 and Romans 8:7–8. He says that "the Reformed position is that spiritual death means 'the elimination of all human ability to understand or respond to God.'" This belief is not stated in Scripture. It is deduced from erroneously equating spiritual and physical death, and it impugns hundreds of invitations to the spiritually dead to repent and turn to God.

Never have I said that men "are *able* in and of themselves to come" to Christ…"outside of the Father's work." We can't even draw a breath without God. But White misinterprets "no man can *come* to Me unless the Father draws him" by overlooking the human action required by "come." White's exegesis of this passage contradicts scores of Scriptures that urge all men to come to God and to Christ without any mention of the Father's drawing. Here is a partial list: Deuteronomy 30:2; 1 Samuel 7:3; Nehemiah 1:9; Isaiah 55:1–7; Hosea 6:1; Zechariah 1:3; Matthew 11:28, 19:14; Mark 10:14; Luke 18:16; John 7:37; Hebrews 11:6; Revelation 22:17. In his book, White deals with *none* of these Scriptures, yet he faults my alleged "failure to interact with the key texts"! At the same time, he claims to "recognize the totality of biblical revelation," yet he gives almost no attention to the Old Testament foundation for the doctrine of salvation.

In light of the many Scriptures like those just listed, "no man can" could not signify *inability* but must mean the *right* to come. Nor does "except the Father draw him" indicate that the Father draws only an elect. Such an interpretation would contradict the many Scriptures revealing that the Father wants all to come to Christ.

White declares that Romans 8:7–8 proves the inability of the natural man to turn to God, thus necessitating his sovereign regeneration before he can believe the gospel. Yet this passage is not addressed to the unsaved but "to them which are in Christ Jesus" (8:1). Paul is not talking about becoming a Christian but exhorting Christians to walk in the Spirit, not carnally in the flesh.

In becoming Christians, those "dead in trespasses and sins" receive eternal life—and eternal life only comes by regeneration. Yet eternal life is by faith; e.g., "That whosoever believeth in him should...have eternal life" (John 3:15); "He that...believeth...is passed from death unto life" (John 5:24); "Every one who...believeth on him, may have everlasting life" (John 6:40); "He that believeth on me hath everlasting life" (John 6:47); "He that believeth in me...shall...live" (John 11:25); "Believing, ye might have life" (John 20:31).

In this chapter alone, I offer at least forty-five passages that clearly refute Calvinism. White responds to *none*. Instead, he rehashes the question: "Can dead rebel sinners exercise saving faith to cause their own spiritual birth?" Who imagines that *receiving* by faith the gift of eternal life *causes* eternal life? And who would suggest that "a man with a heart of stone can...implant a heart of flesh in its place"? We believe. God does the rest: "Through faith...we are his workmanship...unto good works" (Ephesians 2:8,10).

John 1:13 says, "[Believers] were born, not of blood, nor of the will of the flesh, nor of the will of man, but of God." From this, White argues that the new birth involves nothing man can do or any decision of his will, but is all of God. Of course, man can't regenerate himself. But the preceding verse says that those who "received him...that believe on his name...gave he power to *become* [not already *are*] the sons of God" (John 1:12, emphasis added).

This isn't the only clear biblical declaration that God effects the new birth in those who believe the gospel and receive Christ. Scripture refers specifically to regeneration by faith; e.g., "In Christ Jesus I have begotten you through the gospel" (1 Corinthians 4:15); "Begat he us with the word of truth" (James 1:18); "Being born again…by the word of God" (1 Peter 1:23). "Begotten," "begat," and "born again" denote regeneration—and clearly through faith in the gospel. Even R. K. M. Wright, praised by White, admits that "It is the Word…that regenerates."[6] Therefore, the Calvinist "regeneration," without faith, must be something else. It certainly isn't biblical!

"Begotten" "begat" "born again" denote regeneration] through faith in the gospel (!!) ✓

---

1. Charles H. Spurgeon, "The Warrant of Faith," in *The New Park Street Pulpit* (Pasadena, Tex.: Pilgrim Publications, 1978), 3.
2. John MacArthur Jr, "The Love of God," Audiotape, part 5, 1995.
3. John Calvin, *Institutes of the Christian Religion*, tr. Henry Beveridge (Grand Rapids, Mich.: Eerdmans, 1998),Calvin, II: xvii, 1.
4. Spurgeon, "Warrant of Faith," 3.
5. Calvin, *Institutes*, III: iii.
6. R. K. McGregor Wright, *No Place for Sovereignty* (Downers Grove, Ill.: InterVarsity, 1996), 117.

D. HUNT

Final Remarks, by James White

I truly believe that if Mr. Hunt were to recognize just a couple of simple facts, the vast majority of his current objections to the Reformed view of regeneration would evaporate.

First, he confuses terms, such as *salvation* and *regeneration*. In most theological works, *regeneration* is a subset of the larger and broader term, *salvation,* which often includes within it justification, forgiveness, redemption, and adoption. *Sometimes* it can be used in a narrower sense, but in historical discussions of these issues, *regeneration* has a specific meaning that Mr. Hunt normally confuses.

Second, yes, men believe the gospel to be saved. No question about it. I believe it, I preach it, I call men to do it. I just know that no man *will* do it unless and until the miracle of regeneration takes place first. God must open the heart. God must enlighten the mind. God must grant faith. And when God draws one of His elect to Himself, He draws them to Christ through the gospel. The unfailing result of being drawn by the Father is looking to, believing in, coming to (all present tense actions) the Son. It is the *nature* of the new creature in Christ to believe in Him.

Of course, it would help if Mr. Hunt would recognize that Paul was not merely waxing eloquent when he said that we are dead in our transgressions and sins. Paul recognized what this meant, for after he described our state in Ephesians 2:1–3, he pointed us to the only hope for the spiritually dead person:

"But God, being rich in mercy" (v. 4). The Christian message is one of resurrection power. God raises not only the physically dead but the spiritually dead by the same almighty, undefeatable power.

But men's traditions blind them to these truths. Mr. Hunt writes that I overlook the human action of "coming" in the phrase "no man can come to Me." Yet, as the fair reader knows, I not only emphasize the ongoing nature of our coming to Christ but also that every single believer comes, believes, and keeps coming and believing in Christ. I just also believe the undisputed and unrefuted fact that I come to Christ daily because the Father, on the sole basis of His mercy and grace, gave me to the Son in eternity past. Mr. Hunt cannot refute this fact of the text, so he is forced to resort again to the constant refrain; "It cannot mean that, since all these *hundreds* of passages I interpret through the grid of my tradition say otherwise." I can only trust that the reader will consider well the repetitive nature of this kind of defense on Mr. Hunt's part and judge rightly.

First John 5:1 says that we believe because we have been born again. Ongoing faith is *descriptive and definitional* of the new creation. If it were otherwise, we would boast and glory. But since it is not, we can boast only in the Lord.

Final Remarks, by Dave Hunt

Spurgeon opposed those who "assure us that a man must be regenerated before we may bid him believe."[1] Yet, White insists that regeneration precedes faith. But he admits that "men believe the gospel to be saved"; therefore, the regenerated aren't saved! Nor do they have eternal life, because Paul said that those who "believe on [Christ have] life everlasting" (1 Timothy 1:16). Then what "life" is received at regeneration before faith?

White says I confuse *salvation* and *regeneration*. But in the Bible these terms are synonymous. No one can be saved without being regenerated or regenerated without being saved. Spurgeon declared: "A man who is regenerated...is saved."[2] White says that regeneration is "a subset of...salvation." *Subset* isn't a biblical or theological term, but White must resort to it to extricate himself from Calvinism's web of contradictions. A "subset of...salvation" would be "part of" salvation," which White now admits comes by faith, making regeneration by faith also. Having insisted that Calvinism is founded solidly upon exegesis of the entire Bible, White now falls back on *I just know that* "regeneration takes place first." We are still waiting for biblical support. There is no mention of regeneration in the Old Testament, so how could Old Testament saints have had faith?

Calvin, too, contradicted himself. Borrowing from Augustine, he wrote: "The blessed life of the soul...is recover[ed] by the grace of regeneration." Later he declared that "believers, in embracing Christ, are...born...of God

307

(John i.13) [3].... All by whom [Christ] is received in faith will be regarded by our heavenly Father as sons." [4] So in embracing Christ by faith the *believer* is born of God, yet faith follows regeneration?

To the woman with the issue of blood who touched the hem of His garment and was healed, Jesus said, "*Thy faith* hath made thee whole" (Matthew 9:22, emphasis added). To the two blind men, He said, "*According to your faith* be it unto you" (Matthew 9:29, emphasis added). Christ speaks of their faith as though it were their own, not a gift from God. There is nothing about their being regenerated and then given faith to believe. White still hasn't produced even *one* Scripture declaring that regeneration precedes faith. There are none.

Of course, "Paul was not merely waxing eloquent when he said that we are dead in our transgressions and sins." It is equally obvious that God's "resurrection power [is] the only hope for the spiritually dead person." But that doesn't support Calvinism's equating spiritual death with physical death. Christ said that the spiritually dead "hear the voice of the Son of God [and] live" (John 5:25). If we exercised faith, "We would boast"? No, "boasting...is excluded...by the law of faith" (Romans 3:27).

1. Charles H. Spurgeon, "The Warrant of Faith," in *Metropolitan Tabernacle Pulpit*, (London: Passmore & Alabaster), Sermon 531, delivered 20 September 1863 at Newington.
2. Ibid.
3. John Calvin, *Institutes of the Christian Religion*, tr. Henry Beveridge (Grand Rapids, Mich.: Eerdmans, 1998), II: ii, 19.
4. Calvin, *Institutes*, III: xxiv, 5.

D. HUNT

- Chapter Eleven -

TURNING THE BIBLE INTO A CHARADE

by Dave Hunt

Why did Christ command the gospel to be preached to every creature if man is dead and can't believe it and if God has from eternity past predetermined to save only a select group, damning the rest? Why does God command "all men every where to repent" (Acts 17:30) if the elect can't perish and the nonelect can't repent?

It borders on blasphemy to ascribe to God the senselessness and insincerity of pleading for repentance and faith from those who are dead and can neither hear nor respond—those He has from eternity past predestined to eternal torment and from whom He withholds the ability to repent and believe. Why present the elaborate fiction that God loves everyone and that all men have the choice to receive or reject Christ? Why, if God *could* stop all evil and suffering and save everyone, does He allow evil and suffering to grow ever worse and save so few?

In order to maintain the theory of total depravity as the inability to seek or obey God, of an unconditional election that leaves no place for human response, and of an irresistible grace that imposes salvation through sovereign regeneration prior to any faith on man's part, it must be denied that man can choose to believe in and accept Christ as his Savior. Indeed, Calvinism agrees with Luther that man has *no free will*.[1] From that, it follows that man can do nothing on his own initiative, not even evil—and certainly not good. In spite of a plethora of Scriptures to the contrary, the denial of human will remains at the very heart of Calvinism. As Zane Hodges points out, "If there is one thing five-point Calvinists hold with vigorous tenacity it is the belief that there can be no human *free will* at all."[2]

As we shall see more fully in the next chapter, Calvinism follows Calvin's theory that everything that has ever happened or ever will happen, including the vilest wickedness, has all been preordained by God to turn out exactly as He willed: "He has decreed that...all events take place by his sovereign appointment.[3] Everything done in the world is according to his decree...so ordained by his decree."[4] Boettner said, "The basic principle of Calvinism is the sovereignty of God.[5] [He] creates the very thoughts and intents of the soul."[6] In other words, the wickedest sins men commit are conceived, predestined, and caused by God! Sproul agrees: "God wills all things that come to pass."[7] Calvin put it like this:

> We hold that...the counsels and wills of men...move exactly in the course which [God] has destined.... Augustine everywhere teaches...that there cannot be a greater absurdity than to hold that anything is done without [God's] ordination.... No cause must be

sought for but the will of God.... [All] events are...produced by the will of God."[8]

This strange doctrine, so essential to Calvinism, flies in the face of our common sense and daily experience, which tell us clearly that we make hundreds of choices every day and that we can blame none of them on God. Furthermore, as we shall see in the next chapter, the Bible explicitly declares that man acts according to his own will. In fact, he *must* if he is to please and love God. Any Old Testament offering to the Lord was to be given willingly; e.g., "Ye shall offer at your own will a male without blemish" (Leviticus 22:19). And there are dozens of examples of worshipers doing exactly that from the heart; e.g., Exodus 25:2; Judges 5:9; 1 Chronicles 29:9, 17; 2 Chronicles 17:16; 35:8; 2 Corinthians 8:3, 12.

Calvinism turns the Bible and human experience into a charade. Statements by God that command and plead with men to obey abound throughout Scripture, offering pardon from sin for repentance. But if man has no free will, they are all a pretense on God's part, a game He is playing to deceive man into thinking that he can choose to love and seek the Lord. God is misleading men into thinking that anyone can believe in Christ unto salvation, when that privilege is reserved for an exclusive few. In fact, the Calvinist insists that man cannot will anything, that God has predestined his every thought, word, and deed, and yet holds him accountable. This is the Calvinistic charade from Genesis to Revelation.

Boettner declared that "even the fall of Adam, and through him the fall of the race...was so ordained in the secret counsels of God."[9] God commanded Adam and Eve not to eat of the tree of knowledge and told them that if they did, they would die. Yet God really wanted them to eat of that tree, foreordained that they would, caused them to disobey, and then held them accountable and punished them. Calvin states, "The first man fell because the Lord deemed it meet that he should."[10] Sproul agrees, as he must to maintain TULIP: "God desired for man to fall into sin.... God created sin."[11] Also taking his cue from Calvin, Palmer insists, "God ordains sin, and man is to blame.... Sin is...foreordained by God."[12]

Would God not be culpable, at least as a partner in crime, for causing man to sin? No, says the Calvinist, because we can't apply our standards to God. But as we have seen, God put in our conscience the moral standards by which we judge one another. Throwing conscience, common sense, and hundreds of Scriptures aside, the Calvinist insists that "if God decides to predestine or decree any particular evils for any purpose he may intend, who are we to answer back to God (Romans 9:19–24)?"[13]

Of course we dare not judge God. But at the same time, we must have confidence that God is "of purer eyes than to behold evil, and canst not look on iniquity" (Habakkuk 1:13) and "cannot be tempted with evil, neither tempteth he any man" (James 1:13). That being the case, we can be confident that God would not cause man to sin. The very suggestion is contrary to the Bible and repugnant to our God-given conscience. That all sin and wickedness is contrary to God's will and thus could not be willed by Him is so clearly established in Scripture that it needs no further proof here.

The Calvinist takes a few verses out of context and misinterprets them to indict God with causing evil. A favorite "proof" that God is the cause of evil is: "Shall there be evil in a city, and the LORD hath not done it" (Amos 3:6). The Hebrew word there translated evil is *rah*, which is used repeatedly to signify calamity, trouble, suffering, and destruction but almost never moral wickedness. God is warning Israel of His coming judgment upon their sin, and that is the context and subject. This Scripture has nothing to do with God causing moral evil. To do so would violate His holiness.

God cannot will moral wickedness because it is contrary to His will. Repeatedly, God says that Israel's sins have provoked Him to anger and that therefore he has brought evil (calamity, judgment, destruction) upon them; e.g., Deuteronomy 4:25; Joshua 23:15; Nehemiah 13:18; Jeremiah 19:15; 35:17; 36:31. Repeatedly, Jeremiah warns of God's judgment; e.g., "Thus saith the LORD of hosts.... I will bring evil upon this place...because they have forsaken me" (Jeremiah 19:3–4). Yet we are asked to believe that the Lord caused Israel to do evil so He could punish them!

God reminded His people of His pleas for repentance because He did not want to punish them: "I sent unto you all my servants the prophets, rising early and sending them, saying, Oh, do not this abominable thing that I hate" (Jeremiah 44:4). Of course, God never tells His people or even His prophets that He really wants Israel to sin and that He has predestined them to forsake Him, to go into idolatry, and to commit abominable wickedness so He can punish them. That revelation would have to wait until Augustine and Calvin.

God calls Israel's sin "this abominable thing that I hate" (Jeremiah 44:4), yet we are called upon to believe that He foreordained it? We are to believe that God caused Israel to practice things that were abominations to Him? God declared that "this city hath been to me as a provocation of mine anger and of my fury from the day that they built it even unto this day, that I should remove it from before my face" (Jeremiah 32:31), yet Calvinism would have us believe that Israel's disobedience and idolatry were willed and foreordained by God! On the contrary, Paul declared that God has ordained human authorities as his ministers "to execute wrath upon him that doeth evil" (Romans 13:4).

If Calvinism is true, God is mocking man in much of the Bible, pretending to offer salvation from the penalty His law requires for the evil He has decreed that each one commit ("Whatever is done in time is according to [God's] decree in eternity"[14]; "God foreordains everything which comes to pass."[15]). He pretends to be sincere in calling for repentance, while withholding the very grace men need to repent, having foreordained that man can't and won't repent without sovereign regeneration. Calvinism mocks God, His Word, and man himself!

The entire history of mankind becomes a puppet show, with God the puppeteer. He looked down upon men and saw that "the wickedness of man was great.... Every imagination of the thoughts of his heart was only evil continually.... The earth also was corrupt...and...filled with violence" (Genesis 6:5, 11). This situation "grieved [God] at his heart." But, if as Calvinism says, God caused every evil thought, word, and deed, why was He grieved? And how could God be grieved if He could have caused those living in Noah's day to be saints rather than sinners but instead chose to damn them? Yet God *is* love?

White says that God "is able to save perfectly and completely all He desires to save: the fact that not all are saved leads inexorably to the truth of divine election" [i.e., for His good pleasure, God chooses to save only a select number].[16] In the case of the flood, out of the millions and perhaps even billions living at that time, God saved only Noah and his family. Why so few? The Bible says that it was because of the wickedness of everyone's heart, but Calvinism says that God, to demonstrate His justice, caused the wickedness for which He destroyed and damned them. I challenge White to present even one verse that upholds this cold-blooded theory.

Paul said, "We persuade men" (2 Corinthians 5:11). Why, if the elect don't need persuading, having been predestined to salvation, and the nonelect can't be persuaded, having been predestined to the lake of fire? The plain text of Scripture is mutilated in order to fit a theory. Luke writes that Paul and Barnabas "so spake, that a great multitude both of the Jews and also of the Greeks believed." (Acts 14:1). *So spake?* Isn't that misleading? Calvinism says that the listeners' salvation had nothing to do with the apostles' preaching but with God sovereignly regenerating and giving faith to believe. In hundreds of places the plain words of Scripture must be changed to accommodate a man-made theory.

"For God so loved the world" (John 3:16) doesn't really mean the entire world but certain elect sinners in "the particular elective purpose of God.[17] *World* here cannot signify all."[18] "That whosoever believeth on him" doesn't really mean that anyone can believe, but only some. Palmer writes: "It was just because God loved the world of elect sinners that He sent His only begotten Son…. In this passage 'world' does not mean every single person…but…people from every tribe and nation—not only the Jews."[19] A theory is *imposed* upon Scripture.

Calvin presents God as mocking the nonelect: "There is a universal call, by which God through the external preaching of the word invites all men alike, even those for whom he designs the call to be a savour of death, and the ground of a severer condemnation."[20] He calls through the gospel even those He has predestined to eternal doom? Calls them to what? Calvin's God is apparently taunting the nonelect with the gospel, offering a salvation He won't let them have.

Yet Calvin dares to insist:

It cannot be said that he [God] acts deceitfully; for though the external word only renders those who hear it, and do not obey it inexcusable, it is still truly regarded as an evidence of the grace by which he reconciles men to himself. Let us therefore hold the doctrine of the prophet, that God has no pleasure in the death of the sinner: that the godly may feel confident that whenever they repent God is ready to pardon them; and that the wicked may feel that their guilt is doubled, when they respond not to the great mercy and condescension of God. The mercy of God, therefore, will ever be ready to meet the penitent; but all the prophets, and apostles, and Ezekiel himself, clearly tell us who they are to whom repentance is given.[21]

White quotes Calvin regarding 1 Timothy 2:1–4: "God has at heart the salvation of all, because he invites all to the acknowledgment of his truth.... All those to whom the gospel is addressed are invited to the hope of eternal life."[22] How can those predestined to eternal doom be "invited to the hope of eternal life"? What perverseness on Calvin's part to claim that "by the Gospel the mercy of God is offered" to those he declares "are excluded from access to life"![23] Such callousness is chilling!

Calvin claims that "[God] will have all men to be saved" (1 Timothy 2:4) doesn't mean all men but all kinds and races of men[24].... He is speaking of classes.... [Paul's] only concern is to include princes and foreign nations in this number."[25] Calvin's audacity in changing the meaning of Scripture is breathtaking! "Foreign nations" aren't even mentioned. Paul exhorts that "prayers be made for all men." He emphasizes that prayers be made "for kings, and for all that are in authority" and specifies why: "that we may lead a quiet and peaceable life." He then adds, "[God] will have all men to be saved, and to come unto the knowledge of the truth." For turning "all men" into "all *kinds* and *races* of men" and "princes and foreign nations" in order to accommodate their system of theology, Calvinists will answer to God.

So much gets changed! "He is the propitiation...for the sins of the whole world" (1 John 2:2) doesn't really mean the entire world but the non-Jewish elect: "'World' is viewed as intending to transcend a nationalistic Jewish particularism."[26] "The Reformed understanding is...[the "whole world" means] all *Christians* throughout the world."[27] To maintain itself, Calvinism must change the meaning of the text from that which a simple person reading the Bible in his own language would understand. So much of the Bible becomes a charade. God's pleadings with Israel (Isaiah 1:18–20), His offer of salvation to all (John 3:15–17), Christ's "come unto me...all" (Matthew 11:28), and the promise that "whosoever will, let him take the water of life freely" (Revelation 22:17) only *seem* to offer salvation to all. No one can believe the gospel without being regenerated first, and God limits that to the elect. God isn't really offering salvation to all and isn't really calling all men to repentance but only a select few.

Why impose the elaborate fiction upon the Bible of calling all men to repent, of offering salvation to "whosoever believeth," when that isn't what God means? Why raise false hopes with deceptive language? That is the obvious question that Calvinism is unable to answer.

1. Martin Luther, trans. J. I. Packer and O. R. Johnston *The Bondage of the Will* (Grand Rapids, Mich.: Fleming H. Revel, 1999).
2. Zane C. Hodges, "The New Puritanism, part 3: Michael S. Horton, 'Holy War with Unholy Weapons,'" *Journal of the Grace Evangelical Society* 7 (Spring 1994): 12.
3. John Calvin, *Institutes of the Christian Religion*, tr. Henry Beveridge (Grand Rapids, Mich.: Eerdmans, 1998), III: xxiii, 6.
4. Ibid., I: xvi, 6; III: xxiii, 7

5. Loraine Boettner, *The Reformed Faith* (Phillipsburg, N.J.: Presbyterian & Reformed, 1983), 2.

6. Loraine Boettner, *The Reformed Doctrine of Predestination* (Phillipsburg, N.J.: Presbyterian & Reformed, 1932), 32.

7. R. C. Sproul, *Almighty Over All* (Grand Rapids, Mich.: Baker, 1999), 54.

8. Calvin, *Institutes*, I: xvi, 8–9.

9. Boettner, *Reformed Doctrine of Predestination*, 234.

10. Calvin, *Institutes*, III: xxiii, 8.

11. Sproul, *Almighty Over All*, 54.

12. Edwin H. Palmer, *The Five Points of Calvinism* (Grand Rapids, Mich.: Baker, 1999), 100, 116.

13. R.K.J. McGregor Wright, *No Place for Sovereignty: What's Wrong with Freewill Theism* (Downers Grove, Ill.: InterVarsity, 1996), 197.

14. John Gill, *A Body of Doctrinal and Practical Divinity* (Paris, Ark.: Baptist Standard Bearer, 1987), 173.

15. Arthur W. Pink, *The Sovereignty of God* (Grand Rapids, Mich.: Baker, 1986), 240.

16. James R. White, *The Potter's Freedom: A Defense of the Reformation* (Amityville, N.Y.: Calvary Press, 2000), 99.

17. Ibid., 257.

18. John Owen, ed. William H. Goold, *The Works of John Owen*, (Edinburgh: Banner of Truth Trust, 1978), X, IV: 338.

19. Palmer, *Five Points of Calvinism*, 44–5.

20. Calvin, *Institutes*, III: xxiv 7.

21. Ibid., III: xxiv, 15.

22. White, *Potter's Freedom*, 259.

23. Calvin, *Institutes*, III: xxi, 7.

24. John Calvin, cited in White, *Potter's Freedom*, 141.

25. John Calvin, *Calvin's New Testament Commentaries* (Grand Rapids, Mich.: Eerdmans., 1994), 10: 209.

26. John Calvin, cited in White, *Potter's Freedom*, 257.

27. Ibid., 274.

Response, by James White

D ave Hunt's fourth presentation is marked by shrill rhetoric, an incredible lack of understanding of the issues he has chosen to denounce, and a scattergun approach that presents a disjointed collage of false allegations against Reformed theology containing so many basic errors of fact and logic that one could fill a book with in-depth refutations. To say it is disappointing is a gross understatement.

Mr. Hunt does not understand the issues before him. I, along with dozens of others, have attempted over the past couple of years to explain to him the large number of misapprehensions he has about the Reformed faith, but he has refused to listen. This chapter exhibits many of these mistaken assumptions in full color. But what should concern all serious readers is the fact that in his dogged attacks upon Calvinism, Hunt does not provide a coherent, thought-out alternative.

In this chapter, Hunt derisively attacks God's sovereign rulership over all things. But what does he offer? Does he then hold to "simple foreknowledge," the theory that God created the universe, knowing evil would exist, but that He had no *purpose* in its existing? Does he hold to "middle knowledge," the theory developed by the Jesuit theologian Molina? Does he agree with Pinnock, Boyd, and Sanders in promoting "open theism?" We are not told. If God's decree does not include the evil of mankind, that evil has no purpose, and Hunt is left directing us to a God who creates the

319

possibility of evil, starts this universe off on its course, and then tries His best to "fix things" as they fall apart in a torrent of wickedness. This is supposed to comfort us? This is the God who says that He works all things after the counsel of His will? Hardly!

ONCE AGAIN, COMPATIBILISM

Unless harsh rhetoric is to be viewed as a substantive argument (it only functions thus for those with a predilection to such behavior), Hunt does not even *begin* to offer a substantive critique of the Reformed understanding of God's sovereignty and evil or the many passages that illustrate God's control of all things, including man's will (e.g., Genesis 20:6; Joshua 11:20; Judges 9:23–24; Isaiah 63:17). If Hunt is going to present a compelling argument, he is going to have to at least show he understands the belief that God's sovereign decree and man's creaturely will coexist (*compatibilism*) and that since God judges on the basis of the intentions of the heart, there is in fact a ground for morality and justice.

Will Hunt explain why he mocks Calvinists for accepting the truth that God judges men for acting upon the intentions of their hearts even when what they do is clearly part of God's plan (Isaiah 10:5–17)? Will he explain how Joseph's brothers could sin in selling him into slavery and yet God *meant that sinful action for good* (Genesis 50:20)? Will he tell us how Pilate and Herod and the Jews were doing what God has *predestined to occur* when they sinfully handed over the sinless Son of God to crucifixion (Acts 4:27–28)? Will he stop accusing Calvinists of "ignoring" passages when it is he who will not tell us how God could keep Abimelech from sinning against God without violating his "libertarian" free will? And will Mr. Hunt admit that Calvinists believe fully that man has a will and that he uses his will, but that the creaturely will of man, as well as the environment in which it exists, is subject to the ultimate decree of God? When one knows what Reformed theology really is, Hunt's wide-ranging, shotgun attempts to hit the target are seen to be wide of the mark. If the system is so susceptible to criticism, why not aim for the reality rather than a straw man?

WHY PREACH THE GOSPEL?

One of the first things any person honestly studying the Reformed faith comes to understand is that we believe that God ordains *both* the ends *and* the means. God has not only elected a people unto salvation but has chosen to use particular means to accomplish His purpose. Specifically, He uses the preaching of the gospel to bring His elect unto salvation. Since we do not know who the elect are, we are to preach the gospel to every creature, trusting that God will honor His truth as He sees fit in the salvation of His people. Now Hunt may not *like* this view and may not *agree* with it, but upon what basis of logic does he choose to ignore that this is in fact our belief? His opening statement says it all:

> Why did Christ command the gospel to be preached to every creature if man is dead and can't believe it and if God has from eternity past predetermined to save only a select group, damning the rest?

Unregenerate men *are* dead in their trespasses and sins and not only *cannot* believe it but do not *wish* to believe it. They wish to suppress it and every other element of God's truth presented to them (Romans 1:18). We preach first and foremost to honor God in obedience to His command. We recognize the honor of being ambassadors for Christ, and we likewise know that God used the message of the Cross to bring us to faith; hence, we long to see others likewise saved.

Hunt may not like what Ephesians 1:4–7 says, but his dislike of its message of divine election does not make it *false*. What is false is his constant misrepresentation of the Reformed position by speaking of "only a select few" (it is not a part of Reformed theology to believe that the number of the elect is small) and by refusing to acknowledge the fact that those who are condemned never so much as *desired* to repent, reveled in their sin, and will stand upon the parapets of hell screaming their hatred of God in eternity to come, proving the justness of God's condemnation of them. Again, Hunt's tradition may not leave room for the biblical truths he denies, but that does not make them any less biblical truths.

Mr. Hunt asks: Why does God command "all men every where to repent" or perish (Acts 17:30–31) if the elect can't perish and the nonelect can't repent? The command to repent is universal. We need to see that Hunt's position here, while couched in strident, emotionally charged rhetoric, hides a foundational set of beliefs. In this case, Dave Hunt denies to God the very freedom he demands for the creature. This question is based upon two related ideas: first, that God cannot freely choose to show mercy and grace ("the elect can't perish") and that God somehow owes to the fallen and condemned sons of Adam a "chance" ("the nonelect can't repent"). Both are unbiblical ideas derived from Hunt's traditions. The elect *do repent* and the nonelect *do not desire to do so*. The elect are dependent upon God's free grace and mercy to free them from the tyranny of sin. Hunt's constant misrepresentation of this reality is meant to convey the idea that the nonelect *may desire to repent* but that God somehow keeps them from doing so. That is

RESPONSE, BY JAMES WHITE

utterly untrue. This kind of unwillingness to engage Reformed theology in an honest fashion comes out plainly in the following:

> It borders on blasphemy to ascribe to God the senselessness and insincerity of pleading for repentance and faith from those who are dead and can neither hear nor respond—those He has from eternity past predestined to eternal torment and from whom He withholds the ability to repent and believe.

His shrill ad hominem and emotional argumentation aside, how does Dave Hunt deal with the fact that God sent Isaiah to preach a message of judgment even though He said that the people would not believe, and in fact, that He would not allow them to (Isaiah 6:8–13)? Was this a "blasphemous and senseless" thing for God to do, or does He have a purpose in proclaiming His truth even when it results in judgment? Hunt ignores the reality that the message preached to all men has two effects: When joined with the work of the Spirit, it is the very means of salvation for the elect; in all other cases, it brings judgment *to the glory of God*. God is glorified when His justice is done, and when men show themselves to be rebel sons of Adam in their hatred of the proclamation of His truth, His just condemnation of them is honored.

When Mr. Hunt speaks of God "withholding the ability to repent and believe," he is engaging in unfair misrepresentation, for he does not inform his readers that we are speaking of justly condemned rebels who do not desire to repent and believe. This would be like saying that the state is unjust for withholding a pardon from a man on death row who has been justly condemned. A pardon cannot be "withheld" *because it is not owed to anyone in*

323

the first place. Grace cannot be "withheld" because by nature it must be free to be grace. Here again we see how Hunt's belief that grace must be given to all equally denies the fundamental freedom of God.

ALL OVER THE ROAD

The majority of this chapter moves from passage to passage and topic to topic without meaningful interaction. Traditional interpretations of passages are thrown out in quick succession without any attempt to provide an exegetical base. Instead, emotional terms like *audacity, chilling, mockery,* and the like are offered in the place of measured and fair exegesis of the relevant texts. For example, Hunt accuses Reformed theologians of "changing" the Bible. What he really means is that they challenge his traditional understanding of what particular verses mean. When one understands all that the Bible says about the atonement, for example (i.e., that it is truly substitutionary and that it perfects those for whom it is made), Hunt's traditional (and acontextual) interpretation of such passages as 1 John 2:2 have to be reconsidered (the original audience would have understood that to mean that distinct groups, Jews and Gentiles, make up the "world").

With reference to 1 Timothy 2:1–4, rather than dealing with the fact that Paul speaks of *kinds* of men in the immediate context, Hunt chooses the easy road of emotional, ad hominen special pleading, assumes his own meaning of the text, and then writes, "Calvin's audacity in changing the meaning of Scripture is breathtaking!" Calvin "changed" nothing. If Mr. Hunt wishes us to believe that "all men" in the passage is to be taken as "every single individual person," let him explain his basis for saying so. Let him explain why we should not allow Paul's own words in verse 2 define the term (i.e., "kings and those in authority"), and let him then seriously deal with the fact that his

RESPONSE, BY JAMES WHITE

interpretation makes Jesus the mediator for *every single individual,* forcing us to believe the amazing idea that Christ intercedes for those in hell itself! Here we see the love of man's alleged autonomy leading a person to teach that Christ *fails in His work as High Priest* (which is what is in view in 1 Timothy 2:4–6). Upon what basis are we to believe that Paul was promoting such a view? Mr. Hunt does not tell us. He simply assumes the rightness of his tradition, ignores meaningful exegesis, and then caps off his attack with an emotional appeal to his audience using such terms as *audacity* and *changing the meaning of Scripture.* Calvin changed nothing. He worked with the passage beyond the level of mere tradition, which is what Hunt refuses to do.

Unfortunately, the rest of Mr. Hunt's presentations only increase the level of rhetoric while at the same time *decreasing* the amount of meaningful biblical exegesis. Truly we see one fact with clarity: One side presents measured exegesis of the biblical text; one side presents emotionally laden reiterations of traditions. Let the reader decide!

Defense, by Dave Hunt

Hunt "derisively attacks God's sovereign rulership over all things"? No, I simply disagree with Calvinism's unbiblical and irrational idea that "rulership" means that God *causes* every wicked thought, word, and deed. White contends that if God doesn't decree evil, "evil has no purpose." Evil must have a purpose? Yet evil comes from man's heart (Matthew 15:19) and "worketh not the righteousness of God" (James 1:20). God allows evil and can prevent, control, or use it, even for good (Genesis 50:20), but He doesn't even tempt anyone to evil (James 1:13), much less decree it.

I've already dealt with Abimelech, the Assyrians, and the crucifixion. These are special situations where God either sovereignly prevented evil or used evildoers for His purposes according to His "counsel and foreknowledge" (Acts 2:23)—but without *decreeing evil.* Yes, God judges "the intentions of the heart," but Calvinism falsely says that He *causes* the intentions He judges.

I've never said that the universe is out of control, with God trying "His best to 'fix things' as they fall apart." Calvinism limits God to a "sovereignty" that can't handle free will. Sin is not God's will, but the *counsel* of His will allows it for a brief time. God is obligated to no one, but His love provides salvation for all and calls all to repent. White insists that unregenerate man can choose only evil, but no Scripture says so. Reasoning from Calvinism's false analogy, he says that the spiritually dead "*cannot* believe." Then he says that they don't "*wish* to believe." So the dead can *wish?* Jesus said, "ye *will not*" (John 5:40, emphasis added).

God pleads: "I have set before you life and death.... Choose life.... Love the LORD thy God" (Deuteronomy 30:19–20); "If the LORD be God, follow him,: but if Baal, then follow him" (1 Kings 18:21); "Look unto me, and be ye saved, all the ends of the earth"(Isaiah 45:22). God wastes earnest appeals on the *dead* who *cannot* respond?

Of course "God's sovereign decree, and man's...will coexist," but not as Calvinism says, with man able to will only evil as decreed by God. White says, "Calvinists believe fully that man has a will." So they say. But they also deny this. Pink calls the idea of free will "ignorance,"[1] Spurgeon says, "Free will is nonsense,"[2] and Calvin calls it a "frigid fiction."[3] Calvinists from Sproul ("God wills all things that come to pass"[4]) to Calvin ("[all] events are...produced by the will of God."[5]) say that God causes all, yet dare to say that man has a will—it just isn't free. Calvinists contradict themselves and then say that we don't understand them. Yes, they believe in man's will—just as they believe that God loves those He predestined for hell! "Compatibilism" is double-talk.

White says that God "uses the preaching of the gospel to bring His elect unto salvation"—a further admission that regeneration before faith doesn't save. He objects to my likening the elect to a "select few." But Christ said, "Few there be that find it" (Matthew 7:14). *Find?* And *strive to enter* (Luke 13:24)? White's avoidance of such declarations of man's responsibility prevents a proper exegesis of "except the Father draw him."

The nonelect "never so much as *desired* to repent...and will stand upon the parapets of hell screaming their hatred of God"? Not the rich man. He desired the salvation of his brothers (Luke 16:23–30). God's call to "every one that thirsteth" (Isaiah 55:1), His offer to reveal Himself to all who seek Him with all their heart (Jeremiah 29:13), Christ's appeal to any man who thirsts (John 7:37), and numerous other passages refute such a caricature.

Of course, God proclaims "His truth even when it results in judgment." Read Jeremiah! I have never suggested that "grace must be given to all equally." Grace knows no obligation—but if it is not given, it is withheld. I do not deny that all men are "justly condemned rebels" or suggest that it is "unjust" for God not to pardon the guilty. I've repeatedly stated that we all deserve eternal damnation.

Justice, however, is not the *only* issue. Calvinism scarcely mentions God's love and explains away the many declarations that God desires "all men to be saved" (1 Timothy 2:4) and has "no pleasure in the death of the wicked, but wants him to "turn from his way and live" (Ezekiel 33:11).

I'll turn the other cheek to White's characterization of my presentation, which uses phrases like "lack of understanding...scattergun approach... derisively attacks...shrill...strident, emotionally-charged rhetoric...unfair misrepresentation...defying meaningful interaction," and which he caps off by accusing me of "emotional, ad hominem special pleading" because I don't believe that Paul meant "kinds of men" in 1 Timothy 2:1–6.

"Kings and those in authority" (v. 2) are not *kinds* of men, but *one kind*— rulers. Three times we have the word *all*: prayers for *all* men in verse 1, God's desire for *all* men to be saved in verse 4, and Christ a ransom for *all* in verse 6. But "all" means "*all kinds of men*" because verse 2 exhorts special prayer for rulers? Please! Such are the lengths to which Calvin and his followers must go to limit God's love to the elect. White faults me for not allowing "Paul's own words to define the term." That's exactly what I've done.

White argues that if *all* means "all," that "makes Jesus the mediator for *every single individual*.... Christ intercedes for those in hell.... Christ *fails in His work as High Priest* (in view in 1 Timothy 2:4–6)." Christ ceases intercession for those who enter hell. Nor does He fail because billions reject Him. Calvinism puts the blame on God instead of on Christ-rejecting men.

1. Arthur Pink, *The Sovereignty of God* (Grand Rapids, Mich.: Baker Book House, 1984), foreword, unnumbered first page.

2. Charles H. Spurgeon, "Free Will—A Slave," www.the-highway.com/freewill_spurgeon.html.

3. John Calvin, *Institutes of the Christian Religion*, tr. Henry Beveridge (Grand Rapids, Mich.: Eerdmans, 1998), III: xxiii, 6–7.

4. R. C. Sproul, *Almighty Over All* (Grand Rapids, Mich.: Baker, 1999), 54.

5. Calvin, *Institutes*, I: xvi, 8–9.

D. HUNT

Final Remarks, by James White

Mr. Hunt began this section by claiming that Calvinism makes the Bible a "charade." Yet, in his defense of his claims, he continued his straw-man misrepresentations. He wonders if spiritually dead men can "wish." Of course they can. Despite my best effort, Dave Hunt still does not understand that the inability brought by spiritual death is the incapacity of the natural man to do what is pleasing and good in God's sight. He continues to confuse man's enslaved will (John 8:34) with his theory of libertarian free will, all the while still saying that Calvinists deny man has a will. If by this point he cannot see the difference between an enslaved will and his view of free will, no amount of repetition on my part is going to change things.

Despite Dave Hunt's claim that he has read "hundreds" of Calvinists, he shows no knowledge of the literature on compatibilism (and even seems to suggest that I coined the phrase), and yet he has the temerity to say it is "double-talk." I might assign some weight to his assertion if I could bring myself to believe that he understood what it is. But his constant refusal to interact with the "other side," as demonstrated by his use of straw men, has convinced me that no such understanding exists. Indeed, as I listen to Mr. Hunt speak on these issues and read his writings, I fear that he is so intent upon defending libertarianism that at times in his strong reaction against the common view of the Protestant Reformation he goes beyond the positions held by Rome and comes dangerously close to Pelagianism.

Mr. Hunt says that I merely "explain away" such passages as 1 Timothy 2:4, yet the context itself refers to Christ as the mediator between God and men. At what cost do we maintain libertarianism? Hunt tells us that Jesus ceases intercession for those who enter hell. Then does it not follow that His sacrifice and constant intercession on their behalf before the Father failed to accomplish what He desired? Does this not display in its fullness the man-centeredness of the "gospel" being presented, in which Christ, the mighty Creator, the ever-perfect High Priest, *fails in His work of intercession?* Is it Hunt's view that Christ intercedes for all those who end up in hell? If so, what did this intercession accomplish? What was its nature? Is there disharmony in the Godhead, the Son seeking to save but the Father not agreeing with His desires? Or, as it seems more likely, is Hunt here admitting that the Father can seek the salvation of each individual, the Son can die to secure it, and the Spirit come to bring conviction of sin, *and yet the entire desire and work of the triune God collapse because of the unwillingness of the sovereign creature, man?* Yes, this is indeed Mr. Hunt's view, and I simply do not understand its appeal to the person who boasts only in the Lord.

Final Remarks, by Dave Hunt

The Bible says that the spiritually dead can't do "what is pleasing and good in God's sight"? Surely keeping the Passover is "pleasing and good in God's sight," and millions of spiritually dead Jews have kept it. Pagans told Isaac, "We have done unto thee nothing but good" (Genesis 26:29). That "the wicked...hath left off...to do good" (Psalm 36:3) shows that the wicked did good. Jesus said that sinners "do good" (Luke 6:33).

Several times I've refuted the horrific theory that God *causes* the sinful thoughts and wicked deeds for which He punishes man—that He *could* prevent all sin and suffering if He desired but takes pleasure in damning multitudes to "demonstrate His justice." I've challenged White to give even one verse upholding this merciless theory, but he can't.

Yes, God turned into good what Joseph's brothers intended for evil. But if God *caused* the brothers to do evil, compatibilism is double-talk. Christ's "sacrifice and...intercession...failed to accomplish what he desired"? Only Calvinists would say that if His love is rejected, God fails. Then rebellion is what God willed—a view repugnant to conscience!

Scripture repeatedly says that God desires all men to repent, yet He really doesn't? God irrationally mourns and weeps over the multitudes He has predestined to eternal doom and from whom He withholds the ability to repent? White says that man "is free to turn to Christ but not able." That's like saying man is free to fly to Mars! "Father, forgive them" (Luke 23:34) is a "failed" prayer unless only for the elect? The Bible becomes a mockery!

"He that winneth souls is wise" (Proverbs 11:30) becomes meaningless. Those predestined to hell can't be won, and those predestined to heaven don't need to be won. "We persuade men" (2 Corinthians 5:11) is meaningless; there is no persuading the damned, and the saved are regenerated without believing anything. "Come now, and let us reason together" (Isaiah 1:18) is meaningless for the same reasons. The "great white throne" judgment is also meaningless if God has willed every thought, word, and deed. The Bible's call of hope for all —"Choose you this day whom ye will serve" (Joshua 24:15); "Seek ye the LORD while he may be found" (Isaiah 55:6); "Come unto me, all ye that labor" (Matthew 11:28); "If any man thirst, let him come unto me and drink" (John 7:37)—all this and more is made meaningless by Calvinism!

White says, "Since we do not know who the elect are, we...preach the gospel to every creature." But he can't tell "every creature" that the gospel is for him! He says, "We long to see others...saved." That's blasphemy if he means those God has predestined to hell, and nonsense if he means those He has predestined to heaven.

The "entire desire and work of the triune God collapses" if men for whom Christ died reject Him? No, multitudes who responded to His love will be in heaven. Nor can they "boast," any more than could a beggar accepting food.

Chapter Twelve

GOD'S SOVEREIGNTY AND MAN'S WILL

by Dave Hunt

Intending to protect God's sovereignty, Calvinism makes Him the cause of every thought, word, and deed, and thus of sin. This libels God, mocks man, and erases motivation, as well as any meaning of punishment or reward.

The Bible teaches what daily experience proves: Man has a will he must exercise for or against God, and his will does not impinge upon God's sovereignty. If God's work in man "to will and to do of his good pleasure" (Philippians 2:13) is all of God and nothing of man, why doesn't every Christian live a perfect life? If God irresistibly works His grace in the elect to regenerate them while they are totally depraved, why doesn't He do as good a job after they are His born-again children?

The Bible calls upon man to willingly choose to receive Christ.

Calvinism says that no man is able to will to choose Christ but that God must make him willing. How can a man be made willing unless he is willing? Clearly, if the willingness does not come from man's heart, he is not willing. On this point both Calvin and Luther contradicted themselves, as did Spurgeon.

"Man's will has its proper place in the matter of salvation," declared Spurgeon. "When a man receives the Divine Grace of Christ, he does not receive it against his will.... Nor again, mark you, is the will taken away. For God does not come and convert the intelligent free agent into a machine." Yet he also declared, "Where is free will? Man is so depraved, the way of salvation so obnoxious to his pride...that he cannot like it...unless he who ordained the plan shall...subdue his will."[1]

If God must *subdue* our will, why does He ask us to choose (Joshua 24:15)? Calvin declared that "those who...seek for free-will in man...labour under manifold delusion."[2] Yet Jesus said, "If any man will to do his [God's] will, he shall know" (John 7:17). God said to Israel, "If ye be willing and obedient, ye shall eat the good of the land: But if ye refuse and rebel, ye shall be devoured" (Isaiah 1:19–20). Why such language that clearly puts the responsibility on them, if no one in Israel could will unless God did the willing?

White writes, "Life was a gift given to Lazarus, but the giving of the gift did not in any way indicate an ability on the part of the one who received it."[3] Good point. *No* ability is required to receive a gift. But the fact that Lazarus needed no "ability" to "receive" resurrection does not support Calvinism's claim of *inability* on man's part to receive Christ. Lazarus was given *temporal physical* life—a special miracle that cannot be used to prove anything pertaining to *eternal spiritual* life.

Furthermore, a gift analogy is inapplicable here. Lazarus was physically dead. He was given a renewal of the same *physical* life all men receive at natural birth. *Eternal life,* however, is a gift from God, which Scripture specifically declares *must* be received by faith. White also offers John 12:39–40 as proof of man's inability: [4]

> For this reason they could not believe, for Isaiah said again, HE HAS "BLINDED THEIR EYES AND HE HARDENED THEIR HEART, SO THAT THEY WOULD NOT SEE WITH THEIR EYES AND PERCEIVE WITH THEIR HEART, AND BE CONVERTED AND I HEAL THEM."

But the fact that God blinded the eyes and hardened the hearts of these particular individuals proves that by nature all men are not hopelessly blinded and hardened, as the "inability" of Calvinism's doctrine of total depravity claims. Furthermore, Isaiah 6:9–13 is a specific prophecy pertaining to a distinct people during a limited time. It is not, as White treats it, a general statement describing the permanent natural condition of all mankind. Moreover, John 12:42 states that many of these people, even "among the chief rulers," believed on Him.

White also mishandles 1 Corinthians 2:14: "The natural man receiveth not the things of the Spirit of God: for they are foolishness unto him: neither can he know them, because they are spiritually discerned." White argues:

> The natural man cannot *accept and embrace* spiritual things because he himself is not spiritually alive. He may well completely understand the proclamation of the gospel itself: but until spiritual life is given to him, the words are empty.[5]

How can a person *understand* something if for him the words conveying the idea are empty of meaning? White puts *accept* and *embrace* in italics, but these words aren't even in the text. By "the things of the Spirit of God," White means the gospel, but Paul is referring to "the deep things of God" mentioned in the previous verses, which are only understandable to mature Christians.

That the natural man, though dead in sin, is a spirit being with spiritual (though not eternal) life is clear. The mind of every person is nonphysical, as are all ideas and the very process of thought itself. Surely, White does not attribute thinking to brain cells! Clearly the natural man as God created him, though now in a fallen state, is a spirit being living in a physical body, separated from God by sin but capable of believing spiritual truth.

That the natural man has a will that he can turn to God if he so desires is clear from Genesis to Revelation. Indeed, without that capacity, man could not worship God. Repeatedly we read this commandment to *all* the unregenerated children of Israel: "If ye offer a sacrifice...ye shall offer it at your own will" (Leviticus 19:5). The plain meaning of such clear language must be changed in order to accommodate Calvinism. In keeping with this, the adjective *freewill* is used numerous times to describe the attitude with which offerings were to be brought to the Lord. Consider the following: "Speak unto Aaron, and to his sons, and unto all the children of Israel... whosoever he is...who will offer his oblation...for all his freewill offerings" (Leviticus 22:18). The phrase *freewill offerings* is found numerous times; e.g., Leviticus 22:18; 23:38; Numbers 15:3; Deuteronomy 12:6; 2 Chronicles 31:14; Psalm 119:108.

God repeatedly calls upon the Israelites to return to Him. This is certainly an appeal to the will. There is never a suggestion that they can't respond to the call to repentance and salvation without first being regenerated by God and given the will to worship and obey. Numerous Scriptures clearly indicate that man has a will and that God does not coerce him but desires him to freely choose to love, serve, and obey Him. We see this, for example, in those who donated material to build the tabernacle and brought sacrifices to its door: "whosoever is of a willing heart" (Exodus 35:5); "whom his spirit made willing" (Exodus 35:21); "as many as were willing hearted" (Exodus 35:22); "a willing offering...whose heart made them willing" (Exodus 35:29); "perfect heart and with a willing mind" (1 Chronicles 28:9); "who then is willing to consecrate his" (1 Chronicles 29:5); "offered willingly" (1 Chronicles 29:9); "I have willingly offered all these things" (1 Chronicles 29:17); "willingly offered himself unto the LORD" (2 Chronicles 17:16); "princes gave willingly unto the people" (2 Chronicles 35:8).

The New Testament contains many similar phrases: "The spirit indeed is willing" (Matthew 26:41); "Pilate [was] willing"(Luke 23:20); "Ye were willing" (John 5:35); "The centurion [was] willing" (Acts 27:43); "They were willing of themselves" (2 Corinthians 8:3); "a willing mind" (2 Corinthians 8:12); "not by constraint, but willingly" (1 Peter 5:2). Yet we are to believe that these Scriptures actually mean that man has no will and that God causes him to be willing?

Calvinism treats man as a puppet that God makes willing, yet the Bible gives man credit for having a willing heart as though the willingness were his own. The judgment seat of Christ, His promised rewards, the Great White Throne judgment, and the lake of fire are meaningless if all is of God and nothing is from the heart of man. The many statements about the person being willing from his heart become nonsensical.

That man has a will and the ability to choose from his heart (indeed that he *must* in order to please God) is abundantly clear from the repeated references to "heart" throughout Scripture. David tells the Lord, "therefore hath thy servant found in his heart to pray this prayer" (2 Samuel 7:27). Daniel "purposed in his heart" not to defile himself (Daniel 1:8). Christ indicates that God's Word is sown and takes root in the heart (Matthew 13:23). He warns that God does not forgive us unless we from our hearts forgive "every one his brother their trespasses" (Matthew 18:35). Paul refers to the one abstaining from sex as being "steadfast in his heart…[with] power over his own will" (1 Corinthians 7:37). Of the church offerings he says, "Every man according as he purposeth in his heart, so let him give" (2 Corinthians 9:7).

These references to the heart show that the intention comes from deep within the man himself. It does violence to these Scriptures to insist that God created the prayer in David's heart, caused Daniel to purpose in his heart, causes us to forgive others from our hearts, causes us willingly to give—and so forth. These actions are attributed to the very *heart* of each individual.

How odd that *not one* of the many Scriptures I have just cited about the will, about being willing, or about the heart—*not one of them*—is found in White's chapter "The Will of Man"—or in his entire book! Perhaps he will now explain how such Scriptures teach that man actually has no free will[6] but that, as he says, "Unregenerate men…respond to God…in a universally negative fashion."[7]

White devotes several pages to Romans 9:16 ("so then it is not of him that willeth…but of God that showeth mercy"), which he calls "a passage… directly contradictory to…free will."[8] Yet "him that willeth" indicates that man can will to receive God's mercy. "Of God that showeth mercy" simply means that God makes the rules, not that man cannot respond to the offer of mercy.

God's statement "I will show mercy upon whom I will show mercy" (Exodus 33:19) means that His mercy cannot be coerced or merited, not that He offers mercy only to certain ones. He repeatedly offered mercy to all of Israel. The Bible never says that man cannot respond to that mercy. Furthermore, in Exodus 33:18–34:7, God is proclaiming the abundance of His mercy, not its limitations.

We have so many beautiful pictures in the Old Testament of God's love in Christ. Consider only one: the story of Rebecca being wooed to be Isaac's bride, surely a picture of the Holy Spirit wooing a bride for Christ. The servant asks Abraham what he should do if "the woman will not be willing" to come back with him (Genesis 24:5). Our hearts are thrilled when in response to the question, "Wilt thou go with this man?" she replies, "I will go" (24:58). This story loses its drama and meaning if she really has no will and if God causes it all to happen apart from any heart response from her.

John MacArthur Jr. reasons that for man to be able to say yes or no to Christ would mean that the sin that attracts man and man's will are more powerful than God.[9] Whether a person chooses to follow the Lord or to rebel, revels in sin or finds his delight in God and His Word, says nothing about the "power" of either attraction but speaks to the condition of the heart that responds. The Calvinist erroneously imagines that allowing man the right of choice threatens God's sovereignty. Zane Hodges points out that "if God cannot control a universe in which there is genuine free will…then such a God is of truly limited power indeed."[10]

Calvin spends much time trying to refute the "profane," who logically point to the fact that if man has no freedom of choice and if every event has been foreordained by God, every evil done by man must be the carrying out of God's will.[11] Contradicting himself again, Calvin argues that sin, being "contrary to [God's] precepts," cannot therefore be blamed upon God, even though "if he [God] did not will it, we could not do it... Men do nothing save at the secret instigation of God.... What he has previously decreed...and brings to pass by his secret direction...whatever we conceive in our minds is directed to its end by the secret inspiration of God."[12] Then how can man be responsible for anything?

Calvin argues that man "does not admit reason to his counsel, nor exert his intellect; but without reason...follows the bent of his nature like the lower animals.... If the whole man is subject to the dominion of sin, surely the will...must be bound with the closest chains."[13] Then why does God seek to reason with man? And what of God's "secret direction"? In fact, as daily experience confirms, every man's innate ability to abstain from evil and to choose to follow good is what makes him morally responsible.

Calvin disparages those who argue soundly that unless virtue and vice proceed from free choice, it is absurd either to punish man or reward him. He cannot allow any cooperative effort on man's part. Yes, man can't even draw a breath without God, but Calvin won't admit that man is breathing. Instead of seeing obedience as coming from man's volition, Calvin insists that everything is God's doing. Thus, although Paul writes, "Work out your own salvation...for it is God who worketh in you" (Philippians 2:12–13), Calvin insists that God does everything and man nothing. He quotes Augustine: "When the reward shall come, God shall crown his own gifts, not your merits."[14] Then what does Paul mean by "work out your own salvation" and be "labourers together with God" (1 Corinthians 3:9)? Paul explains this partnership by his own example: "For this I also labour, striving according to his working, which worketh in me mightily" (Colossians 1:29). But Calvin will not allow *any* human response, insisting that "believers act (if I may so speak) *passively* [his emphasis], inasmuch as the power is given them from heaven and cannot in any way be arrogated to themselves."[15]

One can only wonder why, if God is doing it all, every Christian doesn't perfectly work out his own salvation without any sin or failure. Calvin quotes Augustine from his book, *De Correptione et Gratia:*

O, man! Learn from the precept what you ought to do; learn from correction, that it is your own fault you have not the power; and learn in prayer, whence it is that you may receive the power.[16]

But what would motivate man to so pray if he is the total slave of sin and such a desire is against his nature?

Calvin caps his argument with these words: "Christ declares, 'without me ye can do nothing'" (John xv. 5).[17] Yet this statement itself implies that there is something we must do, even though we cannot do it without Christ's enablement and as His servants. Calvin contradicts himself again, this time with another quote from Augustine: "The Spirit of God who actuates you is your helper in acting, and bears the name of helper, because you, too, do something."[18] What? Then he goes on to deny that we actually do anything:

As God by his precepts stings the consciences of the ungodly, so as to prevent them from enjoying their sins... So, in his promises, he in a manner takes them to witness how unworthy they are of his kindness.[19]

But what is the significance of conscience if God is the author of every thought, word, and deed? And why stir such emotions if they aren't really the person's but are created by God? The human experience has been reduced to a charade! Calvin continues with regard to the elect: "As our indolence is not sufficiently aroused by precepts, promises are added, that they may attract us by their sweetness, and produce a feeling of love for the precept."[20] *Attract us?* If God sovereignly does all, why the need of attraction? Sovereign regeneration before faith and "attracting" repudiate each other.

One can only cry out in frustration at such irrationality and contradiction. What is the point of "worship" if God causes it and man has no voluntary part in it? And why "stir up believers to supplicate his grace" when God is only "gracious to whom [He] will be gracious"? And if all is, in fact, sovereignly bestowed by God, what could it mean that promises are added because precepts don't arouse us sufficiently? What is the need to *arouse us* if God sovereignly does all?

And what is this about God "attempts to accomplish"? Surely a sovereignty that does whatever it pleases doesn't "attempt" anything! The inconsistency of Calvin's system is betrayed by his many lapses into language that doesn't fit unless man indeed has the power of genuine choice.

1. Charles H. Spurgeon, "God's Will and Man's Will," in *Metropolitan Tabernacle Pulpit* (London: Passmore & Alabaster), sermon delivered 30 March 1862.
2. John Calvin, *Institutes of the Christian Religion*, tr. Henry Beveridge (Grand Rapids, Mich.: Eerdmans, 1998),I: xv, 8.
3. James R. White, *The Potter's Freedom: A Defense of the Reformation* (Amityville, N.Y.: Calvary Press, 2000), 98.
4. Ibid., 106–109.
5. Ibid., 110.
6. Ibid., 91–120.
7. Ibid., 98, 101.
8. Ibid., 166.
9. John MacArthur Jr., "The Love of God," Audiotape, part 4, 1995.

10. Zane C. Hodges, "The New Puritanism, part 3: Michael S. Horton, 'Holy War with Unholy Weapons,'" *Journal of the Grace Evangelical Society* 7 (Spring 1994): 12.

11. Calvin, *Institutes,* I: xvii, 1–3.

12. Ibid., I: xvii., 5– xviii, 4.

13. Ibid., II: ii, 26–27.

14. Ibid., II: v, 2.

15. Ibid., II: v, 11.

16. Ibid., II: v, 4.

17. Ibid.

18. Ibid., II: v, 14.

19. Ibid., II: v, 10.

20. Ibid.

Response, by James White

In his fifth presentation, Mr. Hunt repeats the already refuted theory that Calvinism says man has no will. In other words, if one denies his theory of libertarian free will (the key plank of all of man's religions and a belief he holds in common with Roman Catholicism, historical Arminianism, Mormonism, and all other forms of Pelagianism and semi-Pelagianism), one *must* deny the existence of the will *en toto*. The fact that Reformed literature is filled with references to man's will and that the greatest work on the subject written in English was written by an avowed Calvinist (Jonathan Edwards) does not slow Hunt down in the least bit, for even when he has to admit this, he simply says that we contradict ourselves.

The idea that maybe, just maybe, it is Dave Hunt who has missed the entire point of the debate does not seem to be a viable option. Let us lay aside this canard once for all (and with it a large portion of the arguments presented thus far): Man has a will. Unregenerate man's will is, according to the Lord Jesus Himself, enslaved to sin (John 8:34), but it is still a will. It acts upon the desires presented to it by the fallen and corrupt nature of all those who are in Adam. Regenerate man's will is freed from slavery to sin and is able to choose to do what is pleasing to God, even though we will struggle with the sin that remains a part of our experience until we are glorified, The unregenerate will cannot do so (Romans 8:7–8).

These few basic considerations are not hidden deep in some secret

347

Calvinistic handbook, so why Mr. Hunt continuously ignores them is beyond comprehension. All of his arguments about men willing to do this or that are, of course, utterly irrelevant, for Calvinists believe fully that man wills to do what he does. We just accept *everything* the Bible says about man's will, while Mr. Hunt's traditions banish elements of biblical truth in an effort to limit God's freedom by depicting man as a creature who has the ability to control God's grace and forgiveness. Despite these facts, Hunt writes:

> How odd that *not one* of the many Scriptures I have just cited about
> the will, about being willing, or about the heart—*not one of them*—
> is found in White's chapter "The Will of Man"—or in his entire
> book! Perhaps he will now explain how such Scriptures teach that
> man actually has no free will but that, as he says, "Unregenerate
> men…respond to God…in a universally negative fashion."

How odd indeed! Might it be *because they are irrelevant?* Might it be because Hunt is misrepresenting my position? As for the requested "explanation," I have offered a rather full one in my presentation on man's inabilities.

The next canard to dismiss is Mr. Hunt's objection to God's eternal decree. Please note our contrasting positions: While I used one of my seven presentations to establish the biblical basis of God's kingly freedom, Hunt has given us no positive defense of whatever form of nonsovereign position he is assuming. In this section we are repeatedly told that to believe Ephesians 1:11 or Psalm 135:6 makes God the author of sin. Mr. Hunt dismisses the fact that every single Reformed work on this topic emphasizes (as I stressed in my opening presentation) the reality of secondary causes. And on what basis? He says it is a contradiction. But does he demonstrate why?

No. He dismisses the reality of Reformed belief simply because it is contrary to his Arminian tradition. Since it does not fit in his system and he does not understand it, he must reject it.

THE LAZARUS ILLUSTRATION

I have often used the illustration of Jesus' calling Lazarus from the dead as an image of Christ's awesome power over life and death. Dave Hunt objects to the application of the illustration to spiritual matters, pointing out that Lazarus received physical life rather than spiritual life. While that is quite true, is Christ limited in His capacity so that He can sovereignly bestow only physical life, not spiritual life? When Jesus says that He gives life to whom He wishes (John 5:21) are we to limit this to *physical* life? Surely not. The sovereignty and authority of the Son of God extends to both spheres. It must if Jesus is going to fulfill the will of the Father expressed in John 6:38–39.

THEY WERE NOT ABLE TO BELIEVE

In my response to Norman Geisler, I addressed his comments on the appearance of the telling phrase, "They were not able to believe" in John 12:39. Mr. Hunt makes reference to this and attempts to explain how it is that we see this as a plain assertion of the inability of men to exercise faith (something that Hunt utterly denies throughout his attacks upon Reformed theology). It is highly instructive to see how he handles this text.

First he tells us that just because God blinded the eyes of certain individuals does not mean that all men are blinded. Quite true: We have plenty of biblical testimony as to the universality of spiritual death. The point of the passage is the phrase "They were unable to believe." Is Mr. Hunt admitting that *in this case at least* these men lacked the ability to believe?

Then he tells us that the passage from which John quotes, Isaiah 6, was about a specific people at a specific time. That is true, but it only compounds Hunt's problem—for now we have the same inability posited of the Jews in Isaiah's day *and* the Jews of Jesus' day! The group of those who are *unable to believe* (contra Mr. Hunt's repeated assertions) is growing.

Then Hunt misrepresents my statements in *The Potter's Freedom.* A fair reading of the section shows that I was responding to Geisler's eisegetical errors regarding the passage: I did not base universal assertions upon the text.

Finally, Mr. Hunt points to verse 42 and the fact that even some of the rulers believed in Christ. Quite true. But does this change the fact that others were *unable to believe?* Obviously those who *did* believe were *enabled* to do so (John 6:65).

ROMANS 9 OR JOHN 6—EITHER ONE

A classic example of turning a passage on its head is provided in these words:

> White devotes several pages to Romans 9:16 ("so then it is not of him that willeth...but of God that showeth mercy"), which he calls "a passage...directly contradictory to...free will." Yet "him that willeth" indicates that man can will to receive God's mercy. "Of God that showeth mercy" simply means that God makes the rules, not that man cannot respond to the offer of mercy.

First, Mr. Hunt has misread my work yet again. The quotation he provides is about John 6:44, not Romans 9:16. But it matters little, for both are utterly destructive of any form of libertarian free will. Norman Geisler had taken a passage that begins, "No man is able" and had concluded that the passage teaches free will. In an ironic twist, Hunt now takes Romans 9:16, "so then it does not depend on the man who wills or the man who runs, but on God who has mercy" and concludes that it "indicates that man can will to receive God's mercy." Remember that this verse comes on the heels of "I will have mercy on whom I have mercy" (v. 15) and is followed in context by "so then He has mercy on whom He desires, and He hardens whom He desires" (v. 18). What is the common theme? God is the one who *mercies* (this is an active verb in the original). Does Hunt see this? No, his tradition blinds him to the text. He says that what we see here is that "God makes the rules, not that man cannot respond to the offer of mercy." Where did the issue of man's response come from? The text is speaking of God's freedom to have mercy on some and not on others. But tradition clouds Hunt's sight so much that he writes:

> God's statement, "I will show mercy upon whom I will show mercy" (Exodus 33:19) means that His mercy cannot be coerced or merited, not that He offers mercy only to certain ones. He repeatedly offered mercy to all of Israel.

Here again we have the "X" of Scripture turned into the "not-X" of tradition. Hunt misses the fact that "mercy" is a verb in this passage: God is indeed saying that He will mercy some and harden others. This is the unquestionable teaching of Romans 9:18. But Hunt turns the direct statement of the text on its head. He continues: "The Bible never says that man cannot respond to that mercy. Furthermore, in Exodus 33:18–34:7, God is proclaiming the abundance of His mercy, not its limitations."

See how the tradition of man's alleged autonomy results in this purely eisegetical response? There is no room in Hunt's view for sovereign mercy, and yet Romans 9 is all about just that. God *mercies* whom He wills and *hardens* whom He wills (direct verbal parallels in the original language). Hunt has to reduce this divine freedom to God's offering a universal mercy that either fails or succeeds, depending on man's response. And with reference to Exodus 33, in reality the text cited is about God's freedom to reveal Himself to whom He wills. In every instance we find the role of tradition resulting in the eisegetical errors that fill Hunt's responses.

REFUSING TO LET GOD BE GOD

On November 2, 2002, I debated Dr. John Sanders, one of the leading proponents of open theism. Open theists deny that God knows the future exhaustively and, as self-avowed Arminians, use many of the same arguments against God's sovereign decree that Hunt uses. At one point in my opening statements I said:

> Here again we see the need to allow God's revelation to have its place of primacy in our thinking rather than the philosophical systems of men. Upon what biblical basis are we to say that God's timelessness precludes true interaction with His creatures when we, as time-bound creatures, are supposed to begin our thinking with the recognition that God's ways are not our ways, and His thoughts are higher than our own? How can we intrude ourselves into His eternal existence and say that unless He exists and acts as we do that we will not believe what He says in His Word? His giving of specific predictive prophecies that encompass myriads and myriads of human

decisions shows us clearly that He does indeed have exhaustive divine foreknowledge; His Word tells us that He works all things after the counsel of His will; He tells us that He makes the blind and the lame and the deaf, even illustrating His purposes in the blind man in John 9; He plainly tells us in Amos that if disaster befalls a city, has not the Lord done it? The biblical testimony is vast and wide, and should we not recognize that we are bound to accept God's revelation of these truths always understanding that it is our bent to limit God and to conform Him to our image? Should not this recognition cause us to examine very carefully any attempt to make God ever more like the creature, impressing upon our views of Him very creaturely limitations so as to make Him, we think, more "approachable" or "attractive"?

I believe this is exactly what Dave Hunt is doing in the prosecution of his new campaign against Reformed theology. Just because he cannot understand how God's eternal decree interfaces with time does not, and cannot, result in the rejection of the many passages that do, in fact, teach this divine truth.

Defense, by Dave Hunt

Concerning free will, Calvin declared, "If this frigid fiction is received, where will be the omnipotence of God, by which…He rules over all?"[1] White, too, claims that what he repeatedly decries as "libertarian free will" would "limit God's freedom" and give man "the ability to control God's grace and forgiveness." Sovereignty can't cope with free will?

Sadly, as Hodges says, "This [Calvinist] view of God actually *diminishes…* His sovereign power. For if God cannot control a universe in which there is genuine free will…[He] is of truly limited power…."[2] Calvinism would rob God of the glory He receives through worship and praise from the hearts of those who could have rejected His love, grace, and forgiveness.

At the root of Calvinism is the mistaken belief that man's free will and God's sovereignty cannot coexist. Calvin declared that "the will of God…cannot be resisted by the human will."[3] If so, all wickedness is God's will. Moreover, if man cannot reject God's love, neither can he love God from his heart. In denying genuine freedom of choice, Calvinism renders impossible love or worship from man's *heart*. Thus it is not man's rejection of Christ but God's sovereign decision in unconditional election that causes billions to spend eternity in the lake of fire.

White ignores Scripture's repeated references to "willing heart," which show that man's intention comes from deep within himself, contradicting

355

Calvinism's view of sovereignty. He makes no response to my questions concerning Calvin's statements that God "attempts...to attract and arouse us," a clear contradiction of Calvinism.

When I accept Calvinists' denials of free will, White protests, "Let us lay aside this canard once for all.... Man has a will. It just happens to be enslaved...to sin." Yet Christ taught that sinners "do good" (Luke 6:33), and White admits that even an "unregenerate man can choose not to commit a particular act of sin."[4] So the will is only *partially* "enslaved to sin"? Nor does White explain how "man has a will" yet God wills everything that happens—another contradiction.

White claims to "accept *everything* the Bible says about man's will." Yet he ignores as "*irrelevant*" the Scriptures I cite concerning "freewill offerings"; e.g., Leviticus 22:8,; 23:38; Numbers 15:3; Deuteronomy 12:6; 2 Chronicles 31:14; Psalm 119:108). Repeatedly, God said, "Speak unto the children of Israel, that they bring me an offering: of every man that giveth it willingly with his heart (Exodus 25:2–9)...of his own voluntary will" (Leviticus 1:3). Surely such offerings from unregenerate Israelites pleased God, yet White says that "the unregenerate will cannot do [anything] pleasing to God." To call these Scriptures *irrelevant* is no escape from the contradiction between "freewill offerings" and the dogma that "no cause must be sought for but the will of God."[5]

Desiring a willing response from man's heart, God's "counsel" (Ephesians 1:11) gave man the power of choice. But the Calvinist says that for man to reject God's will would destroy God's sovereignty. Wasn't God sovereign when Satan rebelled? Was He not in control when Adam and Eve disobeyed His command? The Calvinist must say that it was really God who planned, decreed, and caused Satan's rebellion, the sin of Adam and

Eve, and every wicked thought, word, and deed in history.

White says, "Hunt has given us no positive defense of whatever form of nonsovereign position he is assuming. In this section we are repeatedly told that to believe Ephesians 1:11 or Psalm 135:6 makes God the author of sin." *Never* have I taken such positions. Calvinism's extreme view of sovereignty is the problem. It states explicitly that God "creates the very thoughts and intents of the soul" [6;] that "God wills all things that come to pass" [7]; that "[all] events are…produced by the will of God" [8]; and that "God created sin."[9]

When I point out the folly of likening Lazarus's resurrection to salvation, White asks if I limit Christ's capacity "so that He can sovereignly bestow only physical life, not spiritual life." Not at all! His analogy won't work because a physically dead person can't sin or do *anything*. In response, he says that I limit "Christ's awesome power over life and death." Again, this is obviously untrue, as is his claim that I deny "the universality of spiritual death."

Of course, man's will cannot *cause* God to extend grace, but it is essential for *accepting* His grace. Yes, God has mercy upon whom He will have mercy—but Scripture declares that He offers mercy to all. That "mercy is a verb" changes nothing. Yes, He hardens some who are already hardened against Him. If they were "dead" and "unable to respond positively to God," He wouldn't need to harden them, would He?

White admits that John 12:39 pertains to a specific group and a special situation, not to all men at all times, yet he calls it a "plain assertion of the inability of men to exercise faith." If all men have this "inability" to believe, why would God blind them to prevent them from believing?

Fails or *succeeds* are terms inapplicable to grace, mercy, and love. Surely God's love "never fails" (1 Corinthians 13:8), yet billions reject it. Nor does their rejection put them in control, as White erroneously asserts.

To liken my position to "open theism," a view that I repudiate, is irresponsible. So is the claim that I "reject the many passages...that teach...how God's eternal decree interfaces with time." It is the Calvinist who won't let God's sovereignty interface with time except to create every thought, word, and deed. This is the crux of the problem.

1. John Calvin, *Institutes of the Christian Religion*, tr. Henry Beveridge (Grand Rapids, Mich.: Eerdmans, 1998), III: xxiii, 7.

2. Zane C. Hodges, "The New Puritanism, part 3: Michael S. Horton, 'Holy War with Unholy Weapons,'" *Journal of the Grace Evangelical Society* 7 (Spring 1994): 19.

3. Calvin, *Institutes*, III: xxiii, 14.

4. James R. White, *The Potter's Freedom: A Defense of the Reformation* (Amityville, N.Y.: Calvary Press, 2000), 113.

5. Calvin, *Institutes*, I: xvi, 8.

6. Loraine Boettner, *The Reformed Doctrine of Predestination* (Phillipsburg, N.J.: Presbyterian & Reformed,1932), 32.

7. R. C. Sproul, *Almighty Over All* (Grand Rapids, Mich.: Baker, 1999), 54.

8. Calvin, *Institutes*, I: xvi, 8–9.

9. Sproul, *Almighty Over All*, 54.

D. HUNT

Final Remarks, by James White

D ave Hunt writes, "Nor does White explain how 'man has a will,' yet God wills everything that happens—another contradiction." The sovereign King cannot will that men have wills? Of course He can. But here again we see Hunt's main problem: For the will to be a true will from his view, it must be free in the libertarian sense. Otherwise, it is not truly a "will." We have seen how God withheld Abimelech from sinning (Genesis 20:6). Consider these words as well:

> For it was of the LORD to harden their hearts, to meet Israel in battle
> in order that he might utterly destroy them, that they might receive
> no mercy, but that he might destroy them, just as the LORD had
> commanded Moses. (Joshua 11:20)

God hardening hearts to destroy a people? What of their libertarian free will? And recall the promise of God to Israel in Exodus 34:24: He promises to curb the sinful attitude of covetousness in the hearts of Israel's neighbors when the men of Israel faithfully go up to worship Him. Covetousness originates in the very heart of man, the very place that Dave Hunt refuses to allow God to exercise His sovereignty. Is it not a freewill decision of the pagan neighbor of Israel whether he will or will not covet the land of the faithful Israelite? How dare God interfere with their libertarian free will!

Indeed, consider the problem raised by Mr. Hunt's exaltation of the creaturely will to the point where it determines the bounds of God's activities. When God prophesied through Isaiah that Cyrus would let the people of Israel go and restore them to the land, how did God know this? If Hunt answers, "foreknowledge," we face the classic conundrum: Was Cyrus free to do otherwise? If God's foreknowledge is perfect, does it not follow that the future is, in fact, fixed? And if it is fixed, upon what basis did it take the shape it did? Is the outcome of all history merely the fortuitous result of the decisions of free creatures, and if so, how can God claim glory for its final form? Mr. Hunt has not deigned it proper to provide us with a meaningful basis in his theology from which to launch his criticisms of the Reformed confession of God's sovereignty over all things.

One other point must be emphasized: It is untrue to say that Calvinism does not press the responsibility of man upon him. Only by ignoring the body of Reformed literature can such a view be maintained. And if it is urged that we are inconsistent to do so, the answer is clear: We do not know the identity of the elect, so we command men everywhere to repent. We preach the gospel to *all* creatures, knowing that God will honor the proclamation of His Word, either in the salvation of His elect or in the just and proper judgment of those who love their sin and rebellion.

Final Remarks, by Dave Hunt

White simply rehashes arguments I have already refuted. He offers nothing new, just that God prevented Abimelech from sinning, hardened the hearts of Canaanite kings to fight Israel, and kept Israel's enemies from attacking her. I've shown that these are special situations, not proof, as Calvinism asserts, that man has no choice but that God causes every thought, word, and deed.

White says that "man has a will"—it just happens to be enslaved to sin. He adds that "man wills to do what he does." Yet leading Calvinists say that God "creates the very thoughts and intents of the soul"[1]; God wills all things that come to pass[2]; and that [all] events are produced by the will of God. [3] That sounds like man's will is "enslaved" by God! Calvinism won't allow man to act independently of God's will, even to sin.

In Calvinism, all evil and suffering are exactly what God wants. Thus man no more has a "will" than preaching the gospel to those predestined to eternal damnation is a genuine invitation "to the hope of eternal life."[4] This is the double-talk Calvinism offers. Otherwise, says White, man would "limit God's freedom," and the creature would have "the ability to control God's grace and forgiveness." On the contrary, that God's gift is rejected does not control the Giver in any way. God's love, grace, mercy, and forgiveness are not dependent upon whether man receives them.

All through Scripture, God offers the water of life to all who are thirsty (e.g., Isaiah 55:1). Christ claims to be that water of life and offers Himself to all (e.g., John 4:14; 7:37) The Bible ends with renewing the same offer: "Whosoever will, let him take the water of life freely" (Revelation 22:17). The fact that many refuse to drink neither limits God nor changes the fact that the water of life is available to all. "The gift of God is eternal life" (Romans 6:23). By its very nature a gift must be willingly received.

White hasn't explained why God repeatedly calls upon those who can't from their hearts choose between good and evil, between God and Satan. Calvinism creates the contradiction of God pleading with mankind to repent and receive the salvation He offers, while withholding the very grace without which no man can do so—pretending to offer salvation to those He has from eternity past predestined to the lake of fire!

White repeatedly points to a few proof texts of problematic interpretation in the attempt to prove that the spiritually dead cannot heed God's call to repentance. And he ignores the hundreds of verses that in the plainest language call upon man to repent, to come to God, to believe, and to seek the Lord with all his heart willingly and obediently—and that affirm that many have done so.

1. Loraine Boettner, *The Reformed Doctrine of Predestination* (Phillipsburg, N.J.: Presbyterian & Reformed, 1932), 32.
2. R. C. Sproul, *Almighty Over All* (Grand Rapids, Mich.: Baker, 1999), 54.
3. John Calvin, *Institutes of the Christian Religion*, tr. Henry Beveridge (Grand Rapids, Mich.: Eerdmans, 1998), I: xvi, 8–9.
4. Calvin, *Institutes*, III: xxi, 7.

Chapter Thirteen

SALVATION OFFERED TO ALL

by Dave Hunt

Christ commands, "Go ye into all the world, and preach the gospel to every creature" (Mark 16:15). Calvinism voids that mandate by teaching that the nonelect cannot believe the gospel and that the elect are regenerated without it. That belief entangles Calvinists in a web of contradictions. Either the gospel is *not* "the power of God unto salvation to every one that believeth" (Romans 1:16), or Calvinism's "regeneration" leaves one still unsaved until faith is received to believe the gospel.

Both alternatives contradict Scripture and render the gospel superfluous. If God sovereignly regenerates totally depraved sinners without any faith in Christ on their part, the gospel is not needed. Spurgeon complained:

If I am to preach faith in Christ to a man who is regenerated, then the man, being regenerated, is saved already, and it is an unnecessary and ridiculous thing for me to preach Christ to him."[1]

We have already shown that salvation, as many Scriptures declare (e.g., John 3:15, 16, 36; 5:24; 6:40, 47), comes only through believing the gospel. Therefore, Satan attempts to take the Word from the hearts of those who hear it "lest they should believe and be saved" (Luke 8:12). The Calvinist has to admit that Hebrews 10:39 refers to the elect: "We...believe to the saving of the soul." Clearly, faith must precede salvation. Yet Calvinism rejects this cardinal truth.

Unquestionably, salvation and regeneration are inseparable, as Spurgeon said, "saved already, being regenerate."[2] John writes, "that believing ye might have life through his name" (John 20:31). How can the spiritually dead receive life except by regeneration? Yet Calvinism insists that regeneration precedes faith, causing the gospel to be preached to those already regenerated, a proposition Spurgeon rejected as "absurd, indeed!"[3] As a Calvinist, however, he affirmed basically the same error: that only the elect could be saved because Christ had died for them alone.

All of the apostles' hearers surely understood that the good news of salvation was offered to *every one* of them: "We declare unto you [all] glad tidings." (Acts 13:32). But if Calvinism is true, how could the gospel be "glad tidings" to anyone who didn't know that he was one of the elect? And if faith doesn't come until after regeneration, what is the purpose of preaching the gospel either to the unregenerate who can't believe it or to the regenerate who can believe but, being born again and saved, surely don't need it?

Paul preached the same "good tidings of great joy...to all people" announced by the angel of the Lord (Luke 2:10). Yet those predestined to eternal torment find *no* "joy" in knowing that Christ came to save others— but not them! Calvinism limits to an elect the joy the angel said was for all. Pink insists that for anyone to claim that the purpose of Christ's death was to provide salvation for all "is to undermine the very foundations of our faith."[4] This sounds like the apostles' mistaken early belief that the gospel was only for Jews (Acts 11:1–3; 15:1).

The Calvinist claims that the angel didn't mean "all people" but "all kinds of people." For White, "who will have all men to be saved" (1 Timothy 2:4) means "all kinds of men."[5] *Kinds?* Where is that idea in the Bible? Commenting on this text, Calvinists individually contradict themselves and each other. Pioneer missionary and Calvinist Robert Moffat declared that "God our Saviour willeth the Salvation of all."[6] Likewise Spurgeon, contradicting his own stand for particular redemption, declared:

> I was reading just now the exposition of [one] who explains the text so as to explain it away [as] if it read 'Who *will not* have all men to be saved....' [In fact,] the passage should run thus—"whose wish it is that all men should be saved....' As it is *my* wish...so it is God's wish that all men should be saved; for, assuredly, he is not less benevolent than we are.[7]

Yet, like other Calvinists, Spurgeon contradicted himself again in saying that God is able to save all He desires to save. Then He *is* less benevolent than Spurgeon, who desired all men to be saved, and surely less benevolent than Paul, who was willing to be "accursed from Christ" if that would save his brethren the Jews (Romans 9:3).

At Pentecost, Peter called upon *every one* present to "Repent, and be baptized...in the name of Jesus Christ." (Acts 2:38). Similarly, Spurgeon repeatedly pleaded with *every one* to believe the gospel.[8] Peter didn't call upon "some of every *kind* of person" to believe. How would *kind* be defined? "Then they that gladly received his word were baptized" (v. 41). That possibility was open to all.

Arrested for preaching, Peter told the rabbis: "The God of our fathers raised up Jesus...to give repentance to Israel, and forgiveness of sins" (Acts 5:30–31). That *all* Israelites were *always* offered salvation is clear. The Old Testament provides the foundation for biblical understanding of God's salvation. There the word *redeemer* is found all eighteen of the times it appears in the Bible, *atonement* is found eighty of the eighty-one times it appears, and *redeemed* is found fifty-five of sixty-two times. And in the entire Old Testament there is no hint of redemption or atonement being limited to a select group.

Leviticus reveals the various offerings that foreshadowed Christ's coming sacrifice as the "Lamb of God, who taketh away the sin of the world" (John 1:29). The tabernacle (and later the temple) in which these sacrifices were offered "was a figure for the time then present" (Hebrews 9:9). Let us examine the "figure" to understand the fulfillment.

Every sacrifice and feast day under the Old Covenant pictured Christ and was for all Israel, though most Israelites rejected the Lord. This was true of the Sabbath ("There remaineth therefore a rest to the people of God" [Hebrews 4:9]), the Passover ("For even Christ our passover is sacrificed for us" [1 Corinthians 5:7]), the Day of Atonement (By his own blood he entered in once into the holy place" [Hebrews 9:12]), and every sacrifice.

The Old Testament sacrifices that looked forward to the Cross were offered for all who would believe, and it must be so with their fulfillment in Christ. It does violence to the foundation carefully laid in Scripture to suggest that the fulfillment of the Old Testament in Christ's sacrifice at Calvary was only for a select group.

All Israelites participated in killing the Passover lamb and were sheltered under its blood when they applied it to their houses. God provided salvation for all, though many later perished in the wilderness. Yet concerning "my flesh, which I will give for the life of the world" (John 6:51), John Owen insisted that "*world* here cannot signify all that ever were or should be."[9] Otherwise, "Almighty God would have the precious blood of his dear Son poured out for innumerable souls whom he will not have to share in any drop thereof."[10]

Unquestionably, however, the blood of the Passover lambs was shed for multitudes who perished. In fulfillment, the blood of Christ, the true Passover Lamb, must also have been shed for many who perish. Clearly, all of Christ's blood had to be shed even if only one person would be saved. Thus none of it was wasted.

God's prophets always offered repentance and salvation to every Israelite. None of the feasts and sacrifices was only for a privileged elect. But most of Israel rebelled and many went into idolatry. Salvation was therefore both available and offered to many who are now in hell. Stephen indicted the rabbis and all Israel: "Ye do always resist the Holy Ghost: as your fathers did, so do ye" (Acts 7:51).

Philip preached Christ from Isaiah 53 to a high-ranking Ethiopian returning from Jerusalem. The new convert asked, "See, here is water; what doth hinder me to be baptized? And Philip said, If thou believest with all thine heart, thou mayest" (Acts 8:36–37). Again, the only condition for him to be saved, as for anyone, was to believe.

Apparently ignorant that some people have been predestined to eternal life (and need no persuasion because they will be sovereignly regenerated by God without the gospel before they can believe it) and that others have been predestined to eternal doom (and therefore can't be persuaded to believe), Paul *proves* in the synagogue and marketplace that Jesus is the Christ (Acts 9:1). Strangely ignorant of TULIP, he spends the rest of his life attempting to persuade everyone he encounters to believe the gospel (e.g., Acts 13:43; 14:1; 17:17–34; 18:4, 19; 19:8–9; 20:21; 24:25; 26:28; 2 Corinthians 5:11).

The preaching of the apostles sometimes bears much fruit and at other times brings few conversions and much persecution. There is no consistent pattern. As a direct result of Peter's healing a man named Aeneas of the palsy, "all that dwelt at Lydda and Saron...turned to the Lord" (Acts 9:35). Yet when an even greater miracle is done, the raising of Dorcas from the dead, "many [but not all] believed in the Lord" (Acts 9:42). In Iconium, without any credit to miracles, Paul and Barnabas "so spoke, that a great multitude both of the Jews and also of the Greeks believed" (Acts 14:1). But it took an earthquake to cause the Philippian jailer to cry out, "Sirs, what must I do to be saved?" To whom Paul and Silas replied, "Believe on the Lord Jesus Christ, and thou shalt be saved, and thy house." (Acts 16:31).

In every city, Paul went first into the synagogue and offered salvation to the Jews; when they rejected the gospel, he turned to the Gentiles. *Not once* was the idea introduced that only an elect could believe. *Always* the gospel was preached to all and it was up to each one to believe in or reject Christ. To persuade the Jews, Paul used the promises of the coming Messiah given by the Old Testament prophets as proof that Jesus is the Christ (Acts 13:25, 33, 35); and for the Gentiles he added reason, science, and philosophy (Acts 17:22–34).

In the entire book of Acts there are only two places where predestination by God could possibly be the cause of anyone believing the gospel. Even in those cases, however, it is clear that faith precedes and is essential to salvation. Nor is there ever a suggestion that those who believe are part of a favored elect to whom alone salvation is granted. Yes, God opened Lydia's heart, "that she attended unto the things which were spoken of Paul" (Acts 16:14). That need mean only that He gave her the understanding she needed to believe. Why some believe and others don't depends upon the willingness or unwillingness of individual hearts: "The seed is the word of God.... The good ground are they which in an honest and good heart, having heard the word, keep it" (Luke 8:11, 15).

But what of "as many as were ordained [*tetagmenoi*] to eternal life believed" (Acts 13:48)? If it were intended to mean *ordained* or *predestined* or *elected*, the Holy Spirit would have used one of those words rather than this participle of *tasso*. This root, which appears seven other times in the New Testament, is never used for an eternal decree: "Then the eleven disciples went...into a mountain where Jesus had appointed [directed/ordered] them" (Matthew 28:16); "For I also am a man set [placed] under authority" (Luke 7:8); "They determined [directed/ordered] that Paul and Barnabas...should go up to Jerusalem" (Acts 15:2); "It shall be told thee of all things which are appointed [determined] for thee to do" (Acts 22:10); "They had appointed [designated] him a day" (Acts 28:23); "The powers that be are ordained [established] of God" (Romans 13:1); "They have addicted [devoted] themselves to the ministry of the saints" (1 Corinthians 16:15). Nor is an eternal decree intended in Acts 13:48.

Greek grammarians tell us that *tetagmenoi*, a nominative case, perfect tense, passive voice participle of *tasso*, indicates an outside influence upon the Gentiles toward eternal life and believing the gospel. But, as Barnes says, this influence was "not...an eternal decree" but something *present* at the time. Paul's anointed preaching and the conviction of the Holy Spirit would fit the context here and in all of Acts. It would contradict the rest of Acts for 13:48 to mean that certain ones alone were foreordained to salvation by God and sovereignly given faith to believe the gospel. Certainly predestination of an elect group to salvation cannot be proved from this passage.

The context is clear. In verse 46, Paul told the Jews, "Seeing ye put it [the gospel] from you...we turn to the Gentiles." The Jews' rejection came from their own wills; it was not the result of an eternal decree from God. Verse 48 presents the contrast between the Jews who rejected the gospel and the Gentiles who believed it. What influence made the difference? We are not told. The book of Acts provides many examples and options, but a sovereign decree is not among them.

Yes, Paul tells the Thessalonians: "God hath from the beginning chosen you to salvation through sanctification of the Spirit and belief of the truth" (2 Thessalonians 2:13). The meaning of "from the beginning" is the question. Paul uses this expression three other times: "who knew me from the beginning" (Acts 26:5); "from the beginning of the world" (Ephesians 3:9); and "in the beginning of the gospel" (Philippians 4:15). None of these expressions is related to predestination from eternity past.

"The beginning of the gospel" is associated with Macedonia (v. 16), perhaps because Paul received a unique call to that region in a vision of "a man...saying, Come over into Macedonia, and help us" (Acts 16:9). Thus from "the beginning of the gospel" in Macedonia, the Thessalonians, as part of that region, were chosen to hear it. Yet their salvation came only by "belief of the truth," not by Calvinism's regeneration *before* believing the gospel.

Calvinists turn "for God so loved the world" (John 3:16) into "God so loved His elect."[11] But Christ said, "As Moses lifted up the serpent in the wilderness, even so must the Son of man be lifted up: that whosoever believeth in him should not perish, but have eternal life" (John 3:14–15). "Any man, when he beheld the serpent of brass, he lived" (Numbers 21:9). Healing was available to *any and every* Israelite without exception. The parallel Christ makes with His crucifixion for sin cannot be escaped: "Whosoever believeth in him" means *whosoever*.

Calvinists selectively quote Spurgeon, avoiding the many times he contradicted Calvinism. Consider the following:

In Christ's name I have wept over you as the Saviour did, and used his words on his behalf, "O Jerusalem, Jerusalem, how often would I have gathered thy children together as a hen gathereth her chickens under her wings, and ye would not...." [White derided my same application in a radio discussion with him.]

Oh! God does plead with...everyone of you, "Repent, and be converted for the remission of your sins...." And with divine love he woos you...crying, "Come unto me...."

"No," says one strong-doctrine man, "God never invites all men to himself...." Stop, sir.... Did you ever read..."'My oxen and my fatlings are killed, and all things are ready; come unto the marriage.' And they that were bidden *would not come*...." Now if the invitation is...made [only] to the man who will accept it, how can that parable be true? The fact is…the invitation is free…. *"Whosoever will,* let him come…."

"As I live, saith the Lord"—and that is a great oath—"I have no pleasure in the death of him that dieth, but had rather that he should turn unto me and live."

Now…some of you [may] say that I was…Arminian at the end. I care not. I beg of you to…turn unto the Lord with all your hearts.[12]

Calvinism leads to a dead end of conflicting emotions. No humane person would let people he could rescue go to eternal doom—much less predestine them to that for his pleasure! Paul was willing to go to hell if that would save others. As Spurgeon admits, God is no less benevolent than we are. But He takes pleasure in damning multitudes?

Spurgeon is torn. To salvage an irrational and unbiblical system, he attempts to escape the conscience-torturing contradictions with, "This is one of those things we do not need to know."[13] The dilemma dissolves only when one admits that God in His sovereignty has granted man the power to choose—but that is unacceptable because it would destroy Calvinism.

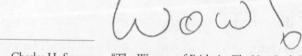

1. Charles H. Spurgeon, "The Warrant of Faith, in *The New Park Street Pulpit* (Pasadena, Tex.: Pilgrim Publications, 1978), 3.
2. Ibid.
3. Ibid.
4. Arthur W. Pink, *The Sovereignty of God* (Grand Rapids, Mich.: Baker, 1986), 260.
5. James R. White, *The Potter's Freedom: A Defense of the Reformation* (Amityville, N.Y.: Calvary Press, 2000), 141.
6. John S. Moffat, *The Lives of Robert and Mary Moffat* (London: T. Fisher Unwin, n.d.), 124.

7. Charles H. Spurgeon, "Salvation by Knowing the Truth," www.apibs.org/chs/1516.htm, sermon preached on 1 Timothy 2:3–4 on 16 January 1880.

8. See, for example, *Metropolitan Tabernacle Pulpit*, 7:148–9.

9. Stanley Gower, in the first of "Two Attestations" to John Owen, book 1 of *The Death of Death in the Death of Christ* (no pub, 1647), in Owen, ed. William H. Goold, *The Works of John Owen* (Edinburgh: Banner of Truth Trust, 1978), IV: 338.

10. Ibid., I: 149.

11. John Owen, cited in White, *Potter's Freedom*, 22–3.

12. Excerpted from Charles H. Spurgeon, "Sovereign Grace and Man's Responsibility," in *New Park Street Pulpit* (London: Passmore & Alabaster, 1859), a sermon preached 1 August 1858.

13. From the opening words of Spurgeon's sermon on 1 Timothy 2:3–4, in *Metropolitan Tabernacle Pulpit*, 26: 49–52.

Response, by James White

I n his sixth presentation, Dave Hunt has again covered a wide range of topics, many of which I have already addressed either in my opening presentations or in previous rebuttals.[1] Other than making some passing comments, I will focus upon two key passages in my reply.

DERISION OR MISCITATION?

When discussing Matthew 23:37 (a passage condemning the Jewish leaders for seeking to keep those under their authority from the ministry of Christ) Hunt says, "White derided my same application in a radio discussion with him." This is an amazing statement. This conversation is available from both our ministries, and anyone who listens to it will discover that what I really did was point out Hunt's miscitation of the passage in the *Berean Call* and then explained his misapplication of it in light of the exegesis I had offered in *The Potter's Freedom*.[2]

Hunt also asserted that the sacrifices of the Old Covenant "were offered for all who would believe, and it must be so with their fulfillment in Christ. It does violence to the foundation carefully laid in Scripture to suggest that the fulfillment of the Old Testament in Christ's sacrifice at Calvary was only for a select group." This is another amazing statement. First we are told that the sacrifices were offered "for all who would believe," and then we are told that the sacrifice of Christ cannot be "for a select group." Did all believe? No.

So, those who believed were a select group, were they not? Of course. The contradiction is obvious. Mr. Hunt's problem is with *who does the selecting*. He has no problem with the sacrifice being for a limited group *as long as it is man who limits it*. His problem is with God's freedom to make that sacrifice truly propitiatory *for those upon whom He sets His mercy*.

JOHN 3:16

Everyone knows John 3:16, and that's the problem. So many are familiar with the verse that very few stop to consider the traditions that have been packed very carefully into its constant and often acontextual citation. It is no overstatement to say that if a more consistent, textually based understanding of the passage can be offered than the one *assumed* by Mr. Hunt in his writings, it follows that his position collapses, so *central* is John 3:16 to his presentation.

There are two vitally important elements in the use of this passage in non- and anti-Reformed writings. First, the term *world* is *assumed* to mean "every single individual human being." Second, the phrase *whosoever* is *assumed* to include within it the idea of "universal capacity and ability." Surely we hear the passage *preached* as if these two things were true. But does serious reflection upon the text provide us with any basis for coming to these conclusions? The answer is a very strong no.

I begin with the meaning of *world*. The wide range of uses of *kosmos* (world) in John's writings is well known. John 3:16 does not define the extent of *kosmos*. However, two things are certain. It is not the "world" that Jesus says He does *not* pray for in John 17:9, a "world" that is differentiated from those the Father has given Him: "I ask on their behalf; I do not ask on behalf of the world, but of those whom You have given Me; for they are

RESPONSE, BY JAMES WHITE

Yours." Neither is it the "world" that is arrayed as an enemy against God's will and truth, as seen in 1 John 2:15: "Do not love the world nor the things in the world. If anyone loves the world, the love of the Father is not in him." Obviously, the "world" we are not to love in 1 John 2:15 is not the world to which God showed His love by sending His Son.

The most that can be said by means of exegesis (rather than by insertion via tradition) is that the world is shown love through the giving of the Son so that a specific, particular people receive eternal life through faith in Him. Since we know that not all are saved by faith in Christ, it is utterly unwarranted to read into *kosmos* some universal view of humanity. How is God's love shown for one who experiences eternal punishment by the provision of salvation for someone else? Surely, then, the use of *kosmos* in John 3:16 is a general one, with more specific uses of the term coming in the following verses. That is, it is the common meaning of *world* that would have suggested itself to the original readers (Jew and Gentile).

There is another issue that should be considered. Verse 17 says that the Son came to save "the world." English usage and tradition again conspire to rob us of the force of the original; that is, many see "but that the world might be saved" as some kind of weak affirmation, when in fact the idea is, "God did not send the Son for purpose X but, instead, to fulfill purpose Y." The clause expresses God's purpose in sending the Son. It does *not* communicate the sense that "God did this, which *might* result in that, *if* this happens." While the subjunctive can be used in conditional sentences, it is also used in purpose/result clauses *without* the insertion of the idea of doubt or hesitant affirmation. The word *might,* then, is not to be read as "maybe," "hopefully," or "only if other things happen" but as in "I turned on the printer so that I might print out this letter." The idea here is purpose, not lack of certainty.

J. WHITE

377

This immediately raises another question, however. Will God truly save the world through Christ? Inserting the concept of "universal individualism" into *world* in verse 16 (as Hunt does continuously), and then insisting (against John's regular usage) that the same meaning be carried throughout the passage, raises real problems. However, there is no need to do this. When we see the world as the entirety of the *kinds* of men (Jew and Gentile, or as John expresses it in Revelation 5:9, where every "tribe, tongue, people, and nation" means world) the passage makes perfect sense. God's love is demonstrated toward Jew and Gentile in providing a single means of salvation for both.

But what about *whosoever*? In the Greek, the phrase "whoever believes" is *hina pas ho pisteuwn*. In the English translation the term *whoever* is meant to communicate "all without distinction in a particular group"; specifically, "those who believe." *Pas* means "all" and *ho pisteuwn* means "the one(s) believing"; hence, "every one believing," leading to "whoever believes." The point is that *all* the ones believing have eternal life. There is no such thing as a believing person who will not receive the promised benefit; hence, "whosoever." This is a common form in John's writings. But as we can see, there is *nothing* in the text that even begins to address universal ability, though Hunt and many others constantly assume this.

One can pour all the emotion one wishes into "but the Bible says whosoever!" but until one deals with what the Holy Spirit actually has given us in the original text and the fact that there is nothing there to support that idea, one is preaching a tradition, not divine truth. It is purely a traditional interpolation to take "whosoever" to mean "there is no election on God's part." All the passage is saying is that all the ones who believe will have eternal life. It does not even attempt to address *who* will believe or any of the related issues like human ability or inability and the nature of saving faith.

J. WHITE

And so we see that John 3:16 does not provide Mr. Hunt with the two absolutely necessary concepts he needs to make his citation of the passage relevant: *World* does not mean "every single individual person" and *whosoever* does not in any way mean "universal ability." Mr. Hunt *must* fully refute these facts if his position is to survive, for they pose a fundamental challenge to its most basic elements.

ACTS 13:48

I have already presented an exegesis of this passage in my discussion of unconditional election, but Mr. Hunt does not discuss most of what I presented. His comments here do not carry weight for the following reasons:

1. His assertion that the Spirit could have used other words in the passage is irrelevant. The issue is what the text means as it stands.

2. Noting that a verb is used in other contexts that are not in any way parallel to this one and that in none of them does the term refer to an eternal decree is likewise irrelevant to the meaning of this passage.

3. To cite nonparallel passages (nonparallel in context, grammar, or syntax), including uses from outside the author (Luke), and then to conclude, "Nor is an eternal decree intended in Acts 13:48" is utterly unwarranted. It is obvious he *does not believe* in an eternal decree; hence, he is doing all he can to avoid "seeing" it here.

4. Thankfully, he does not repeat the errors regarding the meaning of *tetagmenoi* that were central to his comments in *What Love Is This?* (including the adoption of the translation "disposed

themselves"). However, despite having been corrected on these errors (though he does not acknowledge that), he ignores the other contextual and grammatical information provided him and concludes: "It would contradict the rest of Acts for 13:48 to mean that certain ones alone were foreordained to salvation by God and sovereignly given faith to believe the gospel. Certainly predestination of an elect group to salvation cannot be proved from this passage." This is simply wishful thinking. It is not exegesis. His conclusion is left without any foundation whatsoever.

5. He attempts to say that it was Paul's preaching that "influenced" them to believe. But this ignores the fact that the periphrastic construction refers to an action that *precedes* this event. How could Paul's preaching *precede* Paul's preaching? Hunt's explanation ignores the text itself.

6. He insists that the Jews willfully rejected the gospel, which is quite true (his constant misrepresentation of the Reformed position notwithstanding). But Luke does not use the same term for their rejection that he uses for the ordination to eternal life. Sinful men do not "ordain" themselves to eternal life. God alone chooses His sheep.

7. He concludes his section: "What influence made the difference? We are not told. The book of Acts provides many examples and options—but a sovereign decree is not among them." This is not what he said in *What Love Is This?* There he insisted that these men *disposed themselves* to eternal life. Thankfully, he seems to have abandoned this error. But upon what basis are we

to believe that "a sovereign decree" is not behind the phrase "as many as were appointed to eternal life believed"? We are given nothing other than Mr. Hunt's word on the matter. And that is simply not enough.

Acts 13:48 shows us how much of a "given" God's sovereign work of election was to the apostles. Luke did not have to expand the thought or explain his meaning: The person who understands the power of sin that binds the unregenerate heart knows well the necessity of God's work to "open the heart" and "draw" one to Christ. What made one person believe and another remain in disbelief? "By *His doing* you are in Christ Jesus" (1 Corinthians 1:30).

---

1. For example, Hunt writes, "The Calvinist has to admit that Hebrews 10:39 refers to the elect: 'We...believe to the saving of the soul.' Clearly, faith must precede salvation." As we have pointed out, this involves a confusion of terms: Salvation is a multifaceted work of God, and in this passage that term is being used of final salvation, not regeneration, as Hunt seems to assume.
2. I provided a full exegetical discussion of Matthew 23:37, 1 Timothy 2:4, and 2 Peter 3:9 in the sixth chapter.

Defense, by Dave Hunt

I have given a great deal of biblical evidence to which White doesn't respond. He fails to explain how one can be regenerated without faith or what the difference is between regeneration and salvation. Nor does he address the many Scriptures declaring that life (i.e., regeneration) is only by faith.

He agrees that Old Testament sacrifices pointing to Christ were for all Israel, including rebels. Then why isn't the Cross the same? Christ's likening His death upon the cross to the serpent lifted up for all Israel is conclusive. White avoids it. Nor does he respond to believing "in the heart" or that the good soil is "an honest and good heart."[1]

Referring to Christ's lament over Jerusalem (Matthew 23:37), White says that He was "condemning the Jewish leaders for seeking to keep those under their authority from the ministry of Christ." That's not what Christ says. Of the scores of God's laments over Jerusalem through His prophets, not even *one* is addressed to the leaders alone but rather to all Judah and Israel.

Yahweh's continual pleading with Israel refutes Calvinism. Would He plead for repentance from those He has predestined to eternal doom and from whom He withholds essential grace and faith? Surely not. Yet Calvinism creates such contradictions.

Although only one time is recorded in the gospels, Christ's "How often would I" indicates that He pleaded with Jerusalem countless times. Clearly,

He is speaking as Yahweh, the One who repeatedly called Israel to repentance, but White must either deny this powerful declaration of Christ's deity, or admit God's desire for all to be saved. Spurgeon applied Christ's words to all of Israel.[2] So does John MacArthur, but he also says "[God] sometimes expresses a wish for that which He does not sovereignly bring to pass"[3]—another contradiction of Calvinism.

Making one phrase of mine, "for all who would believe," mean "a select group," White ignores the fact that the Levitical sacrifices were for all Israelites, though most rebelled. That only those who believed were saved does not mean salvation was offered only to them. I do not limit "God's freedom to make that sacrifice truly propitiatory." It is Calvinism that limits it to the elect. But for *anyone* to be saved, His sacrifice had to be propitiatory for "the sins of the whole world" (1 John 2:2).

White limits *world* in John 3:16 because in John 17, Christ prays "not for the world" (v. 9). John 3 is about salvation; John 17 concerns the unity and purity of those already saved. Yet White says that Christ is praying "specifically about the salvation of the elect."[4] That is incorrect. Christ's prayer is for believers (v. 20) and would be inappropriate for the world of unbelievers, but that does not limit who can believe. Nor is *world* in John 3:16 the same as *world* in 1 John 2:15–17. The former refers to the people of the world ("whosoever"); the latter describes the world system, "the things that are in the world...that passeth away."

Agreed, God's love is *not* "shown for one who experiences eternal punishment by the provision of salvation for someone else." That is why Calvinism's "unconditional election" and "particular redemption" are unbiblical. But God's love to all mankind *is* shown in His giving His Son as "the Lamb of God, who taketh away the sin of the world" (John 1:29).

Multitudes reject Christ, but love spurned is still love. To support Calvinism, White changes the plain meaning of John 3:16–17 as understood by the vast majority of evangelicals.

Concerning John 3:17, White admits that "the subjunctive can be used in conditional sentences," but claims it *isn't* so used here. Why? Because that would refute Calvinism, a theory not derived from Scripture but imposed upon it. There was "no doubt" as to the desire of God's love. That all are not saved is due to the very nature of love: It must be received from the heart and can also be rejected.

White asks us again to accept Calvin's belief [5] that *world* means *all kinds of men*. *Kosmos* occurs seventy-six times in John's gospel, and *never* does it mean that! Try it: *All kinds of men* knew him not" (1:10); "Show thyself to *all kinds of men*" (7:4); "*All kinds of men* cannot hate you" (7:7); "The Spirit of truth; whom *all kinds of men* cannot receive" (14:17); "I pray not for *all kinds of men*" (17:9); "my kingdom is not of *all kinds of men*" (18:36).

White says that all John 3:16 is saying is "that all the ones who believe will have eternal life. It does not even attempt to address *who* will believe or any of the related issues like human ability or inability and the nature of saving faith." Precisely. He says that *whosoever* puts "all…those who believe…in a particular group." Okay, but "those who believe" become part of the group by *believing*, not by *predestination*.

Whosoever occurs 183 times in the Bible, from "Whosoever slayeth Cain, vengeance shall be taken on him sevenfold" (Genesis 4:15) to "Whosoever will, let him take the water of life freely" (Revelation 22:17). It is found in warnings such as "Whosoever eateth leavened bread…shall be cut off" (Exodus 12:15) and in promises of reward, such as "Whosoever smiteth the Jebusites first shall be chief" (1 Chronicles 11:6). It always means *whosoever*!

Yet whenever it involves salvation, Calvinists say it means a select group.

As for Acts 13:48, the Bible is its own interpreter. It would be unreasonable for this *one* verse to contradict hundreds of others offering salvation to all. Moreover, predestination/election is always on the basis of God's foreknowledge (Romans 8:29; 1 Peter 1:2). Therefore, even if White's interpretation were correct, those "ordained to eternal life" were those God foreknew would believe the gospel.

1. Luke 8:15.
2. Charles H. Spurgeon, "Sovereign Grace and Man's Responsibility," in *New Park Street Pulpit* (London: Passmore & Alabaster, 1859), 1 August 1858.
3. John MacArthur Jr., *The MacArthur Study Bible* (Nashville, Tenn.: Word Publishing, 1997), 1437.
4. James R. White, *The Potter's Freedom: A Defense of the Reformation* (Amityville, N.Y.: Calvary Press, 2000), 265.
5. John Calvin, "Commentary on 1 Timothy," in *The Comprehensive John Calvin Collection* (Ages Digital Library, 1998); *Institutes*, III: xxiv, 16; cited in White, *Potter's Freedom*, 259–60.

D. HUNT

Final Remarks, by James White

T hree items beg comment in Mr. Hunt's response. First, we have a simple error of grammar that might leave some confused. Hunt writes:

Concerning John 3:17, White admits that "the subjunctive can be used in conditional sentences," but claims it *isn't* so used here. Why? Because that would refute Calvinism, a theory not derived from Scripture but imposed upon it.

No, Mr. Hunt, because the Greek language says otherwise. Anyone even slightly familiar with the original language understands the function of *hina* as introducing a purpose or result clause. The same use of *hina* is seen in verse 16 as well, "in order that all the ones believing might have eternal life." The point is that this clause tells us *why* God gave the Son. This is basic, first-year material. It does not introduce some conditional element, and the very suggestion speaks volumes concerning Dave Hunt's view of the gospel, not to mention his ability to engage the text in a meaningful manner. On May 12, 2001, Mr. Hunt said in a conference in Indianapolis, "I know nothing about Greek. It might as well be Chinese. But I can read English." That is fine, but why make a statement that is unsubstantiated by any Greek scholarship and then use it to accuse Calvinists of mishandling the text of Scripture?

In a similar vein, Mr. Hunt's capitulation on Acts 13:48 is instructive. I invite the reader to review the relevant section of *What Love Is This?*, compare the presentation in this book, which was written *after* I posted an open letter pointing out the many errors in Hunt's position (including the presentation of a "better" translation, which is actually that of the *New World Translation* of Jehovah's Witnesses), and then consider the final comments offered here, which basically say, "Well, okay, but it just can't mean they were sovereignly ordained to eternal life because of the *hundreds* of other verses I think teach otherwise." And there is always the "foreknowledge" escape hatch, despite the fact that I have shown the difference between the verbal use of *foreknow* and the noun form and the fact that Hunt has no grounds upon which to base exhaustive divine foreknowledge of future events outside of God's decree, which he denies.

Finally, continuing the pattern of simply ignoring the exegetical information presented, Hunt refers to Matthew 23:37, which he has errantly "paraphrased" before and identified with Jesus' weeping, insisting that it was not, in fact, directed to the leaders of Jerusalem. Yet, the context is clear and compelling: Were all the woes of Matthew 23 directed to all Judah and Israel, Mr. Hunt? And what of the simple fact, neglected in Hunt's errant "paraphrase" of the text, that the ones Jesus sought to gather together were *not* the ones He was addressing, but their "children"? If Jesus makes the differentiation, why doesn't Hunt?

Final Remarks, by Dave Hunt

White denies *omniscience* in his repudiation of any "grounds upon which to base exhaustive divine foreknowledge of future events outside of God's decree." If God must decree the future to know it, He's not omniscient.

White's rejection of God's oft-expressed desire for the salvation of all is shocking. Those in John 3:16 "who believed were a select group"? No! *Anyone* could believe. The Passover, which Calvin called "shadow...made substance,"[1] the Levitical sacrifices, the serpent lifted up for *all* Israel—all these White labels "irrelevant"! This brings to mind Spurgeon's criticism of "our older Calvinistic friends" who explained 1 Timothy: 3–4 "so as to explain it away":

> I thought when I read [one]...the text [was], "Who *will not* have all men to be saved..." but as it happens to say, "Who *will* have all men to be saved," his observations are...out of place....
>
> Does not the text mean that it is the wish of God that men should be saved...? As it is *my* wish...*your* wish...so it is God's wish that all men should be saved.... He is no less benevolent than we are.
>
> As to weeping over sinners as Christ wept over Jerusalem...these brethren...had no sympathy with such emotions, and feared they savoured of Arminianism.[2]

389

Of that incident (Matthew 23:37), White says that "the ones Jesus sought to gather together were *not* the ones He was addressing, but their 'children.'" Yes, Jesus said, "thy children," but Jerusalem's *children* simply means her inhabitants, as Spurgeon understood.[3] That Christ meant Jerusalem's nonadults is absurd. "Children of Israel" occurs 644 times and "children of Ammon," eighty-nine times, and the word *children* never means nonadults. Here are a few of the many times *children* means Jerusalem's inhabitants: "the children of Judah at Jerusalem" (Joshua 15:63); "in Jerusalem dwelt...children of Judah" (1 Chronicles 9:3); "children of Israel...present at Jerusalem" (2 Chronicles 30:21); "the children of Israel...gathered...to Jerusalem" (Ezra 3:1); "all the children of the captivity... unto Jerusalem" (Ezra 10:7); "the gate of the children of the people...the gates of Jerusalem (Jeremiah 17:19); "Jerusalem which now is...in bondage with her children" (Galatians 4:25).

Surely Paul didn't mean just the nonadults, nor did Christ. Was it the nonadults who had killed the prophets and whose house would be left desolate? Clearly, Christ is speaking as the God of Israel who, through His prophets, repeatedly wept over Jerusalem. That Yahweh continually pleaded with Israel to repent refutes Calvinism.

In the New Testament, Christ expresses this passion only once. Yet He says, "How often," implying that He had wept over her countless times. Clearly, He claims to be Yahweh, who repeatedly called Israel to repentance—a claim to deity White denies to protect Calvinism!

1. John Calvin, *Institutes of the Christian Religion*, tr. Henry Beveridge (Grand Rapids, Mich.: Eerdmans, 1998), II: ix, 1–4.

2. Charles H. Spurgeon, "Salvation by Knowing the Truth," in *Metropolitan Tabernacle Pulpit*, 26: 49–52; 27: 600.

3. Charles H. Spurgeon, "Sovereign Grace and Man's Responsibility," in *New Park Street Pulpit* (London: Passmore & Alabaster, 1859), a sermon delivered 1 August 1858.

D. HUNT

- Chapter Fourteen -

BIBLICAL ASSURANCE
OF SALVATION

by Dave Hunt

Biblical assurance of salvation is by faith in God's word. Eternal life is offered as a free gift to all who believe on the basis of Christ having fully paid the penalty for sin demanded by God's infinite justice. One's security for eternity lies not in performance but in God's faithfulness. Only believe!

In Calvinism, however, assurance of heaven is not in believing God's promise of forgiveness and eternal life but rather in being one of the predestined elect to whom alone salvation is granted. How to know whether one is in that favored company troubles many Calvinists. If man's depravity and spiritual death make it impossible to have saving faith without sovereign regeneration, how could one be certain that his faith came in that manner? Might not faith in Christ be in vain because one is not among the elect?

Moreover, how could perseverance to the end be proof of election if the non-elect, as Calvinists admit, are also capable of good works?

Once I had thought that I agreed with at least one Calvinist point, the perseverance of the saints. I learned, however, that this fifth point of TULIP offers an unbiblical basis for eternal security: that of being one of the elect. Piper and his pastoral staff write, "We believe in…the eternal security of the elect."[1] Such security, however, brings comfort only to one who is certain that he is in that select group. Yet how to be certain has troubled many.

Calvinists can't agree among themselves on this vital point. Amazingly, Pink protested, "We have no sympathy whatever with the bald and unqualified declaration 'Once saved always saved.'"[2] Thus, "according to Puritan belief, the genuineness of a man's faith can only be determined by the life [he lives]."[3] No wonder that "nearly all of the Puritan 'divines' went through great doubt and despair on their deathbeds as they realized that their lives did not give perfect evidence that they were elect."[4] Louis Berkhof says that this fifth point "requires careful statement [being] liable to misunderstanding."[5] Joseph Dillow warns that "the Reformed doctrine of the perseverance of the saints…is not only absent from Scripture but could, if not carefully stated, compromise the freeness of the grace of God."[6] In fact, as Vance says:

> It is the Calvinists who reject the biblical teaching of eternal security. The fifth point of the TULIP, *as it was originally formulated and commonly interpreted*, is at enmity with eternal security. Perseverance of the Saints…is not the same thing as eternal security.[7]

Dillow points out that this doctrine often results in "continual introspection and doubt as to whether or not one is…really accepted in God's family."[8] He explains that it was "Theodore Beza [Calvin's successor at Geneva and "more Calvinistic than Calvin"[9]], with his doctrine of limited atonement, who made the quest for assurance based upon works a necessity. Since Christ did not die for all men... according to Beza, assurance must be based on works."[10] But does *assurance* by works differ from *salvation* by works?

The Calvinist great, John Owen, called "our own diligent endeavor...an indispensable means of securing our salvation: unless we use our diligent endeavors, we cannot be saved."[11] Whose "diligent endeavors" could meet God's standards? This is a solemn question in light of Pink's statement: "Those who persevere not in faith and holiness, love and obedience, will assuredly perish."[12]

Piper agrees: "Our final salvation is made contingent upon the subsequent obedience which comes from faith."[13] Likewise, Hodge said, "The only evidence of our election [and] perseverance is a patient continuance in well-doing."[14] Murray insisted that "we may entertain the faith of our security in Christ only as we persevere in faith and holiness to the end."[15] But Calvin said of reliance upon works for assurance: "nothing will be weaker or more uncertain."[16]

How could anyone be certain that his "obedience" and "well-doing" would satisfy an infinitely holy God? Moreover, God's Word is clear that it is "not by works of righteousness which we have done, but according to his mercy he saved us" (Titus 3:5). As works can't save, neither can they prove we are saved. Though we are "created in Christ Jesus unto good works" (Ephesians 2:10), a man's works could all be burned up at the judgment and yet he "shall be saved...as by fire" (1 Corinthians 3:15).

Here the Calvinist mimics the Arminian. Doing sufficient good works to be assured of being one of the elect would justify the very boasting Scripture warns about: "not of works, lest any man should boast" (Ephesians 2:9). Similarly, the doctrine that we must keep our salvation gives those who get to heaven cause to boast.

Seeming to bypass both faith and works (and certainly contrary to the belief of evangelicals today), Calvin suggested that we "recall the remembrance of our baptism...so as to feel certain and secure of the remission of sins."[17] Remember, he was referring to the infant baptism into the Roman Catholic Church, which he and most of the early "Protestants" had experienced and defended: "Wherefore...all the godly may...recall...their baptism [to] assure themselves of that sole and perpetual ablution which we have in the blood of Christ.[18] In baptism, the Lord promises forgiveness of sins: receive it, and be secure."[19]

Similarly, Augustine (Sproul declares that "Augustinianism is presently called Calvinism or Reformed Theology"[20]) argued that "infants, unless they pass...through the sacrament [baptism] which was divinely instituted for this purpose, will undoubtedly remain in this darkness."[21] Nor was baptismal regeneration, as we've seen, the only false belief taught by Calvin. White's book nevertheless praises him as a great exegete of Scripture,[22] referring admiringly to "Calvin's doctrine" and "Calvin's belief" six times on one page.[23]

Calvin also said, "If we are in communion with Christ, we have proof sufficiently clear and strong that we are written in the Book of Life."[24] Yet Christ warned that false prophets can delude themselves into thinking they are not only in communion with Him but doing great works in His name (Matthew 7:21–23). Instead of warning about the self-delusion Christ referred to, Calvin libelously claimed:

But the Lord the better to convict them, and leave them without excuse, instills into their minds such a sense of his goodness as can be felt without the Spirit of adoption. Still…the reprobate believe God to be propitious to them, inasmuch as they accept the gift of reconciliation…. Nor do I even deny that God illumines their minds…that they recognize his grace.[25]

How, then, can anyone be sure that his faith and communion with Christ are not a *delusion from God?* R. T. Kendall raised the question that "if the reprobate may believe that God is merciful towards them, how can we [the elect] be sure our believing the same thing is any different from theirs?"[26] Citing Romans 8:9, Calvin declared that Christ "holds out the hope of a blessed resurrection to those only who feel His Spirit dwelling in them."[27] *Feel?* But Calvin admitted that feelings could be deceiving. Calvinism creates confusion and breeds uncertainty.

Calvinists can't agree among themselves on the question of eternal security. Warfield divorces faith from obedience and makes it depend upon "the element of assent…of the intellect."[28] But Bultmann equates faith with obedience.[29] Robert L. Dabney, whom Dillow disagrees with yet praises as "one of the best minds the Reformed faith has ever produced,"[30] accused the "early" Reformers and their "modern imitators" of "error" with regard to their doctrine of eternal security and disagreed with Calvin.[31] Boettner suggested that because faith "is not given to any but the elect [therefore] the mere presence of faith, no matter how weak it may be, provided it is real faith, is a proof of salvation."[32] But how can one be sure of having "real faith," considering Dabney's warning about "false faith" and Sproul's statement that "there are people in this world who are not saved, but who are convinced that they are."[33]

Most of Calvinism's errors are rooted in its extreme view of God's sovereignty, which allows man no freedom even to sin, much less to accept Christ (see chapter 12) and assures salvation only to those sovereignly regenerated and given faith to believe. Calvin wrote, "If this frigid fiction [of man's will] is received, where will be the omnipotence of God?"[34] In fact, it belittles God's sovereignty to suggest that it would be threatened by human choice.

White claims: "God has wisely and perfectly decreed whatsoever comes to pass in this universe."[35] He is not saying that God *allows* rape, murder, war, and evil thoughts or that He merely *uses* man's evil at times for His own purposes, but that God is the *cause* of all. He limits God's sovereignty by denying His ability to give man the power of choice.

White offers "three scriptural witnesses" to prove his thesis.[36] He cites God's use of Assyria as "the rod of mine anger" to punish Israel (Isaiah 10:5); Joseph's statement to his brothers, "Ye thought evil against me; but God meant it unto good" (Genesis 50:20); and the crucifixion of Christ, "Both Herod, and Pontius Pilate, with the Gentiles, and the people of Israel...[did] whatsoever thy hand and thy counsel determined before to be done" (Acts 4:27).

In fact, none of these Scriptures supports White's thesis. God did not decree that Israel would be disobedient, rebellious, idolatrous; He did not decree that Assyria would be wicked, destructive, and cruel; He did not decree that Joseph's brothers would be evil, jealous, and murderous; He did not decree that Herod and Pilate would be self-serving and unjust in their judgment, that the rabbis would be blind to the truth, wicked, and jealous of Christ, and that the Jewish rabble would prefer Barabbas to their Messiah.

White's examples simply show that God can use the wickedness of man for His purposes. Of the Assyrian, God said, "I will send him.... Howbeit...it is in his heart to destroy and cut off nations not a few" (Isaiah 10:6–7). God *uses* the evil intent of the Assyrian to His own ends. He has not *decreed* his wickedness. As for Joseph's brothers, the very statement "ye thought evil against me; but God meant it unto good" (Genesis 50:20) shows that God did not decree the evil in their hearts but used it for His purposes. The same is true of the crucifixion of Christ: "Him, being delivered by the determinate counsel and foreknowledge of God, ye have taken, and by wicked hands have crucified and slain..." (Acts 2:23). God *foreknew* each person's evil intent—He did not *decree* it but *used* it. God *delivered* Christ into their hands, He did not *cause* them to hate, mock, and crucify His Son. To teach that He did libels God.

Indeed, these very examples contain all the evidence we need that the men involved in each situation acted out their own evil intentions without realizing that God was using them for His purposes: "For they that dwell at Jerusalem, and their rulers, because they knew him not, nor yet the voices of the prophets...have fulfilled...all that was written of him" (Acts 13:27, 29).

On the other side, we have already given many Scriptures clearly supporting the fact that God has given man the right of choice. The testimony of Scripture as well as our God-given conscience amply prove that God does not decree every thought, word, or deed but that "out of the abundance of the heart the mouth speaketh" (Matthew 12:34) and "out of the heart of men, proceed evil thoughts, adulteries, fornications, murders, thefts, covetousness, wickedness, deceit, lasciviousness, an evil eye, blasphemy, pride, foolishness: All these evil things come from within, and defile the man" (Mark 7:21–23).

White writes, "Are we to believe that [those] totally separated from God can come up with...repentance toward God...simply from themselves?"[37]

Men can't even breathe "simply from themselves." But White can give no Scripture showing that man cannot willingly respond to the work of the Holy Spirit in his heart. Nor is any sinner "totally separated from God" until he is in hell.

"The sins of the elect people of God were nailed to the cross of Christ *and no others*,"[38] says White. In fact, no sins were nailed to the cross. Christ was nailed there who bore "our sins in his own body on the tree" (1 Peter 2:24). The law that condemned all mankind was nailed to the cross by Christ fulfilling it and paying its full penalty for sin (Colossians 2:14).

White asks, "How can we be 'free' in heaven and yet not able to fall?" Neither Lucifer nor any angels who fell were redeemed by the blood of Christ and indwelt by the Holy Spirit, as are Christians. Nor were any of them "in Christ...a new creature" (2 Corinthians 5:17) or "created in Christ Jesus unto good works" (Ephesians 2:10). Their minds were not "renewed day by day" (2 Corinthians 4:16), they did not "have the mind of Christ" (1 Corinthians 2:16), and they were not members of the church, which is Christ's body (1 Corinthians 12:27; Ephesians 1:23; 4:12).

The Calvinist handles "freedom" by saying that God *causes* the elect to do His will *willingly*. The Westminster Confession states that the elect are "made willing by his grace."[39] It is an oxymoron to say that someone is *made* willing. The Synod of Dort also taught that man's will is "sweetly and powerfully" bent to God's will.[40] If "bent," then man's will remains, leaving the Calvinist with the same possibility that the "bent" will might one day rebel in heaven.

It is inconceivable that those who have been "crucified with Christ" (Galatians 2:20), for whom Christ is their life (Colossians 3:4), who are not their own (1 Corinthians 6:19), and who in heaven have become "like him; for [they] see him as he is" (1 John 3:2) could ever choose to rebel. On earth the truly saved are heartbroken if they yield to temptation. They long for release from their bodies of sin and this evil world. In Christ's presence the redeemed are free of all that could tempt them to the sin that grieves them now.

All the righteousness we need is in Christ, who "is made unto us... righteousness" (1 Corinthians 1:30) and who *is* "OUR RIGHTEOUSNESS" (Jeremiah 23:6; 33:16). This righteousness becomes ours not by works but by faith: "To him that worketh not, but believeth on him that justifieth the ungodly, his faith is counted for righteousness" (Romans 4:5).

Our assurance is not in baptism, good works, or denial of choice. John declares, "These things have I written unto you that believe on the name of the Son of God; that ye may know that ye have eternal life" (1 John 5:13). Believing in Christ is our assurance.

1. John Piper and Pastoral Staff, *TULIP: What We Believe about the Five Points of Calvinism* (Minneapolis, Minn.: Desiring God Ministries, 1997), 24.
2. Arthur W. Pink, *Eternal Security* (Grand Rapids, Mich.: Baker, 1974), 11.
3. Zane C. Hodges, author's preface to *The Gospel Under Siege* (Kerugma, 1992), vi.
4. R.T. Kendall, *Calvin and English Calvinism to 1649* (London: Oxford University Press, 1979), cited by Bob Wilkin in *The Grace Report*, July 2000.
5. Louis Berkhof, *Systematic Theology* (Grand Rapids, Mich.: Eerdmans, 1941), 545–6.
6. Joseph C. Dillow, *The Reign of the Servant Kings: A Study of Eternal Security and the Final Significance of Man* (Schoettle., 1993), 14.
7. Laurence M. Vance, *The Other Side of Calvinism* (Vance Publications, 1999), 555, 562.
8. Dillow, *Reign*, 13.
9. Philip Schaff, *History of the Christian Church* (Grand Rapids, Mich.: Eerdmans, 1910), 8:873; Alan Sell, *The Great Debate* (Grand Rapids, Mich.: Baker, 1982), 1, passim..
10. Dillow, *Reign*, 269.
11. John Owen, cited in Arthur Pink, *An Exposition of Hebrews* (Grand Rapids, Mich.: Baker, 1968), 600.
12. Pink, *Eternal Security*, 28.
13. John Piper et al., *What We Believe*, 25.

14. Charles Hodge, *A Commentary on Romans* (Edinburgh: Banner of Truth Trust, 1972), 292.

15. John Murray, *Redemption Accomplished and Applied* (Grand Rapids, Mich.: Eerdmans, 1955), 155.

16. John Calvin, *Institutes of the Christian Religion*, tr. Henry Beveridge (Grand Rapids, Mich.: Eerdmans, 1998), III: xiv, 19.

17. Ibid., IV: xv, 3.

18. Ibid., IV: xv, 4.

19. Ibid., IV: xv, 15.

20. R. C. Sproul, *The Holiness of God* (Chicago: Tyndale, 1993) , 273.

21. Augustine, *On the Merits and Forgiveness of Sins and on the Baptism of Infants*, www.la.utexas.edu/phl354db/AugBaptism.html,1:35.

22. James R. White, *The Potter's Freedom: A Defense of the Reformation* (Amityville, N.Y.: Calvary Press, 2000), 28. From the Introduction by R. C. Sproul, Jr.

23. Ibid., 20.

24. Calvin, *Institutes*, III: xxiv, 5.

25. Ibid., III: ii, 11–12.

26. Kendall, *Calvinism*, 24.

27. Calvin, *Institutes*, III: ii, 39.

28. Benjamin B. Warfield, "Faith," in *Biblical and Theological Studies* (Grand Rapids, Mich.: Eerdmans, n.d.), cited in Dillow, *Reign*, 272.

29. Cited in Dillow, *Reign*, 273.

30. Ibid., 286.

31. Ibid., 286–7.

32. Loraine Boettner, *The Reformed Doctrine of Predestination* (Phillipsburg, N.J.: Presbyterian & Reformed, 1932), 308.

33. Quoted in Philip F. Congdon, "Soteriological Implications of Five-point Calvinism," *Journal of the Grace Evangelical Society* 8 (Autumn 1995):15.

34. Calvin, *Institutes*, III: xxiii, 6–7.

35. White, *Potter's*, 45.

36. Ibid., 45–51.

37. Ibid., 102.

38. Ibid., 270.

39. Westminster Confession of Faith (London: no pub., 1643), X:1.

40. Cannons of Dort (1619), reproduced in Vance, *Other Side*, 607–26.

Response, by James White

I am thankful that Dave Hunt chose to address the "fifth point" in his opening statements, because it does indeed help to bring out the ramifications of the two positions to consider this important topic.[1] I do not believe that any person who rejects the sovereign decree of God and the perfection of the work of Christ in providing a *real atonement* (that perfects those for whom it is made) has a basis to believe in any form of "eternal security." Those who limit God's freedom through asserting some form of libertarian free will are completely inconsistent in claiming that once a person "accepts Christ," he somehow loses the free will that got him to that position in the first place and is now "secure" from falling. If Christ's work of salvation is dependent upon our cooperation to be effective, there is no reason to believe it is eternally secure *at any point.*

First and foremost, as has been the case throughout this work, Dave Hunt fails to give any positive support to the position he *assumes* to be true. This is joined with liberal misunderstanding of the position he excoriates, resulting in a number of straw men. For example, we read:

> How could anyone be certain that his "obedience" and "well-doing"
> would satisfy an infinitely holy God? Moreover, God's Word is clear
> that it is "not by works of righteousness which we have done, but
> according to his mercy he saved us." (Titus 3:5)

No one is suggesting, of course, that our obedience "satisfies" God: Our sole righteousness is that of the imputed righteousness of Christ. Our obedience shows our nature and glorifies God. It does not make us "more saved." Hunt then says that a doctrine that teaches we must "keep our salvation" gives us a ground to boast. Yet we believe that Christ saves His sheep perfectly: We do not "keep" our salvation; Christ keeps us, and we persevere in faith as a result. Indeed, it is hard to avoid pointing out that it is Mr. Hunt and his libertarian free will that introduce ground for boasting—not the Calvinist!

But leaving these issues aside, what exactly is Mr. Hunt objecting to in the Reformed view? And how does he suggest that we fulfill Paul's command in 2 Corinthians 13:5: "Test yourselves to see if you are in the faith; examine yourselves! Or do you not recognize this about yourselves, that Jesus Christ is in you—unless indeed you fail the test?" Hunt's main objection is found in these words:

> In Calvinism, however, assurance of heaven is not in believing God's promise of forgiveness and eternal life but rather in being one of the predestined elect to whom alone salvation is granted.

Of course, only the elect truly believe God's promise of forgiveness and eternal life, so the entire assertion shows no understanding of the position being criticized. But even if one defined the "elect" as those God "sees" will believe, doesn't Mr. Hunt have to face the same questions? He says that the problem with the Reformed view is that people have to try to determine if one is of the elect. Yet, how does his view provide something "better"? Even if you do not believe in the elect (2 Timothy 2:10), you still have to answer

J. WHITE

the question about false faith. It seems Hunt does not believe that one can *have* a false faith, or that any faith, even if it is temporary, results in salvation anyway. He seems to believe that it is wrong for a person to grow in confidence of his salvation as he sees God working in his life.

The Bible speaks much of faith, and it clearly shows us that some have a false faith, a faith that does not result in salvation. There are those who "believe in vain," and anyone who holds a non-Reformed position must struggle with this fact. The parable of the soils (Matthew 13:1–8) includes those who exhibit only temporary faith, something the disciples saw often during the ministry of Christ. John had to address the issue of those who "went out" from the Christian fellowship because they were not truly *of* that fellowship (1 John 2:19). Obviously, those who went out had at one time professed faith in the truth.

One of the most striking illustrations of the reality of false faith is found in John's gospel. John presents a striking contrast between ongoing, active, living faith and point-in-time, temporary faith.[2] Those who have ongoing faith have eternal life (John 6:40). But those who have one-time, temporary faith do *not* receive eternal life. These are described in John 2:23 as "believing" in Christ, but notice Christ's response:

Jesus, on His part, was not entrusting Himself to them, for He knew all men, and because He did not need anyone to testify concerning man, for He Himself knew what was in man. (John 2:24–25)

Theirs was a false faith, just as the Jews who "believed" in Christ in John 8:30 ended up trying to stone Him by the end of the chapter. Yes, they "believed," but that faith was not ongoing, and hence was not living. It was the kind of faith James decries in James 2:14, a kind of faith he says "cannot save."

Apostasy is a common topic in the New Testament, so the fact that there will be those who will claim to be Christians and even profess an orthodox faith but who are *not* truly in Christ and heirs of eternal life (Acts 20:29–30) is a fact of biblical revelation. Calvinists and Arminians have to deal with this reality. The Calvinist says that saving faith is a gift of God and that those who do not have that faith must have a *false faith* that is not focused on the true Christ and the true gospel. The Arminian, however, who believes everyone is capable of exercising saving faith, has a real problem. That is why historically Arminians have always rejected "eternal security." There is no place for it in their system.

If we are not to gain encouragement and growth in assurance from the observation of the work of God in our lives, and if we are to be unconcerned about false professions of faith and hypocrisy in the church, why does a large portion of the New Testament give us guidance about how we are to live? Why is 1 John even in the Bible if what Mr. Hunt is saying is true? Indeed, Hunt again shows the traditional and eisegetical nature of his position when he writes:

> Our assurance is not in baptism, good works or denial of choice. John declares, "These things have I written unto you that believe on the name of the Son of God, that ye may know that ye have eternal life" (1 John 5:13). Believing in Christ is our assurance.

Assurance is a Spirit-borne blessing, and He can use *means* in giving us this blessing, including the realization that God is working in our lives through our desires, our reactions, and our attitude toward sin and holiness. But I refer to the misuse of 1 John 5:13. In its context, what are "these things" that John has written? He is referring to everything that came before in his epistle, that is, all of 1 John, which includes such faith-testing things as "if you hate your brother you are a liar" and "if you love the world the love of the Father is not in you." These are the "things" John refers to that give us assurance that we have eternal life. Hunt has misread the passage as if it were saying, "Since you believe on Jesus, you know you have eternal life, and all the rest does not matter." That would make the entirety of John's epistle superfluous.

Dave Hunt asks:

If man's depravity and spiritual death make it impossible to have saving faith without sovereign regeneration, how could it be certain that one's faith came in that manner? Might not faith in Christ be in vain because one is not among the elect? Moreover, how could perseverance to the end be proof of election if the nonelect, as Calvinists admit, are also capable of good works?

As we have seen in John, the Bible contrasts the saving faith of some with the nonsaving faith of others. Saving faith is the work of the Spirit in the heart, which is why it perseveres to the end. Hence, Hunt thrashes another straw man when he posits the idea of a man who has faith in Christ but is not one of the elect. That is not a possibility, because unregenerate men cannot do *truly* good works. Moreover, it is irrelevant to the Lord's words, "The one who endures to the end, he will be saved" (Matthew 24:13). One either interprets that passage to be *prescriptive*, meaning that one's endurance brings about one's salvation (the view of most works-salvation systems), or as *descriptive*, meaning that the saved endure (the Reformed view). How does Hunt understand these words? We are not told. His objection is pragmatic, not theological or biblical. And given the fact that he does give us a positive statement of his position to examine, we can hardly test his views by the standards he sets for others.

THE REALITY

The perfection of Christ's work of salvation—from the reality of God's eternal decree, to the deadness of man in sin, to the effectiveness of His substitutionary death in behalf of the elect, to the application in time by the Spirit of God—is the only basis of any consistent doctrine of perseverance, or "eternal security." Every system that reduces the work of Christ to the hypothetical level must abandon the solid rock of assurance that comes only from recognizing His awesome power. Reduce Jesus to the role of making us "savable," and you no longer have the slightest reason to believe that, once a person is in Christ, he will remain there. But strip man of his pretended autonomy, recognize his utter dependence and God's unparalleled power, and accept the truth of the eternal nature of Christ's saving work (and its inability to fail), and you will find a firm and necessary foundation. My hope is built on nothing less than Jesus' blood and righteousness: He will never fail to do the Father's will (John 6:38–39), and that is my hope.

---

1. Unforunately, he addressed almost every other element of Reformed theology as well, leaping from one topic to another. He attempts to respond to compatibilism but demonstrates a complete misunderstanding of the concept, misrepresenting the straw men he continues to attack in the process. He attempts to answer the question of

whether libertarian free will is definitional of humanity but fails to offer a meaningful defense. He attempts to address the extent of the atonement but continues to present a hypothetical versus real atonement. Indeed, at one point Hunt writes of me, "He can give no Scripture showing that man cannot willingly respond to the work of the Holy Spirit in his heart." Since the work of the Spirit in the heart is to bring regeneration, how could it be otherwise? The Reformed position says that once the Spirit frees us from our bondage to sin and brings us spiritual life, we willingly cling to Christ! And sadly, ignoring the fact that I'm a Reformed Baptist, he again attacks Calvin's views on paedobaptism and then notes that I referred to "Calvin's doctrine" many times on one page of *The Potter's Freedom,* as if this were relevant. The page was on how Geisler rejects Calvin's doctrinal positions and yet calls himself a Calvinist. But as no one is aided by this kind of scattergun approach, I have chosen to address only the issue of assurance in this response.

2. Specifically, he often contrasts *believe* in the present tense (i.e., saving faith) with *believe* in the aorist tense (temporary, transitory faith).

Defense, by Dave Hunt

White says that non-Calvinists "reject the sovereign decree of God." No, we reject Calvinism's false view of sovereignty, which White failed to justify from Scripture in his first chapter (see my response). God could keep all mankind from ever sinning? If *you* could, wouldn't *you* stop all sin, suffering, and death? Yet God, instead, brought this horror upon humanity for His good pleasure?

White calls "libertarian free will...ground for boasting!" *Libertarian?* Free will is God's sovereign gift, and receiving a gift gives no reason to boast. Without free will, we could neither love God or one another, nor willfully sin. Calvinists say that free will would "limit God's freedom." They limit God! An unbiblical denial of free will, which White calls the "central issue of the *entire Reformation*,"[1] creates most Calvinist errors.

By "sovereign decree" Calvinists mean that God *causes* every thought, word, and deed, whether good or evil. We reject this defamation of God's holy character. Evil proceeds "out of the heart" (Matthew 15:19), and the heart is not changed by "power" but by persuasion. We love God, not because He sovereignly made us love Him but because "he first loved us" (1 John 4:19).

Calvinism's *real atonement* comes not from Scripture but from reasoning that if Christ came to *save* sinners, His death didn't just make us "savable" but actually saved the elect. If so, they were never dead in sin but were saved before they were born. "Believe…and thou shalt be saved," "Whosoever will, let him take," and many other Scriptures show that salvation is *offered to all* but is effective only to those who believe and receive. Nor do I reduce "the work of Christ to the hypothetical level." He fully saves all "that come unto God by him" (Hebrews 7:25).

God offers salvation; man can only accept or reject it. Yet Calvinism says that the right to choose puts man in control. How is the recipient of a gift in control?

I've never said that "once a person 'accepts Christ,' he somehow loses the free will that got them to that position in the first place and is now 'secure' from falling." White says I fail to provide "positive support" for my position. In fact, I fully explain the biblical basis of assurance, and he doesn't respond to it.

I asked for a clear statement in Scripture that man is "unable" to respond to the work of the Holy Spirit in his heart. Instead of Scripture, White reiterates "the Reformed position" and asks "How could it be otherwise?"

White tries to minimize Calvin's influence by stating that he only refers in his book to "Calvin's doctrine" six times on page 20 to show that Geisler isn't a true Calvinist. What better proof of Calvin's influence! (See also pages 25, 71, 77, 85, 103).

As a "Reformed Baptist," White disagrees with Calvin's paedobaptism? Why hasn't he warned about this and Calvin's other false doctrines, such as his claim that infant baptism (even by an unbelieving Catholic priest) [2] or that being born of elect parents[3] gives certainty of one's election?

That Paul told the Corinthians to examine themselves as to whether they were "in the faith" doesn't justify Calvinists looking to works as evidence of being among the elect. Paul didn't say to examine their "works," but their "faith." To those who look to works instead of faith, Christ says, "I never knew you; depart from me" (Matthew 7: 23).

I believe in biblical election, "according to the foreknowledge of God" (1 Peter 1:2), not in Calvinism's "unconditional election." White refers to the "parable of the soils" as proof that "saving faith is a gift of God." No gift of God is mentioned. The "seed" is the Word; the "soil" is the heart. Christ emphasizes choice, understanding, and responsibility: "Sown in his heart...root in himself...understandeth (Matthew 13:19, 21, 23); "An honest and good heart" (Luke 8:15).

To show that faith is the gift of God, Calvinists cite Ephesians 2:8: "For by grace are ye saved through faith; and that not of yourselves: it is the gift of God." This is the *only* verse in the Bible containing both the word *faith* and the word *gift*. But *gift* refers to *that*, which is neuter, while *faith* is feminine. Many Calvinists agree that faith is not the gift. Calvin himself said, "Paul...does not mean that faith is the gift [but that] salvation is given to us by God."[4]

Many Scriptures (e.g., John 4:14; 6:27; 10:28; 17:2; Acts 26:18; Romans 5:18; Galatians 3:14; Hebrews 9:15; 2 Peter 1:3; Revelation 2:7) tell us that salvation, eternal life, and justification are the gift of God ("the gift of God is eternal life" [Romans 6:23]). *Never* is it said that God sovereignly gives faith; faith is *always* credited to the individual. Scripture refers to "thy faith" eleven times and to "your faith" twenty-four times. It refers as well to "our faith...my faith...their faith,...his faith"—but White avoids these Scriptures in his book.

Why is White so concerned with "faith" if one is regenerated *without* it? The real issue is whether a person is among the elect. If faith is a choice, he can look into his heart with God's help and know whether his faith is real.

But how can he examine the genuineness of his faith if it was sovereignly given by God, especially considering Calvin's warning that God gives to some a false assurance the better to damn them?[5]

White misapplies Matthew 24:13. "He that shall endure unto the end, the same shall be saved" is a promise that those who survive the Great Tribulation will be saved by the return of the Messiah.

His comments about Arminians are irrelevant since I'm not one and am not defending them. I'm "unconcerned about false professions of faith and hypocrisy in the church," in spite of my many books expressing concern? Please!

1. James R. White, *The Potter's Freedom A Defense of the Reformation* (Amityville, N.Y.: Calvary Press, 2000), 34.
2. John Calvin, *Institutes of the Christian Religion*, tr. Henry Beveridge (Grand Rapids, Mich.: Eerdmans, 1998), IV: xv, 1–6.
3. Ibid., IV: xv, 22.
4. John Calvin, *Calvin's New Testament Commentaries* (Grand Rapids, Mich.: Eerdmans, 1994), 11:145.
5. Calvin, *Institutes*, III: ii, 11–2.

D. HUNT

Final Remarks, by James White

An unbiblical denial of free will, which White calls the 'central issue of the *entire Reformation*,' creates most Calvinist errors." So writes Dave Hunt.

We have noted that the only references to "free will" Hunt can find are to "freewill offerings," which are obviously irrelevant to the biblical discussion of the nature of the will and its relationship to sin, since in this context they are referring merely to offerings that are not demanded by law with reference to sin but instead flow from the desire of the Israelite to give something to God. The very fact that Hunt presses into service such references shows how very extrabiblical the tradition of libertarian free will is. Indeed, in examining the effect of Hunt's tradition upon the text of Scripture, we have seen the phrase "are not able" turned into "everyone is able" or "are not willing (but are still able, if they choose)" a number of times. So while the Calvinist clearly says that man does as he desires and pleases, we recognize that the will, acting upon the desires of the fallen nature of man, is enslaved to evil, in need of being freed by the grace and mercy of God.

But if Mr. Hunt is denying that this issue was, in fact, central to the Reformation, he is very much in error. I remind him of the words Luther wrote to Erasmus in their debate over the bondage of the will long ago:

Moreover, I give you hearty praise and commendation on this further account—that you alone, in contrast to all others, have
attacked the real thing, that is, the essential issue. You have not wea-
ried me with those extraneous issues about the Papacy, purgatory,
indulgences and such like—trifles, rather than issues—in respect of
which almost all to date have sought my blood (though without success); you, and you alone, have seen the hinge on which all turns,
and aimed for the vital spot.[1]

To what does Luther refer? To the issue of the bondage or freedom of
the will. All the religions of man require the creaturely will of man to stand
sovereign over God, so that no matter how much weight is given to God
and His grace, in the final analysis, it is man who is in control of the final
decision regarding his salvation. This is fundamental to Roman Catholicism:
The entire sacramental system is based upon the concept of free will. All
systems that deny the perfection of Christ as Savior and present any form
of works-salvation likewise hold to this view. And on this issue, along with
the resultant belief that God's grace tries but fails to save, Dave Hunt stands
shoulder-to-shoulder with Rome *against* the Reformation. As the reader
may recall, that was the first thing I pointed out to Dave Hunt when we
first discussed this issue, and it is still at the heart of the matter.

---

1. Martin Luther, *On the Bondage of the Will: A New Translation of* De Servo Arbitrio
    (1525) Martin Luther's Reply to Erasmus of Rotterdam, trans. J. I. Packer and O. R.
    Johnston (Grand Rapids, Mich.: Fleming H. Revell Company, 1957), 319.

J. WHITE

Final Remarks, by Dave Hunt

Freewill offerings...not demanded by law with reference to sin [that] flow from the desire...to give something to God...are obviously irrelevant to the biblical discussion of the nature of the will," says White. An astonishing statement! No less puzzling is his assertion that it is "extrabiblical" to cite *from the Bible* the numerous references to freewill offerings and willing obedience to God.

White decries free will as "enslaved to evil," unable to do what is "pleasing and good in God's sight." Yet freewill offerings, good and pleasing in God's sight, are approved seventeen times for spiritually dead Israelites. And the exercise of one's "own voluntary will" (Leviticus 1:3), "own will" (Leviticus 19:5; 22:29), "own freewill" (Ezra 7:13), or gifts and sacrifices offered "willingly" (Ezra 3:5; 7:16) are also recorded.

Scripture refutes White's claim that the "will is enslaved to evil" and that those dead in sin cannot turn to God in faith without being regenerated. Man *voluntarily* yields himself to sin (John 8:34; Romans 6:16–17, 19). A sinner *can seek* "the LORD while he may be found" and *can call* "upon him... [and] forsake his way, and the unrighteous man his thoughts: and...return unto the LORD, and he will have mercy upon him" (Isaiah 55:6–7). *All* are invited to do so.

Of course, "this issue was...central to the Reformation," and Calvinism took the wrong side. Its extreme view of sovereignty, leading to the denial of free will, is the root of its many other errors.

415

Non-Calvinists *do not* "require the creaturely will of man to stand sovereign over God" so that man "is in control of the final decision regarding his salvation." That is like saying that because a criminal broke the law, he stands sovereign over the judicial system and controls his own sentence!

That man can accept or reject the "gift of…eternal life" (Romans 6:23) is required by the very nature of a gift and the fact that to be saved one must believe in the heart (Acts 8:37; Romans 10:9). Amazingly, White persists in the claim that salvation by faith is a "form of works-salvation." In fact, faith is the very antithesis of works (Romans 4:5). It is Calvinism that in effect offers salvation by works because it looks to works for assurance of salvation. Biblically, assurance comes by faith in the promise of eternal life in Christ made by "God, who cannot lie…before the world began" (Titus 1:2).

For man to be able to reject the gospel means that "God's grace tries, but fails, to save"? Christ failed because those who heard His "gracious words" tried to kill Him (Luke 4:22, 29)? Grace, like love (1 Corinthians 13:8), by its very nature *never fails,* even when rejected, but it does not force itself.

The final insult is to say that I stand "shoulder-to-shoulder with Rome"— after all I have done to oppose Rome! That incredible accusation is further proof of White's failure to support his position with Scripture and reason.

FINAL AFFIRMATION

by James White

I have engaged in this attempt at dialogue out of my love for God's truth and my firm conviction (one that grows through every encounter like this) that the consistent testimony of God's Word is that God is sovereign and free in salvation, that His grace is powerful, and that what is called "Calvinism," at least as it is defined by those who hold to it, is the most consistent representation of the gospel of Jesus Christ. I have come to this conclusion because I believe that the Bible is God-breathed, that it is consistent with itself, and that when we bow to its authority and engage its text through doing God-honoring exegesis, we come to know His truth with ever greater precision. I am a Calvinist because the exegesis of the text of Scripture leads me to that conclusion.

I am also a churchman. As an elder in a Reformed Baptist church that unashamedly proclaims the doctrines of grace, I believe I have a duty to protect the flock. Part of that duty involves warning about those who oppose the central tenets of the gospel we hold so dear. This is why, in response to Dr. Norman Geisler's *Chosen But Free*, I wrote *The Potter's Freedom*,[1] despite the fact that *Chosen But Free* was published by my own publisher and was edited by the same fine folks who have edited most of my books. I knew that Dr. Geisler's book would cause confusion but that it would also provide an

417

opportunity to explain and defend the doctrines of grace to a wide audience.

There is a substantial difference between Dr. Geisler's work and Dave Hunt's recent anti-Calvinist work, *What Love is This?* Both, sadly, show a strong dedication to an extrabiblical tradition, to be sure. Neither can be said to have accurately represented the position they both seek to undermine. But on the spectrum of scholarship, accuracy, "rhetorical temperature," and cogency of argumentation, *Chosen But Free* is light years removed from *What Love Is This?*

Dave Hunt chose to engage in a crusade to warn people about the dangers of Calvinism despite the consistent and widespread warnings of people with whom he had worked in ministry, in some cases for decades. Early on we discussed the issue on a radio program, the recordings of which are made available by our respective ministries. But what strikes me is that while Mr. Hunt has surely expanded the number of his arguments since then, *the fundamental misunderstandings of the position he decries have not changed.* This is highly significant, for just as his initial objections were based upon his particular brand of evangelical tradition, *the same is true now.* That is, I see no evidence that Mr. Hunt has grown at all in his understanding of the system he feels is so dangerous and dishonoring to God. I and the many others who have sought to expand his understanding so that he is at least disagreeing with *real* Calvinism, have met with abject failure.

This has come out in this attempted debate. No matter how often a straw man is put down, it comes right back up again in another chapter on a different topic. Such constant errors as saying that Calvinism denies that man has a will, denies that faith is important in salvation, and denies the use of the gospel in calling men to salvation have all been refuted, and yet they appear in Hunt's final presentations just as they did in the initial ones.

So why engage in this exchange? My initial inclination was against the idea. I would prefer a multiparty, face-to-face, moderated, public debate, as I believe the cross-examination of such a debate would allow the inconsistencies of Mr. Hunt's position to be fully exposed in a fashion a written debate simply cannot provide.[2] But I eventually acquiesced because I felt this book could accomplish a few important things.

First, I believe that this work will be read by an audience that would not otherwise ever consider this topic. As such, I hope it will spark an interest in further reading and, confident of the rightness of my position, will only advance the truth. Second, since I had engaged Mr. Hunt previously and exhorted him not to publish *What Love Is This,* I was at least in a position to consistently undertake the project as a published representative of "Calvinism."

But most importantly, I return to a theme I have struck many times in this dialogue. At one point in our radio dialogue, Mr. Hunt offered an interpretation of a verse that bore no connection to the context at all. I pointed out that it came from his tradition, not from the text. His reply was, "James, I have no traditions." And as I said then, so I have had to say repeatedly in this debate: The person who does not know he has traditions is the person most enslaved to them.

Dave Hunt's denial of Calvinism is not based upon careful, consistent exegesis of the biblical text. It is based upon his traditions, which then determine the meaning of the biblical text and therefore (and this is very important) cannot be *tested* by that biblical text. Those traditions become infallible in and of themselves, *even if they are contrary to the actual meaning of the text.* We have seen this come to light a number of times but especially in Hunt's insistence that the plain words of John 6:44 simply *cannot mean what they mean.* He cannot begin to argue from the basis of the text itself that "is not able" actually means "is not willing," but that is what he insists it *must* mean. And upon what basis? Because his tradition tells him that is what the Bible teaches; therefore, even the Bible itself must be made to "fit" the demands of tradition.

This encounter has illustrated the role of extrabiblical tradition in a way almost no other could. It is one thing to see it functioning openly, as it does in Roman Catholicism. But here we see how it works among those who deny its existence in their own ranks. When we honestly seek to discipline ourselves to engage in meaningful, consistent, and in-depth exegesis, we are showing due honor to God and the Scriptures, for we are seeking to hear His voice in His Word *alone.* And it is my hope that all who read this exchange will, as a result, seek to examine their own traditions under the bright light of the God-inspired Scriptures.

A LAST WORD FROM SPURGEON

Throughout this debate a constant source of frustration has been the repeated misrepresentation, *in the face of offered correction,* of the position being denied. This is not the first time caricatures and straw men have been thrown at the Reformed platform. Spurgeon experienced it in his day as well. Few people could communicate with the clarity and force of Charles Haddon Spurgeon, and given that Mr. Hunt cited him often, I feel it would be proper to let him close this encounter.[3] The great British preacher who proved you can be a Calvinist and passionate in preaching the gospel, poignantly commented:

And now, having made these remarks upon terms used, we must observe that there is nothing upon which men need to be more instructed than upon the question of what Calvinism really is. The most infamous allegations have been brought against us, and sometimes, I must fear, by men who knew them to be utterly untrue; and, to this day, there are many of our opponents, who, when they run short of matter, invent and make for themselves a man of straw, call that John Calvin and then shoot all their arrows at it. We are not come here to defend your man of straw—shoot at it or burn it as you will, and, if it suit your convenience, still oppose doctrines which were never taught, and rail at fictions which, save in your own brain, were never in existence. We come here to state what our views really are, and we trust that any who do not agree with us will do us the justice of not misrepresenting us. If they can disprove our doctrines, let them state them fairly and then overthrow them, but why should they first caricature our opinions and then afterwards attempt to put them down?[4]

A more fitting conclusion to our debate could hardly be written.

1. James White, *The Potter's Freedom: A Defense of the Reformation* (Amityville, N.Y.: Calvary Press, 2000).
2. Indeed, I hope this kind of exchange will take place as an addition to this book.
3. Indeed, Mr. Hunt has very badly handled Spurgeon, accusing him of all sorts of inconsistencies when, in fact, it is just Mr. Hunt's refusal to listen to Spurgeon that causes his problems.
4. Charles H. Spurgeon, "Exposition of the Doctrines of Grace," sermon preached 11 April 1861.

FINAL DENIAL

by Dave Hunt

White says that "evangelicals have adopted...sentimental traditions regarding God's character and love" It is not "sentimental traditions" but His Word that assures us of His love for all mankind—a love that Calvinism denies. This is the issue!

Calvinists claim that God predestined multitudes He could save to the lake of fire: "Let us not decline to say with Augustine, 'God could change the will of the wicked into good.... Why, then, does he not...? Because he is unwilling.'"[1] "Every man...is either predestined to life or death[2]...by the secret council of God's will[3]....their doom was fixed from all eternity."[4] Any humane person would rescue everyone he could from disaster, yet God predestined to eternal doom multitudes He *could save*? Is this the God who "*is* love" (1 John 4:8)—or is He being libeled? The answer to that question decides this debate.

White accuses me of "personal attacks upon...Calvin [and] Augustine." I give the facts: torture and execution for heresy. He said he would "refute the calumnies launched at...Calvin [and] Augustine." We're still waiting.

Calvinism claims that "the Father loves the human race, and wishes that they should not perish,"[5] but that "the elect alone are they whose eyes God opens."[6] What a contradiction! Yet, White agrees with Calvin that it is *love* to grant a brief respite on earth to those predestined to eternal torment.[7]

John MacArthur Jr. also agrees.[8] Not *one verse* affirms Calvinism's claim that God takes pleasure in damning *anyone*. He has no pleasure in the death of the wicked (Ezekiel 33:11), loves all (John 3:16), and provides salvation for all who believe (Romans 1:16).

Calvinism limits God's love, grace, and mercy to the elect. In obeying Christ's command to be merciful "as your Father also is merciful" (Luke 6:36), Calvinists can only be merciful and loving to the elect—even though they can't know who they are. MacArthur acknowledges Christ's command to love our enemies "'that you may be the sons of your Father...in heaven' (Matthew 5:45, NASB)."[9] But how does loving, forgiving, and doing good to all mark Christians as children of a Father who loves only the elect? Are we to be more loving than He?

Non-Calvinists who believe that God has "mercy upon all" (Romans 11:32), that His "tender mercies are over all his works" (Psalm 145:9), that He sent His Son "that the world through him might be saved" (John 3:17), that He laid on Christ "the iniquity of us all" (Isaiah 53:6) and desires "all men to be saved" (1 Timothy 2:4) must be loving and merciful to *all*. What a difference!

White relies on a few passages of arguable interpretation. His strongest case that God predestined only an elect to salvation comes from Acts 13:48 and 2 Thessalonians 2:13. Yet his interpretation does not fit God's character as so clearly established throughout all of Scripture. Hundreds of Scriptures (I have cited scores of them) declare in the clearest terms that God loves and desires the salvation of all. Some of these White explains away by interpreting *world* as *elect* and *all men* as *all classes of men*. *Whosoever* suffers a similar fate, along with God's love. But dozens of Scriptures to which I called his attention won't allow such mishandling, so he neither responded to them in this debate, nor referred to them in *The Potter's Freedom*.

Calvinists say that they preach the gospel so that the elect (whom no one can identify) will hear and believe. They can't tell anyone, "Christ died for *you*." But Paul tried to *"persuade* men" (2 Corinthians 5:11) to believe in Christ. Paul, not being a Calvinist, didn't know that the elect *don't need* to be persuaded and that the nonelect *can't be* persuaded. Nor can White rebut the fact that Paul desired to be eternally damned if that would save the Jews (Romans 9: 3). How dare Paul long for the salvation of those whom God "for His pleasure" predestined to eternal torment![10] Was Paul not inspired of God?

White claims to go by all of Scripture, but he repeatedly cites the same few texts. That Abimelech and the Assyrians were kept from sinning is offered several times as "proof" that God causes men to do good or evil and could stop all sin if He so desired. Pointing to God's sovereignty as justification for His predestination of multitudes He *could* save to damnation, White refuses to consider the hundreds of Scriptures in which God pleads with Israel and all mankind to repent and turn to Him.

How can God be sincere in pleading with and offering salvation to those He has from eternity predestined to eternal torment? Spurgeon, whom I am accused of misunderstanding and misquoting, said, "Now, was God sincere....? [U]ndoubtedly...He sent his prophets, he entreated the people of Israel to lay hold on spiritual things, but they would not."[11] This is only one of several instances of Spurgeon contradicting limited atonement—and himself. If limited atonement is true, God is "sincerely" offering salvation to those for whom Christ didn't die.

MacArthur likewise affirms limited atonement yet declares, "Surely His pleading with the lost, His offers of mercy to the reprobate, and the call of the gospel to all who hear are all sincere expressions of the heart of a loving God."[12] When we call this a contradiction, Calvinists say that we can't judge God by our standards, though God has put His standards in man's conscience and calls us to "reason together" with Him (Isaiah 1:18).

In hundreds of verses the Old Testament offerings and feasts of Israel lay the foundation for the sacrifice of Christ, the Lamb of God "who taketh away the sin of the world" (John 1:29). *None* of these, from the Passover to the Levitical offerings to the Day of Atonement, was for an elect class within Israel but for *all* Israel. In his book, White deals with none of these foundational Old Testament examples. Nor would he respond to my references to them in this debate. He avoided the entire sacrificial system in the Old Testament, the system that laid the foundation for the Cross.

Of the brazen serpent, God said, "Every one that is bitten, when he looketh upon it, shall live" (Numbers 21:8). Christ uses this event to explain that He also will be lifted up for sin so that "whosoever believeth in him should not perish, but have eternal life" (John 3:15). But White avoids these verses in his book and wouldn't respond to my references to them in this debate. In neither place does White deal with *any* of the key passages in the Old Testament that contradict Calvinism and provide the foundation for the Cross. When I called his attention to them, he dismissed them as "irrelevant."

White refers several times to John 6, Romans 8 and 9, and Ephesians 2 as "proof" that man is dead and cannot choose to receive Christ. Yet he ignores the hundreds of verses in which "God...commandeth all men every where to repent" (Acts 17:30). Does God command repentance from those who can't hear Him, from whom He withholds the grace to repent, and whom He has already predestined to the lake of fire?

White selectively offers Paul's use of Psalm 14 in Romans 3:11 ("There is none that seeketh after God') as proof of man's *inability* to seek God. Yet he sidesteps scores of exhortations for men to seek God, assurances that if they sincerely seek they will find Him, and the many examples of those who have sought and found.

White has no rebuttal for Christ's exhortation to "strive to enter in at the strait gate" (Luke 13:24), for the prodigal's repentant "I will arise and go to my father" (Luke 15:18), for good ground being an "honest and good heart" (Luke 8:15), or for faith being attributed to individuals (Matthew 9:22; 15:28; Mark 10:52; Luke 7:50; 17:19.)

Non-Calvinists can assure all men, "God loves *you*; Christ died for *your* sins." We know that all who believe His promise to "whosoever will" are saved eternally.

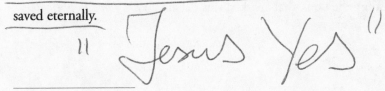

1. John Calvin, *Institutes of the Christian Religion*, tr. Henry Beveridge (Grand Rapids, Mich.: Eerdmans, 1998), III: xiv, 13.

2. Ibid., *Institutes*, III: xxiii.

3. Ibid., II: xxii, 11.

4. Ibid., III: iii, 4.

5. John Calvin, trans. William Pringle, *Commentary on a Harmony of the Evangelists* (Grand Rapids, Mich.: Baker, 1979), 123, cited with approval in John MacArthur Jr., *The Love of God* (Dallas: Word, 1996), 17.

6. Ibid., 125, cited with approval in MacArthur, *Love of God*, 18.

7. Calvin, *Institutes*, III: xxiv, 17.

8. MacArthur, *Love of God*, 15–8, passim.

9. Ibid., 15.

10. Calvin, *Institutes*, III: xxiii, 1.

11. Charles H. Spurgeon, "Sovereign Grace and Man's Responsibility," in *The New Park Street Pulpit* (London: Passmore & Alabaster, 1859), a sermon delivered 1 August 1858.

12. MacArthur, *Love of God*, 17.

Dave Hunt can be contacted at:

www.thebereancall.org

or 1-800-937-6638

where his books and videos can be purchased,

including the book that sparked this debate, *What Love Is This?*

James White can be contacted at:

www.aomin.org

or 1-602-973-4602

where his books and videos can be purchased,

including his book, *The Potter's Freedom*.

WANT TO UNDERSTAND 9\11?

Bible prophecy states that tiny Jerusalem will play a pivotal role in the world's destiny. This stunning documentary explains why.

ISBN 1-92912-532-1